Alexander Games has been the comedy critic of the London *Evening Standard* since 1996. He is also the author of *Pete & Dud*, a study of the creative partnership of Peter Cook and Dudley Moore. He is married with two children and lives in London.

Also by Alexander Games

Pete & Dud: An Illustrated Biography

BACKING
into the
LIMELIGHT

The Biography of Alan Bennett

Alexander Games

review

First published in 2001
by HEADLINE BOOK PUBLISHING

First published in paperback in 2002
by REVIEW

An imprint of Headline Book Publishing

10 9 8 7 6 5 4 3 2

ISBN 0 7472 6661 1

Typeset by Avon Dataset Ltd, Bidford-on-Avon, Warks

Text design by Jane Coney

Typeset in Garamond

Printed and bound in Great Britain by
Mackays of Chatham plc, Chatham, Kent

HEADLINE BOOK PUBLISHING
A division of Hodder Headline
338 Euston Road
London NW1 3BH

www.reviewbooks.co.uk
www.hodderheadline.com

CONTENTS

Introduction

The chocolate in the canteen at the British Library has a suitably literary theme. There are seven small bars in one block, each illustrated with the portrait of a writer. The first six are Noël Coward, William Shakespeare, Beatrix Potter, Oscar Wilde, Dame Agatha Christie and Charles Dickens. All look impeccably writerly, as one would expect: faces upturned to show off their literary credentials, shrewdly comfortable with their status on the conveyor belt of destiny. The seventh figure is a half-length portrait, painted by Tom Wood in 1993, of a man with fair hair, sitting at a table, with his chin resting in his palm. He is wearing a gunmetal-blue shirt with buttoned-down collars. There is a three-pin plug on the table, and also, for some reason, a brown-paper bag, as if he had turned up for the sitting on his way back from the corner shop. The painting hints at accessibility, the absence of airs and graces for which, as a Yorkshireman, he is well known. But as he stares at a point well past the observer's right shoulder, the familiar rumpled parting and owl-like expression hint at a reserve which has always been part of his make-up. The figure in the portrait is, of course, Alan Bennett, a man whose face is so well known that it can be used to sell chocolate. Not bad for the son of a Leeds butcher who believed at the age of seven that he had already seen the best that life could offer.

Alan Bennett's popularity is a phenomenon. He is among the most widely praised writers of his generation. He has written – as well as having acted – for and on radio, TV, theatre and film. Geographically, his work is set mostly in the heart of northern or southern England, with rare trips to Paris and even Moscow. It ranges in time from present-day to post-war Britain and back to the Hanoverians. He has put words into the mouths of working-class mothers as well as kings and queens. He has decoded other people's lives for film and theatre. But what seems equally fascinating to people is the running commentary which he has been conducting on his own life for the last twenty years. Those reading it are bound to come away feeling that they have learned something about him. They must also feel curious about the parts that Bennett has chosen to withhold. Guy Burgess, the spy whom he so brilliantly sketched in *An Englishman Abroad*, declared: 'If I wore a mask, it was to be exactly what I seemed.' To George III, whose madness he also sketched, he gave the line: 'I have remembered how to seem.' Alan Bennett has never forgotten how to seem like Alan Bennett. Which is exactly what makes him so difficult to know.

Alan Bennett is popular across many different generations and for many different reasons. His own generation have followed him, and have witnessed the most remarkable transformation from the shy, donnish-looking owl in *Beyond the Fringe* through his various renaissances, from sketch-show star to playwright and beyond. Young listeners know his voice from tapes of *Alice* or *Pooh*; the highbrow still think of him as a don *manqué*; others still admire his *Talking Heads*. He is the mascot of the *London Review of Books*, as well as the spirit behind such fly-on-the-wall adventures as *Dinner at Noon* and *The Abbey*. A lover of art galleries, a habitual visitor to country churches, he has dedicated much of his life to keeping a part of old Yorkshire free of improving makeovers. Architecturally conservative, politically liberal, Alan Bennett is cherished by the British for representing a view of England which many can find only in old photograph albums.

Bennett made his name in the revue *Beyond the Fringe* in 1960. At the back of the published scripts are three essays that first appeared in 1987. Two, of two pages each, are by Peter Cook and Dudley Moore. Jonathan Miller, who felt he had said enough on the subject long before, made no contribution. But the longest essay, running to three pages, is by Alan Bennett. It is a remarkable reversal of the roles that the four enacted during the run of the show, when Bennett felt awed into silence by the fluency of Cook and Miller, and it proves beyond doubt that Bennett had flourished as a writer. This book charts, in part, that change in their respective fortunes, as Bennett went from being laconic to loquacious, at least in print. Having felt awed into silence by Peter Cook's logorrhoea during the *Fringe* years, Bennett's writing and performing credits were roughly double those of Cook's thirty years later. And for all his ambivalence about his own contribution to that famous show, the jokes in Bennett's later plays were to prove some of the most keenly anticipated – and contested – areas of his work.

Some critics take the view that if he were less concerned with being funny, his plays would have a more serious purpose. But at the same time few doubt that he writes some of the best jokes in the business. And look where those flawed plays have got him. He already occupies half a column in the *Oxford Companion to the Theatre*. (Doubtless he will occupy more in the long-overdue new edition.) He has fourteen entries in the *Chambers Dictionary of Quotations*. Compare that with two for Peter Cook, one for Jonathan Miller and none for Dudley Moore. Alan Bennett flowered a little late, but when he did so, he didn't stop.

Of course, he has done his best to evade the easy pull of categorisation, most notably when it has been conferred on him by the media, and any study of Alan Bennett has to include his run-ins with the press. This book has reheated many of those doorstep battles: too many times, some might feel. But, having worked on a newspaper myself, I cannot conceal an interest in those yellowing, multiply folded, time-blistered columns of newsprint. They are eyewitnesses to a certain moment in history, after all, even when they don't come out of it terribly well. Some, especially newspapermen and women, feel that Alan Bennett has tried to have it both ways: importuning the press with one hand while brushing them off with the other. Many celebrities have played cat and mouse with the media, though few as skilfully or for as long as Bennett. As the actor Sir Nigel Hawthorne wrote in a letter to me, 'I think, without in any way wishing to seem critical, that the phrase "backing into the limelight" might well apply to him.' The phrase was first used by Lowell Thomas, in fact, about T. E. Lawrence, but despite that it became the working title of this book, and one that eventually made its way on to the cover.

Luckily, there is a lot more to say about the life and work of Alan

Bennett than the question of when he felt his privacy was being disrupted. He has written over sixty individual works. He has touched on themes of loneliness, madness, ambivalence, treachery, exile and patriotism; love, longing, finding and not finding. He has written about single people, couples and families; about happiness, unhappiness, broken dreams and fresh starts. He has fed amply on the peculiarities of his own family, as well as speculating on the lives and motives of people with very different backgrounds from his own. His constant complaint is that his family and childhood were not in the least interesting. And yet what an acreage of work those dull origins fuelled.

This book is really the work of an eavesdropper. It is positive, celebratory and sympathetic, and most certainly not dirt-dishing, but it is not official, approved or authorised. I wrote to Bennett, obviously, but he declined to cooperate. So did his closest friends (see Postscript). I could, I suppose, have spoken to a friend of the gaffer on the film set next to the one where they shot *A Private Function*, or to someone who knew someone who knew someone else who had once worked at the Queen's Theatre around the time when one of Bennett's plays was being performed there, but there didn't seem much point, for two reasons. First, there is so much of Bennett to write about, and so much accompanying text, be it interviews, profiles or news stories, that I felt I had my hands full just coping with this material. Second, it struck me that there was some poetic justice in the writer and star of *On the Margin* being viewed from the margin. So I have stuck to the margin, and in the process have missed out on a lot of kindly but repetitive stories about what a lovely man he is. I hope this will suffice.

I am proud to have dug up some examples of Bennett's earliest writing, from school and university, which I imagine very few people will have seen. And I was delighted to devote an entire chapter to his 1966 TV series *On the Margin*, which now, sadly, exists only in script. That, for me, was a work of preservation. But there is much since then which Bennett fans may be grateful to be reminded of, such as the series of TV plays that was published as *The Writer in Disguise*, as well as highlighting some of his less well-known contributions to the *London Review of Books*. Bennett has been very busy for the last forty years. And he has kept me busy too.

It has been a strange experience to be researching and then writing about Bennett for the past year. I have thought long and hard about which sort of people are likely to be interested in reading a biography of the man who has variously been described as an owl, a tortoise, a teddy bear and whatever animal it is that shuts itself away when it has caused a stir and refuses to speak to anyone. At times I have felt somewhat shy, embarrassed even, when revealing the subject of my study. 'Oh, it's, er, well, it's Alan Bennett,' I say to someone painfully fashionable, or academic, or young. But as soon as the words leave my lips, I have been almost blinded by the smile that the sound of his name produces. 'Alan Bennett!' they say. 'Oh, I just . . . love him.' All sorts of people, it seems, have a special reason for liking him.

And yet which Alan Bennett do they love? There are certain works – one thinks of *Kafka's Dick* or *Prick Up Your Ears* – which I would hesitate to be seen reading in public. So what is the voice of Middle England up to? Not fitting an image that others have constructed for him, you might say. Or being something of a paradox. That is, I suppose, one of the reasons why writers write.

Bennett's women are a subject of much controversy too. He has either been praised as writing some of the best parts ever written in that unjustly neglected field, or else been accused of sandwiching them into ham roles, all of which are in some way variations of his mother. He has been charged with being 'in the closet', and yet has written at length, and sympathetically, about issues of homosexuality. He has been described as a snob and a man of the people, an old-fashioned Tory and a Camden leftie, a rooter-out of humbug and a producer of the same. How can he fit all these categories? The answer would seem to be that you will find in Bennett some reflection of your own tastes and preferences. The only thing you cannot expect to find in his work is a straightforward answer to the question of who he is. His work is his explanation, and it is no bad thing to be thrown back against that every so often.

My interest in Alan Bennett probably dates from some indefinable moment in the late 1960s when, not yet into double figures, I first heard his famous parody of a sermon entitled 'Take a Pew' on a radio programme and decided that his voice sounded funny, without being quite sure why. When, years later, I read a transcript and then acquired a recording of *Beyond the Fringe*, I relished not just the humour but the reaction it provoked from the audience. It seemed to be opening a door to a room previously thought locked. Once out, of course, there was no chance that the door might be closed again, only that the vibrancy would fade in others' hands. From four Oxbridge-educated men making clever jokes about their contemporaries' behaviour and attitudes in the early 1960s, we have had to watch until 'satire' evolved into a bunch of lads doing impersonations of various second-rate TV stars in the late 1990s: not a great leap for political comedy. The appeal of listening to Bennett and his colleagues is to study a group of people who were at the watering hole early on, and who made good use of it.

On 4 March 1986 I joined about a hundred adults, and almost as many querulous children, to hear Bennett read from *Winnie-the-Pooh* at the Tricycle Theatre in Kilburn, north-west London. Bennett recalled this occasion in *Writing Home*: 'I battle against the crying of babies and the shouts of toddlers and end up screaming and shouting myself hoarse. It is *Winnie-the-Pooh* as read by Dr Goebbels.' I don't remember Bennett shouting, but I do remember seeing a lot of very misty-eyed mums and dads, who all seemed to be relishing the twin pleasures of hearing one national treasure declaiming the words of another. And I also remember that one of Bennett's shoelaces was trailing as he walked out on to the stage, which seemed entirely in character.

Some short time later, I was walking up an unfamiliar crescent-shaped street in Camden Town, full of early Victorian houses with top floors shaped like turrets. It was dark, and it was raining. Suddenly, I noticed a figure step out in front of me. Tall, bespectacled, fair hair, a crumpled shirt collar: it had to be Alan Bennett. It was. Before I had time to compose a sensible remark, I remembered that I had heard him just recently on the radio and shouted out: 'I heard you on the World . . . um, Service, last . . .' But he was already retreating. Ducking inside the lapels of his coat, he dived down a pathway, keeping a polite but firm distance before turning round. (To be fair to him, it was raining quite hard.) I heard the words, 'Thank you for your support', and then he was gone.

As I stood, puzzled but not entirely surprised, on that street corner, staring at the front door which had now slammed emphatically shut, I wondered why my offer of praise had made him scuttle up the path with even greater haste. This book started as an investigation into what might have made him run away. I think I can now state with some degree of confidence that it was nothing personal.

Part One

The *Fringe* And All That

1

Not quite like other families
Childhood, 1934–1946

To the young Alan Bennett, the experience of growing up in Leeds was not unlike that of someone growing up in a fifteenth-century Italian city-state. The arms of the city – the owls and the lamb in the sling and the motto 'Pro rege et lege' ('For king and law') – were stamped everywhere, on school books, library books, at the tram stop, the market, over the entrance to the Central Library. In 1994 Bennett wrote that if they'd left Leeds alone, and not ripped the heart out of it by tearing down many of its old buildings and plastering the city centre with high-rise blocks, raised shopping malls, one-way streets and inner-city motorways, 'Leeds today would have been one of the architectural showplaces of the kingdom, a Victorian Genoa or Florence, on the buildings of which many of its banks and commercial properties . . . were modelled.'

Some observers were not so sure. J.G. Kohl, writing in 1844, thought that 'Leeds is perhaps the ugliest and least attractive town in all of England.' And when J.B. Priestley, a native of neighbouring Bradford, made his *English Journey* in the autumn of 1933, he slightingly described Leeds – belatedly upgraded to city status in 1893 – as 'the shopping and amusement centre of the West Riding', adding: 'It has not the authentic, queer, carved-out-of-the-Pennines look of Bradford and some of the other towns. It is a large dirty town that might almost be anywhere, and mostly built of sooty brick.'

That soot was the sweat of a staggering industrial puberty. Leeds underwent a huge expansion during the nineteenth century. Between 1841 and 1900, as the Industrial Revolution took hold, its population soared from 88,000 to 178,000, bringing many immigrants to the city and changing its complexion permanently. Leeds was a busy trading centre. It was in an open market in Leeds in 1884 that Michael Marks, a Jewish refugee from Poland, first opened a household goods, haberdashery, toy and sheet-music business known as Marks' Penny Bazaar before teaming up with Thomas Spencer to create Marks & Spencer. By the end of the Second World War, Leeds was the sixth largest city in England. The *Yorkshire Post* described it as 'the industrial capital of the north' and 'the geographical and strategical centre of Britain's greatest workshop'. With its roots in the cloth industry, Leeds was the world's largest ready-made clothing centre, employing about 56,000 people. Alongside the cloth was a considerable trade in livestock. The daily Wholesale Meat Market and Abattoir covered about two acres near the Kirkgate General Market and was probably the most important in Yorkshire. To be a butcher in Leeds in the early twentieth century was a secure and respectable, if not romantic, way to earn a living.

'By 1832,' wrote the historian R.J. Morris, 'over a fifth of the population could claim middle-class status.' The definition of 'middle class' is a notoriously tricky one: but the trade unions could have struck a blow for workers' rights over a case involving a young couple who wished to marry. The groom was a butcher who had worked for the local Co-operative since 1919, but the Co-op was unwilling to set a dangerous precedent by appearing lax, and insisted that he had to be at work at 8.15 a.m. The local vicar, the Revd Herbert Lovell Clarke, had to inform the groom, Walter Bennett, that he was unable to read out the wedding vows until eight o'clock in the morning. The church was unyielding on this point, and the Co-op proved to be so too, refusing to allow their employee to be fifteen minutes, let alone half an hour, late for work. Fortunately, the vicar came up with an ingenious solution, reading up to but not including the vows by eight o'clock, and then, on the stroke of eight, marrying the young couple. And so Walter Bennett and Lilian Mary Peel, he twenty-five, she twenty-four, were married at Armley Church early on the morning of 29 September 1928, and the happy couple celebrated in the evening by going to the Grand Theatre to see *The Gondoliers*, or *HMS Pinafore*, depending on which version you read.

In any event, they would certainly not have wanted a big, fancy wedding. Walter, who was born at home in Holbeck, one of the villages clustered round the centre of Leeds, on 28 January 1903, was a shy man, who preferred playing his violin to any more overt show of emotion. His mother was born Fanny Maria Noble, and his father, Henry Bennett, was a gas worker. Fanny Bennett died when Walter was five, and her place was taken by a woman whose hostility to Walter so horrified the family that her real name was scrubbed from history, and she was consigned to perpetual ignominy as 'the Gimmer', a contemptuous term for a sheep that has had no lambs. She made life utterly miserable for Walter, telling tales about him that got him into trouble with his father. Alan Bennett told Terry Coleman of the *Guardian* in 1989 that his father's stepmother was 'straight out of a fairy story, who starved him, made him practise his violin in the dark, and put him to butchery. He never had a bad word for anyone except her. The day of her funeral everybody was happy.' The real identity of 'the Gimmer' looks likely to remain a Bennett family mystery for a while yet, since no trace of this woman, or of her marriage to Henry Bennett, has surfaced in publicly available records.

Lilian Mary Peel was born, also at home, in Greetland, just south of Halifax, on 4 February 1904. Her father, William Peel, was a draper's assistant, and her mother's name was Mary Ann Peel, née Smith. Lilian was the youngest of three sisters, the others being Kathleen and Lemira, or Myra. There was also a brother, Clarence, who died, aged twenty, on 21 October 1917, in Flanders. When she moved to Leeds with Walter, they made their home in Halliday Place, Armley. It was a small street in a respectable working-class area. George Kelly, a police sergeant, lived at number 2; George Wilkinson Jr, a foreman, at number 6. There were also three clerks, a station attendant, a 'traveller', a railwayman and a joiner. The Bennetts were accustomed to taking a summer holiday in the traditional coastal resorts like Morecambe, Flamborough or Filey. For many, summer holidays were opportunities for relaxation. For others, they were also an opportunity to get on with other business, and so, on 9 May 1931, a son, Gordon, was born at home. With uncanny accuracy, again on 9 May 1934, and nine months after another successful annual summer holiday, another son was born at home whom they named Alan.

When Gordon was born, Walter's occupation was described as butcher's storekeeper. By the time Alan was born, Walter – slowly making his way up the Co-op hierarchy – was described as a butcher's manager. His salary in the early years of the war was £6 a week. The residents of Armley Lodge Road, the branch where he worked, had rather more colourful professions. They included a fried fish dealer, a boot repairer, a stone polisher and a prison officer.

Impressions of the young Alan Bennett's life come from throwaway remarks in his diaries and, occasionally, interviews. Grandma Peel lived at 7 Gilpin Place in Wortley, also in Leeds 12, where she kept the piano that his Great Aunt Eveline practised before accompanying the silent films at the Electric Cinema in Bradford. (The apparition of Joyce Chilvers, accompanied by her mother, rising up through the floor while playing the cinema organ in *A Private Function* must have been a familiar sight to him.) There were musical evenings in the front room every Sunday, when Great Aunt Eveline would duet with Walter. It's likely that Bennett first heard many of the songs that have cropped up in his plays and films – from 'Pedro the Fisherman' in *Afternoon Off* to 'I've Got Sixpence' in *Rolling Home* and 'My Alice Blue Gown' in *Talking Heads* – during these early years. Uncle George, Walter's brother, who was a bricklayer 'and has a fine voice and a face as red as his bricks', would sing. The songs would include standard favourites like 'Bless This House' and 'Where'er You Walk'. Such evenings would last until Grandma Peel died in 1950.

As well as being a modest carpenter capable of turning his hand to fretwork, Walter Bennett took up the double bass some time in 1942. It was to prove a fad, along with his enthusiasm for home-made herb beer which 'regularly explodes in the larder', but for a while the Bennett family were dragooned into hearing him play in a band 'somewhere in Wortley', just one of the 'schemes Dad has thought up to make a bit of money'. Bennett later wrote that 'I already knew at the age of five that I belonged to a family that without being in the least bit remarkable or eccentric yet managed never to be quite like other families.'

The young Bennett was surrounded by voluble northern women, each with her own idiosyncratic storytelling methods. He would spend hours listening to them chatting. His long-suffering father frequently ran out of patience with them. 'I wouldn't care, but you're no further on when she's done,' he would say sometimes, laughing about it at the same time. Whether or not he thought them particularly funny at the time, Bennett's ear was tuned from an early age to the folkloric filter through which the most humdrum of daily events could be projected.

The Peel women were proud of their name. There is a story, probably apocryphal, that Lilian's family were distant relatives of Sir Robert Peel, the great Tory Prime Minister who took over, for three months only, from the Duke of Wellington on 10 December 1834, a hundred years before Alan Bennett was born. Peel's second term of office was more successful, lasting from August 1841 to June 1846 before he lost to the Whig Lord John Russell, whose grandson Bertrand would form the subject of one of Alan Bennett's most notable early parodies.

Asked about his father by Hugh Hebert of the *Guardian*, Bennett described him in 1986 as 'a very gentle man. A man who scratched the pigs' backs with a stick, and was afraid of bulls.' Intensely musical, he had perfect pitch, sometimes playing outside in the coal cellar, where he could concentrate better, away from the chattering hordes inside. The young Bennett remembers taking the route to the coal cellar through the cold room, which was full of great beasts' heads oozing blood, and a smell that, when it was recreated on the set of *A Private Function* to the horror of the film crew, felt to him like home.

Bennett senior didn't have a large wardrobe, just 'my suit and my other suit', he used to say. But young Bennett enjoyed accompanying his mother into the centre of Leeds's still impressive shopping area, with its large department stores like Hitchen's, Marshall and Snelgrove, and Matthias Robinson's. Like many children who enjoy watching the daily rhythms of the adult world, Bennett would join her for tea in Betty's Café on Commercial Street, or Hitchen's tobacconist on Otley Road. One tradition that he enjoyed was the occasional visit of the chiropodist. 'There was this ceremony of spreading newspaper on the floor, to catch the clippings,' he reminisced. The clippings resurfaced in *A Private Function*, and chiropody returned in 'Miss Fozzard Finds Her Feet', from *Talking Heads 2*.

The Bennett family's experience of war was comparatively brief. On the day war broke out, anticipating a blitz centred on Armley, Bennett's parents evacuated themselves from Leeds and took their two sons by bus to Pateley Bridge, out in the Yorkshire countryside. Walter Bennett knocked on several doors until he found a farmer who was kind enough to take them in. The boys saw out the tense opening months of the war on the farm, before Bennett's parents, realising that the threat of air strikes had passed, welcomed them back. For the boys, of course, it was a time of great excitement. Bennett junior felt personally slighted that 'the longed-for rain of bombs' never came. While the skies over Sheffield and Liverpool were black with Heinkels, Leeds was overlooked. Bennett learned 'the useful lesson that life is generally something that happens elsewhere'. From time to time, he remembered in *Telling Tales*, 'the sirens went and my brother and I were wrapped in blankets and hustled out to the air-raid shelter that stood outside our suburban front door', but they waited in vain. The explanation, says Bennett, was probably quite logical. 'The city specialised in the manufacture of ready-made suits and the cultivation of rhubarb, and though the war aims of the German high command were notoriously quixotic, I imagine a line had to be drawn somewhere.'

Bennett and his family picnicked in summer and sledged in winter on the hill at the top of the Armley Grange estate, facing Baptist's Field and now, of course, built over. The young Bennett had a rigid hierarchical knowledge of every street, knowing, for example, that the half-built houses in Armley Grange were a cut above the Hallidays, but that the Hallidays were superior to the Edinburghs across Moorfield Road. Bennett maintains that there was nothing unusual about this. 'Every child carries in its head a finely contoured social map of its surroundings, one that would put to shame the most conscientious sociologist,' he wrote in the *Yorkshire Evening Post* on 10 April 1992.

Most funny people born between the wars have a long list of their favourite radio comedy programmes, usually including *ITMA* (*It's That Man Again*) and, post-war, *The Goon Show*. Bennett told John Bird in March 2000 that he hated the star of *ITMA*, Tommy Handley. He also hated Tommy Trinder, because they were both 'relentlessly cheerful'. The only *ITMA* character he liked was Monalott the charlady. Sure enough, he brought a charlady, Mrs Swabb, to life in his stage play *Habeas Corpus*. Bennett preferred the characters who seemed to him to relate to his own life. These were the northern comedians whom he'd see annually at pantomimes. They were people like Albert Modley and Frank Randle, whose style was quirky but conversational. Another one was Norman Evans. 'He'd have no teeth in and have a very prominent chin. He'd be saying things like: "Ooh, there's that cat again. Oooh, get it inside. I could taste it in the custard." This was very real because you would actually see women like this and you had heard them talk and so the humour was wedded to real life.'

After the family moved from Armley, Bennett's local cinema was the Headingley Picture House on Cottage Road. Bennett junior also had a particularly sensitive ear for music. He never forgot the day when, as a sixth-former, one of his schoolfriends hummed the opening bars to Brahms's Second Piano Concerto as they sat on a tram at West Park, and every Saturday night – or so it seemed – he and his friends went to hear the Yorkshire Symphony Orchestra at the Town Hall. They used to pay sixpence and sit behind the double basses at the back of the orchestra, listening to music like Sir William Walton's First Symphony. Covent Garden used to visit once a year for a two-week season, which was how he came across operas like *Der Rosenkavalier*. 'It was always very difficult to get in, and I remember I stood in the gods to hear,' he told Roy Plomley on *Desert Island Discs* in 1967. However, he recalled years later in *Telling Tales*, 'I note, at the age of ten, a fully developed capacity not to enjoy myself, a capacity I've retained intact ever since.'

Bennett junior's favoured reading haunt was Armley Library at the bottom of Wesley Road, which he described as 'a grand turn-of-the-century building with a marble staircase and stained-glass swinging doors'. The Junior Library used to be in the basement, and Bennett remembers it being 'presided over by a fierce British Legion commissionaire, a relic of the Boer War'. The books were 'uniformly bound in stout black or maroon covers', so that '*The Adventures of Milly Molly Mandy* was every bit as forbidding as *The Anatomy of Melancholy*'. The serious and the farcical often stand together in Bennett's work.

Bennett junior's other source of inspiration was the Church. Bennett told Janet Watts in the *Observer* in 1988 that he was 'fervently religious' from his confirmation until his twenties. Bennett's confirmation at St Michael's, Headingley, by the Right Revd Henry Handley Vully de Candole, the Bishop of Knaresborough, one evening in 1949 was a deeply significant moment. He later joined the Crusaders, an evangelical Bible class for grammar school boys held on Sunday afternoons in the parish room of a Congregational church in Cumberland Road, Leeds. Easter at St Michael's meant 'great lilies on the altar, the copes and the candles and the holy ladies plummeting to their knees at any mention of the Virgin's name'. Bennett told Humphrey Carpenter that he was 'devoted to the language of the 1662 Book of Common Prayer; years later it was still "the only work of literature of which I know large sections off by heart" '. Bennett's fascination with the trembling chalice was almost Wildean. As a teenager, he never doubted that he would become a clergyman. Though he later abandoned strict religious faith, he never shook off the feelings of awe that overtook him each time he attended a properly conducted traditional church service, and there can be few country churches whose doors have not creaked slowly open to a visit from Alan Bennett. And, of course, when it came to parodying the voices and verses that had inspired him for so much of his teens, his own efforts put those of most of his contemporaries into the shade.

Years later, in *Dinner at Noon*, Bennett recalled summer holidays spent cringing in coastal bed and breakfasts, his parents' unease when away from home compounded by his mother's insistence on ordering a pot of tea in a cafeteria and then stealthily passing round pre-buttered bread below the table. Much of their food would be brought with them from Leeds in a bulging cardboard box tied with string, and Walter Bennett would invariably mistime the moment for the handover of the shilling tip to the porter, offering it while the facilities were still being explained, for example, which turned it into 'an unwelcome interruption'.

He attended Upper Armley National School, now Christ Church School, from the age of five. Nineteen forty-four ranks as the 'lost year', when the entire Bennett family decamped to Guildford; Walter had seen an advertisement in the *Meat Trades Journal* to manage a family butcher's shop in the town. Both boys went to the Royal Grammar School, and Bennett here experienced, for the first time, children who called their parents 'Mummy' and 'Daddy' instead of 'Mam' and 'Dad', and life seemed rather closer in substance to the mystical worlds that made up his childhood reading list. In 1989 Bennett told Michael Hickling of the *Yorkshire Post* that he and his parents 'lived a rootless sort of life in hotels. When Dad became quite ill, my mother, who was a woman of no education and very shy, had to find a new flat, get us into school and organise things, which, looking back, must have been quite intimidating.' It didn't help, Bennett added, that his mother suffered from depression. Gordon joined the cadets, but the Bennetts soon returned to Yorkshire, the dreams of escape extinguished.

Back in Leeds, they moved out to Headingley, living above Walter's new butcher's shop – his own, this time, not the Co-op's – at 92a Otley Road. Bennett, still keenly conscious of social distinctions, was always embarrassed that there was no hallway or vestibule, and that one simply opened the front door and walked into the living room from outside, 'as indeed a couple did one night, thinking it was a pub'.

As the eleven-plus loomed, he took the entrance examination for Leeds Grammar but was confused by a question about the biblical character Job. Thinking it was a reference to the other word for 'occupation' rather than 'Book of . . .', he answered along those lines. There must have been an imp of the perverse about the younger Bennett that strengthened him to indulge himself in such ways. Years later, in the programme notes for his first West End show, Bennett described not so much a real incident as the sort of person he felt he used to be. 'As a boy he achieved high office in the Wolf Cubs but never graduated to the Boy Scouts through a deep-seated inability to skip backwards the requisite thirty-three times.' Leeds Grammar turned him down, of course. If the slightly older Bennett discerned a suspicion of authority in the slightly younger Bennett, that was balanced by a wave of religious devotion which coloured the remainder of his teens, leaving him far better qualified to answer questions about any number of biblical prophets. By then, the chance to enter Leeds Grammar had been and gone, but he found the admission procedure for Leeds Modern Boys' School more straightforward, and he took his place there in 1946.

2

We want to see *you* at the CU

Leeds Modern Boys' School, 1946–1954

Leeds Modern was founded in 1845 by Sir Edward Baines as the Leeds Mechanics' Institute School. In 1931 it moved to Lawnswood, just west of the city centre, where, now renamed Lawnswood High and fully comprehensive, it still stands. Early photographs show an architecturally imposing building, reminiscent of an Oxbridge college, with columns and stone steps, and row upon row of windows. Latin was compulsory, and gowned masters roamed the corridors.

Its aim was to give 'a liberal training for boys who intend to enter the professions or engage in one of the local industries'. Apparently uncowed by its older, more famous rival, Leeds Grammar School, which predated it by over 300 years, 'Modernians' were encouraged to believe that they inhabited the best of all possible worlds, striving to 'challenge stout spirits' in fulfilment of the school motto, 'Fortem posce animum'.

According to Frank Holland, who replaced Dr G.F. Morton as headmaster in 1948, the attraction of Leeds Modern was that it aimed to educate 'the whole boy'. Progress towards that holistic ideal could be assessed in the pages of the school magazine, *The Owlet*. Edited by the staff but with contributions drawn from the length and breadth of the school, *The Owlet* gives the impression of a body of pupils striving ceaselessly to expand their horizons. Boys aiming to take the school motto literally were encouraged to join school treks to Italy (Passo San Giacomo, 1926) and Austria (Oberammergau, 1934). But it wasn't only the future Axis powers that were visited. Loch Carron and Loch Monar were crossed in 1935, and a photograph from 1939 shows a party of boys on the road to Achiltibuie. Any novelty, one felt, could be tolerated so long as a young writer could compose a suitably dignified method of describing the experience in prose or verse. Thus, in 1951 S.A. Hardy from form III.L recorded in excited tones a journey taking in 'London – New York – London . . . by Plane'. A few years earlier, in the summer of 1949, P.N. Brooks of VI.A.2 took up a page fulminating at 'what loathsome conveyances trams are'. The pages of *The Owlet* were elegant and extremely well turned, with lots of confident young voices keen to advertise their skills. Even by these high standards, though, the voice that arrived in issue 129 in summer 1948 was distinctive.

Under the headline 'Cinderella – 1948 Version' a small conceit began to unfold itself. 'Despite popular belief that Cinderella "lived happily ever after",' began the writer, 'she was very unhappy with the prince and, very soon obtaining a divorce from him, she returned to her two sisters and her drudgery.

'Cinderella, whose real name was Ethel Higgins, lived in a small house in a suburb of London. With her lived her two ugly sisters, Pearl and Ruby.' The piece went on in a similar, whimsical vein. It was signed 'A. Bennett, IV.A'.

During the next few issues, A. Bennett concentrated on work, passing his Higher Certificate in English, English Literature, French, History and Latin, but by the winter of 1949 he had, for the time being, moved on from writing parodies. Instead, we find in issue 133 the first public expression of a theme that would occupy him from then on. The article is called 'Relics of Old Leeds'. It comprises a brisk tour of the few remaining interesting (i.e. old) buildings in what he calls 'the Victorian ugliness' of Leeds. Bennett laments the nineteenth century, when 'row upon row of back-to-back slum houses was erected where formerly half-timbered and graceful Georgian houses had stood'. He concludes: 'It is possible to find these bits of old Leeds if one is observant, and almost every month we read of some relic discovered in the course of building or the strengthening of foundations. Only a few months ago there was discovered the beautiful mosaic on the front of Denby & Spinks, upholsterers, in Albion Street. These mosaics showed that this building was once the Music Hall. Unfortunately, part of these mosaics has been covered up again. Leeds is sadly lacking, however, in objects and buildings of historical interest, and those we have should be jealously preserved and any attempt to pull them down or destroy them should be fiercely resisted.' The piece was signed 'A.B., VI.A.1'. Thus spoke the future chairman of the Settle Conservation Society.

The conservative tinge was not confined to architecture. In the summer of 1950, with *Beyond the Fringe* still ten years off, he penned a sonnet called 'Ah Music, What Crimes Are Committed In Thy Name!':

> From out the room, by melody one claimed,
> Erupt vile sounds of music, sadly maimed,
> Of trumpets hot (their players sooth are steaming),
> Of tubas fat and clarinets a-screaming.
> The zealots now, with rapt attention,
> Blare out their musical dissension.
> Piano too joins in the fray,
> Trombone discordant then begins to bray.
> At 'scrannel scrap' and viol chivied
> Poor Handel on the walls is livid;
> Discord on dat chord pounded out,
> Til Beethoven is put to rout.
> Pray tell me, Muse, what name this clatter has?
> Euterpe, anguished, sobs 'The name is Jazz!'

If the tone of young Bennett's poem seems callow or pompous to modern ears, it should be read against the climate of the times. Even so, 'Discord on dat chord' is, by most standards, a pretty good pun.

Bennett seems to have been a popular and well-liked boy, and greatly in demand for school plays, to judge from this review of *The Taming of the Shrew* from the spring edition of *The Owlet* in 1950: 'The main characters of Katharina and Petruchio, on whom so much depends, were well acted; and all the other parts followed their fine example. The play was most enjoyable and was well supported on each evening.' The part of Katharina, so praised by the reviewer, was played by A. Bennett.

A few months later, Bennett had earned the right to be described as one of 'our two seasoned actors'. Appearing before the guest of honour, Lord Scarborough, for the winter term's Speech Day, 'J.G. Scaife and

A. Bennett gave us able versions of Lorenzo's speech and Tennyson's "Ulysses" respectively, both of which made great demands on intelligence of interpretation and subtleties of rhythm'. In fact, Bennett was one of the recipients of those prizes, carrying off both the Declamation Prize and the Leeds Institute Sixth Form Prize. Bennett's pace was beginning to hot up.

It didn't end there. By the winter of 1950, Bennett had become honorary secretary of the Literary and Historical Society, and so was charged with writing up the minutes. The future trustee of the National Gallery recorded that there had been three meetings so far that term, and that the subjects covered had ranged from a film strip in the Geography Room about Michelangelo to a discussion on modern poetry, and finally a round of Any Questions in which 'A panel of four members answered a number of questions ranging from politics to an abstruse question on rugby'. Writing in the *London Review of Books* almost fifty years later, one of Bennett's few criticisms of its editorial line was 'too much football'. Bennett's sporting career was never as distinguished as his academic record.

His activities were not limited to secular matters. Describing a busy term in the life of the Junior Christian League in the summer of 1951, the apparently ubiquitous A. Bennett wrote that 'Meetings were, as a whole, well attended. We have built up an active nucleus of regulars, including Swallow, Bushell, Sharpe and Norton.' He even rounded off his summing-up with an unexpected and uncharacteristic attempt at arm-twisting. 'Our meetings, which have included film strips, Bible study and talks, are open to all in the Junior School – and don't forget – we want to see *you* at the CU [Christian Union].'

He was on safer ground with his continuing commitment to the Literary and Historical Society. In their second meeting, Bennett combined several of his interests by proposing the motion 'That Private Enterprise is more likely to further the cause of Christianity than a society based on the economic doctrines of Communism'. The motion was carried by a small majority. Their third meeting 'consisted of a series of discussions on various topics, ranging from Mr Brymer's modest assertion that he was a fried egg, defying anyone to disprove it'. Ten years later, in *Beyond the Fringe*, philosophy again featured prominently. Jonathan Miller as Bertrand Russell, for example: ' "Moore," I said, "have you any apples in that basket?" "No," he replied, and smiled seraphically as was his wont. I decided to try a different tack. "Moore," I said, "have you then *some* apples in that basket?" . . . and from that day forth we remained the closest of friends.' And so on.

By Christmas 1951 Bennett was a senior prefect, no doubt singing the school song, 'Forty Years On', as lustily as any others. His face is clearly seen in a photograph of scholarship winners, preferring to look, grinning shyly, at his fellow winners than straight at the camera. He is, of course, on the margin, behind a well-groomed head of hair, parted on the left. He won a Senior City Scholarship, as well as emerging from the General Certificate with a scholarship in History and Latin. As if these were not garlands enough, he also won the Leeds Institute Sixth Form Prize for English and the Templeton Scripture Prize. When HMQ declares in *A Question of Attribution* that 'For me, Heaven must be something of a comedown', Bennett may have been thinking of his own experiences as a sixth-former.

Alan Bennett has always talked dismissively of himself as an adolescent. In an article written years later for his college magazine, he described himself, on leaving school, as 'authoritarian, High Anglican and, it shames me to say it, an unthinking Tory'. It was only, he says, 'a saving streak of silliness that stopped me from turning out to be John Selwyn Gummer'. Years later, he talked equally dismissively about Leeds Modern, telling Humphrey Carpenter: 'It wasn't old. It wasn't new. There was not even a kindly schoolmaster who put books into my hands. I think one may have tried to, but it was not until I was sixteen, and a bit late in the day.'

In one of the very few references anywhere to his teachers, Bennett recalled for his Oxford college register how he had 'a moment of revelation one afternoon in French when the master, faced with some persistent obtuseness in the class, had suddenly laid his head on the desk and cried, not at all comically, "Oh, why am I wasting my life in this godforsaken hole?" ' Bennett says that he 'saw for the first time that the teachers were people with lives not unlike my own' who might well see the school – 'which I'd never thought very much about one way or another' – as a prison. If that was the case, why, then, all this straining after secretaryships and debating societies? Why the enthusiastic contributions to the school magazine? Perhaps because, like any writer in training, he was using the school's abundant facilities simply as a scratch-board on which to sharpen his own skills.

In *Telling Tales*, Bennett admits that as a child he got on better with his mother than with his father. Spending all his time either in church or the library, he felt his father had little time for him, perhaps because 'there are none of the conventional rows he's had with my brother at the same age and who is already asserting his independence in the stock ways, smoking on the quiet, coming home tipsy once or twice'. But what Bennett's choleric descriptions of his early life generally omit is the picture that emerges of him from the pages of *The Owlet*: of an opinionated, articulate, naturally intelligent and communicative young man. He seems extremely self-possessed, and nowhere near as hunched or crab-like as he has made himself out to be. His jokes are funny, his seriousness commands attention, and his academic success is remarkable, relentless and apparently effortless. Of course, something had to give. While most adolescent boys would have been focusing their energies on a faltering and ultimately futile examination of the opposite sex, or their own, Bennett was looking beyond that, gazing out at the world and deciding which bits of it he belonged to, and which bits he did not. Of course, he may well have been indulging in adolescent fumblings too, but the pages of *The Owlet* were no place for the display of such trophies. What matters is that Bennett made many friends at Leeds Modern, besides covering himself in academic glory.

The Owlet always recorded examination results in full, and those winning places to university were habitually entered in the column marked 'School Successes', but in the summer of 1952 even the death of George VI could not restrain a note of pride creeping into the prose. 'This is the largest number of successful entries to the older Universities in the history of the school,' it declared. The total number was five: small, perhaps, compared with Leeds Grammar's fourteen, but significant none the less. Continuing the school's slight preference for Cambridge over Oxford, only Bennett's pal Tony Cash had gone for the Dark Blues, winning a place at St Edmund Hall. For the others, Tetley and Brenan were off to Emmanuel, and P. Lancaster, who seemed to be good at most things, had won an open exhibition to Selwyn. Bennett was down to go to Sidney Sussex.

In the meantime, he underwent national service. Having enlisted at Pontefract Barracks, Bennett spent his thirteen months in the Intelligence Corps at Cambridge translating Chekhov and Dostoevsky, and then went on to Bodmin. 'It wasn't like being in the army at all,' he told Roy

Plomley in 1967. 'We didn't wear uniforms. We used to live in a country house just outside Cambridge, and it was one of the happiest periods of my life.' For many of a religious persuasion, the rituals of basic infantry training come as no shock to the system. 'I actually didn't even mind the drill,' he told Paul Vallely in 1977. Training also included being transported from Pontefract to Totley, south-west of Sheffield, to practise their gun skills. 'You knew you were coming to Sheffield because you could taste it in your mouth, it was so gritty and sooty,' he said years later. With relations between Britain and the Soviet Union at an all-time low, Bennett was selected for the Joint Services Russian Language course, presumably with the intention that he might be able to unpick the martial intentions of the Communist invaders if it came to that. Rather than wear out their heels doing square-bashing, the best minds, including Bennett's, were sent to study Russian, up to A-level and beyond, at Cambridge. In Stephen Gilbert's unofficial biography of Dennis Potter, *Fight and Kick and Bite* (1995), Bennett described the selection process. 'You knew to say "Can I be on the Russian course?" because it was a fairly cushy number and otherwise you might be on the front line. That was urgent when I went in because the Korean War was going on and a lot of people in my intake were sent East. You didn't even have to do a test to go on the course; you just had to have School Certificate. They tested you after six or eight weeks, and if you passed high enough you were issued with a Woking suit [i.e. civvies], which was poor quality, and you went on to university. There were some people who were so agin the army in every respect they wouldn't wear their own nicer clothes in the army's time. That was the hard-line approach.' During the course he was treated as an officer cadet, but when it was over he went to Mons officer training school, where he was failed. He returned to England, this time to Maresfield in Sussex.

The absurdities of army life have brought out the best in many a humorist. When he wrote his own programme notes for *Beyond the Fringe*, he summed up his experiences as a conscript by claiming that 'psychological maladjustments dogged his army career, when he failed his commission for persistently folding his blankets badly'. Many survived their call-up years by finding a like-minded soul with whom to share the joke. Bennett made friends with another bright young lad, born in 1933, educated at Kingston Grammar School and on his way to Emmanuel College, Cambridge, called Michael Frayn. The two collaborated in the writing of mess-room cabarets, in the course of which, as Frayn told Humphrey Carpenter, Bennett used to impersonate 'a minor canon at a provincial cathedral, taking morning muster parade . . . Alan just imagined that they would do the same at cathedral [as they did in the army] – would check all the dons and minor canons.' And he did so in a 'preposterous' ecclesiastical accent.

'I think that if I'd become an officer I would have been much more a fully fledged member of the establishment than I ever became,' he told Terry Coleman in 1989. When the conscripts went back to the Intelligence Corps, Bennett was a private, while Michael Frayn was an officer. Bennett remembers the last few weeks at Maresfield as being 'much worse than basic training. I remember a sergeant made me scrub out a urinal with my bare hands.'

The upper limits of the academic world were pretty binary in those days. Michael Frayn went off to Cambridge, where he would begin his distinguished journalistic career by editing the student newspaper *Varsity* (and handing it over to, of all people, Michael Winner). Perhaps Bennett wished, with the arrogance of youth, to find his own way to university rather than be guided there by school. Or maybe he felt he was now mature enough to win an award – with all the financial advantages to his parents that would accrue if he did. Possibly he felt he had been 'robbed' of an award the first time, and wanted to prove himself right. Or, as he himself said, he genuinely thought that 'having had a taste of Cambridge, however much I liked the place, it might be sensible to go to Oxford instead'. He also admitted later that 'I had a hopeless crush on one of my fellow officer cadets, who was bound for Oxford', which partly explained why he decided to switch from Cambridge to Oxford. He took the examination in December 1953, and won an Open Waugh scholarship to Exeter College to read History. Oxford was to be his home for the rest of that turbulent decade.

3

Mr Bennett, Mr B. and Mr G. were drunk last night: Oxford, 1954–1960

On 6 June 1957 the undergraduate newspaper *Cherwell* asked its sketch-writers to compose lightning portraits of Oxford's colleges. Lincoln, for example, described itself as 'one of the friendliest colleges in the university'. Trinity said: 'We refuse to take life too seriously.' Christ Church let forth the perennial lament of the ludicrously overprivileged that it was 'more maligned and misunderstood than any other college'. The Exeter College sketch-writer seems to have got it about right when he wrote: 'There is nothing particular about us but we are exceptional.'

Exeter College was not one of the colleges which sapped too many of the resources of the *Cherwell*'s editorial staff. Exeter men – and in the days before mixed colleges they all were men – rarely felt tempted to broadcast their affairs to the wider world, and so most college events were for the consumption of college members alone. Nor had Exeter College detained the writer of the *Baedeker Guide to Great Britain*, H.A. Piehler, for very long on his visit to Oxford. In the course of a routine trot around the sixteenth-century front quad, he notes Sir George Gilbert Scott's 1857 chapel, in the style of the Ste-Chapelle at Paris, and the view of the Bodleian and Divinity School from the Fellows' Garden, and then strides stiffly out, to write in greater length about Jesus College.

Exeter College was founded in 1314 by Walter de Stapledon, Bishop of Exeter, as the first college for laymen. Through the gatehouse entrance in the north-east corner of the quad, one can still see part of the old 1432 gate tower, known as Palmer's Tower, and on the south side is the very fine hall, with its collar-beam roof of Spanish chestnut divided into six bays. College alumni included R.D. Blackmore, the author of the Victorian bodice-ripper *Lorna Doone*, as well as the artist William Morris and *The Hobbit* and *Lord of the Rings* author J.R.R. Tolkien, but in 1954 its most famous past member was undoubtedly Roger Bannister, who ran the four-minute mile that year. It also boasted the then Archbishop of Canterbury, Geoffrey Fisher, who proceeded at a slower pace. There were one or two left-wing firebrands in the college itself, such as Philip French, the future film critic of the *Observer*, whose speeches in the Union attracted appreciative write-ups, but in general the college was a pretty inward-looking place. The bursar admitted in 1956 that 'the financial outlook for a college so poorly endowed as Exeter is never completely free from anxiety'. The *Cherwell* sketch-writer added: 'We are mostly heartless and the bar is the centre of college life.' This was probably true of most colleges, especially in those less promiscuous days, though the good fellows of Exeter at least admitted what few others dared. The bar is the barometer of most colleges, and the junior common room is its natural spill-tray. In the junior common room, or JCR, men would sit, chat, browse through newspapers, head off to the bar, get drunk, come back . . . Thus was the pace of college life regulated.

Nowadays, it's hard to disagree with Philip French that the JCR of Exeter College 'looks like the waiting room at Kinshasa Airport', but in the 1950s it had the sedate grandeur of a gentleman's club. It was a long room, with fireplaces at either end and panelled booths in between. One of the best-read volumes in college was also one of its most heavily annotated: the JCR Suggestions Book. It looked like a Victorian ledger: nearly 200 heavy foolscap pages bound in leather. Members would write on the right-hand page, almost always in fountain pen, and with a formality – and a grammatical and syntactical accuracy – so lightly worn as to be unthinkable fifty years later.

Just as the JCR book served as a steam valve wherein gentlemen could plea for small, life-improving changes, the right of reply lay with the JCR secretary, who would answer every suggestion, usually with a simple 'Noted', at other times with a longer, though always pithy, entry. Of course, even the word 'Noted' can imply several shades of humour, depending on the vehemence with which the suggestion has been put forward.

Most of the suggestions are pretty humdrum, and reading them now you could be forgiven for thinking that what most of these men were really appealing for was their mother, or a woman to take her place. 'Sir, There is no towel in the Fourth Quad, Yours etc . . .', reads one, or 'Sir, May we please have new nail-brushes? Yours etc . . .' 'Dear Sir, Could we please have some brown boot polish and the brushes wherewith to rub it off and put it on.' 'Sir, There were no tumblers for my milk at tea-time today. Can we have some please?' All were signed. Writing anonymously in the book was most definitely 'Not On', or even 'Off'.

Bennett's first entry, from Michaelmas Term 1954, is brief, serious, cautious and slightly pompous: 'Sir,' he wrote, 'In view of the abysmally low standard of university literature, could the JCR not purchase weekly a copy of *Granta* – the journal of another – and certainly more literate – place? Yours etc. A. Bennett.' So much for that, but the following entry picks up his point. 'Sir,' wrote M.B.,* 'If Mr Bennett thinks he is entitled to continue to satisfy, at the JCR's expense, the craving for lofty literature which he acquired as a Pongo in some Fenland barrack, I see no reason why I should not also have my "Dandy", which I have missed ever so much since demob.' It is one thing to write in a Suggestions Book. But to see oneself referred to as a 'Pongo' ('an English serviceman', Eric Partridge, *Dictionary of Slang*) suggests that one has reached a certain status.

Later, Bennett wrote a tart – and, even in those golden days of unlocked doors and unchained bicycles, doubtless futile – request that whoever stole his Bush portable wireless return it, and a rather indignant note 'thanking' whoever 'borrowed' his gown for 'returning' it.

In a memoir of his college days, written years later for the Exeter College Register, Bennett mentions some of the places and characters with whom he shared his days. One was the shop Vardoc – gone now, of course – which satisfied his hunger for 'ties in bright plain colours'. (In fact, every representation of Bennett in the Suggestions Book portrays him as wearing a bow tie, though this may of course be whimsical.) Bennett describes Exeter as a 'cosy' college. He notes its unexceptional

*Since it was difficult to reach some of the contributors to the Suggestions Book, I have decided to refer to them by their initials.

sporting and academic record, but also remembers the JCR as being full of 'jokes and bawdy', more Inner Temple than Athenaeum, with a 'tolerance, geniality and indolence' which he found 'intoxicating and highly addictive'. All this despite saying in his opening remarks that 'the place inspires little nostalgia (and indeed I find myself reluctant to recall it)'.

Bennett's memoir is of a man about to sit at high table. He notes the presence of distinguished dons like Professors Dawkins and Mavrogordato, as well as the gregarious Nevill Coghill. He met a former college member or old Exonian, Joel Sayre, who had known Scott and Zelda Fitzgerald, which left him amazed and awe-struck that his little world had somehow clashed with that of the author of *The Great Gatsby*. It was a certainly a step on from what he had until then assumed would be his only literary claim to fame, that he had delivered meat on his bicycle in Leeds to a Mrs Fletcher, the future mother-in-law of T.S. Eliot.

In the summer of 1955 Alan Bennett made his first contribution to *The Owlet* as an Old Modernian. The writer apologised for leaving the writing of his letter until the last night of term, but 'Dear Mr Editor', the letter began, in traditional style, 'it is only at such times as this . . . that I realise how slowly, how imperceptibly the university binds one to herself, and to her peculiar way of life'. No doubt one of the reasons he loved his new life was that 'Oxford is the place where the unexpected is always happening in a rather grand way . . . Last term I came round the corner into Radcliffe Square to see the Emperor of Abyssinia strolling into the Bodleian, with nothing to show for it except a rather large car and a few people idly watching; or again, I remember being rushed off to Blenheim by someone I'd only met ten minutes before, to spend a glorious afternoon looking round the house, and dashing back to Oxford, writing an essay on the way to arrive just in time for my tutorial.' When Philip French, Bennett's contemporary at Exeter, says that the two books on every undergraduate's reading list were *Brideshead Revisited* and the recently published – and diametrically opposed – *Lucky Jim*, it looks as though Bennett had found Evelyn Waugh's unashamedly sentimental version of Oxford more seductive than Kingsley Amis's more austere, post-war version.

For many students, a holiday job is important not just as a source of income but also of anecdotes, though most would probably find that one period spent working in a crematorium would furnish them with all the stories they needed. Bennett spent not one but two Oxford vacations cutting the grass at Leeds Crematorium. Cemeteries and graveyards have always figured prominently in his northern plays. In his third year he moved out to Summertown, where he lodged with Richard Wortley, who would go on to be a producer at the BBC. Their landlady, a Mrs Munsey, had a middle-aged daughter called Dulcie, 'who was excessively shy and who bolted noisily into the back room if she ever heard one coming'. He also remembered 'a large old cat which used to crap in the bath. In the way of things when one is young, none of this seemed at all strange to me.'

Mrs Munsey used to prepare a huge breakfast every morning for her two lodgers, of fried egg, two rashers of bacon, baked beans and a slice of fried bread. Bennett, who preferred a more skeletal 'cup of tea and a bit of toast', hadn't the heart – or the nerve – to tell Mrs Munsey that her hearty daily offerings were not being gratefully wolfed down, and so 'I eventually evolved a routine whereby I parcelled the lot up in yesterday's *Times* (stolen from the JCR), which I deposited in the used-ticket receptacle at the bus stop in Banbury Road. So skilled did I become at this daily deposition that I could punt the parcel in as I cycled by without even slowing down.' In essence, it recalls one of Bennett's best-known stories of when he was dining at Magdalen high table a few years later and found to his distress that, as soon as the Fellows had sat down, his chair leg had become caught up in one of the batwings of his BA gown. (This gown was a bigger version of that dandyish item, the scholar's gown, 'something with a swing to it', which was, he claimed, the only reason he had wanted a scholarship to Exeter in the first place.) In a story that is so visually appealing that it must have been 'improved' for posterity at some point, Bennett – his arms helplessly pinioned and too shy to explain his predicament or to appeal for assistance – recalls waving away dish after appealing dish from the college servants, simply because he couldn't reach any of them, whereupon his neighbour said softly to him: 'You know, if you're a vegetarian, they'll do you something special.'

Bennett says he owes his academic success at Exeter to a series of forty or fifty correspondence cards, on to which he had written all his headings and quotations. He says he carried half a dozen or so of these cards with him wherever he went, so that he soon knew the contents off by heart. He also did what all students who mean business do, and looked long and hard at old examination papers until he had 'reduced the type of questions to a set of formulae and practised turning any question round so that it fitted the material I had on my cards'.

The technique recalls a playful piece he wrote for *The Owlet*, entitled 'Examinationship (or the art of succeeding at examinations without actually cheating)', which appeared in the summer of 1951, with a nod to Stephen '*One-Upmanship*' Potter, when Bennett was seventeen. It was the sort of essay that only someone who had real confidence in his abilities – what his mother would have referred to as 'a swot' – would have dared write. (And had he sent it to *Punch*, the editor would have had no excuse but to print it.) First, he wrote, 'it is essential to appear completely unconcerned at the prospect of the examination. Though you may be on the verge of a nervous breakdown, let your outward appearance give no hint of the inner turmoil.' He also suggests ways to, in the modern parlance, 'psych out' your fellow examinees. 'At some singularly inopportune moment . . . stiffen suddenly, bang down knife and fork, slap your neighbour vigorously on the back and ejaculate "Oedipus theory".' This, Bennett assures us, guarantees impressive results: 'not only is your rival incapacitated during the afternoon, and prostrated with indigestion (and thus can do no revision), but the seeds of an inferiority complex are sown. These seeds can be cultivated until the poor unfortunate comes to regard himself as the lowest and most ignorant worm crawling on the face of the earth.'

During the examination itself, he advises making 'frequent (and unnecessary) journeys for extra paper'. And the final and most devastating blow is 'to finish five, if not ten minutes before time, loudly ask permission to leave and make a carefree exit'. However, he cautions, this tactic 'is to be used only by the more experienced and knowledgeable – its use by someone less so implies not so much the simplicity of the paper as one's inability to answer it'.

It is an ingenious piece of writing: elegant, well paced and, clearly, the sort of thing that holds up a mirror to the tactics to which all clever students feel they have access. The more helpless creatures can only think of various ways of wrecking exams for everyone by falling asleep, feigning collapse or screaming out loud once outside the examination hall. Bennett was one who knew better, and that knowledge is not unattractive.

Bennett the undergraduate also makes his fair share of 'serious' comments in the JCR Suggestions Book. But whereas his first note, concerning *Granta*, was written with a sober hand, his second was anything but. Bennett has clearly been drinking, and is possibly, too, shaking from laughter: 'Sir,' he writes, 'I protest. Someone is in my room at 11.45 p.m. and I can't get in. Why? (And who?)' The response from the JCR secretary is the typically terse 'Throw them out'. The following note, not by Bennett, gets to the heart of the problem. 'Sir, There are WOMEN everywhere, not only in 3.1. Have you anything to say about that?' The secretary, the admirably pithy S.K. ('Suchie') Guram, responds: 'I'm SORRY – it won't happen again.' Which, no doubt, it did.

These entries have a timeless quality. Not because they are not of their time – they most certainly are – but very few of them are ever date-stamped, so, reading them now almost fifty years later, one never knows quite where one is. Several pages could have been covered in a single night, depending on how high-spirited everyone was feeling. Or it's possible – though unlikely – that the book could have been left untouched for several days. The Suggestions Book was the great seductress of college life. Almost everyone – at least, anyone who fancied he was funny – wanted a bit of it. It was, if you must, a fountain-pen version of an Internet chat room, with comments and suggestions whistling in from all over the place, and members no doubt queuing impatiently to have their say. References could be to something written a few lines back, or several pages earlier, or to something entirely new. What makes the book so interesting is when it runs off the rails – which it does regularly – and into territory well beyond the limited scope of suggestions.

Years later, Bennett made much of feeling tongue-tied in the presence of the rapid-fire verbal wit of Peter Cook or Jonathan Miller, preferring to go away and write his thoughts down. The Suggestions Book was surely, then, the perfect arena for him. It reads like a slow-motion transcript of a college 'smoker' (a late-night college revue), many of which were staged regularly in the JCR, and to which Bennett eventually became a real-life contributor.

Occasionally, men felt sufficiently moved to draw pictures to illustrate their point. Some rare creatures seemed equally comfortable with words and pictures. One such was the great college cartoonist

Derek Whitelock. Take this entry, which starts off as a humble proposal and ends with an intriguing cartoon: 'Sir, May we have a college brothel under the bar?' The suggestion, which certainly puts paid to the hint that undergraduates in those days had higher thoughts on their minds than sex, picks out various college 'characters', and each sentence is illustrated with a hilarious little line drawing. 'One can imagine the scene: Mr G. is dancing with a bad lot; Mr T. finding joy at last; Mr Philip French [glowering, and with a spiky beard] talking to a Rumanian journalist gone wrong.' The final picture is of 'Mr Alan Bennett being whipped by a Nubianne'. There follows a picture of a huge, Amazonian (albeit African) woman with giant breasts and a flowery dress, brandishing a cat-o'-nine-tails. And there is Alan Bennett, with an exaggeratedly long chin, a bow tie and round spectacles. He is on all fours, looking hungrily and nervously up at her, with his bottom in the air. The cartoon appeared in Michaelmas (i.e. winter) Term 1956, the first term of Bennett's third year.

The book certainly seems to have borne witness to the huge amount of pent-up sexual energy circulating in that all-male preserve. Of course, the hard core of the book was a clique: perhaps twelve names, with about fifteen more making cameo appearances. But in a small college like Exeter, that was a representative sample of undergraduates. It certainly presents a recognisable picture of Alan Bennett.

Take the physical descriptions of him. To some he is 'Bennett, the Bohemian portraitist'; to others he is 'A certain flaxen-haired youth'. His 'beautiful blond hair' is once described as 'the colour of a ripe octogenarian grapefruit out of season'. Was Bennett some sort of college pin-up? Certainly his features were instantly recognisable. His fair hair, glasses and young-fogeyish style of dressing were notable even then – and many years before the press took an interest in him. Bennett's looks are commented on with more regularity than almost anyone else in the JCR clique, and yet the tone throughout remains so overwhelmingly – at times almost stiflingly – ironic that one can never be sure one has mastered the sub-text of what game these clever young men are playing. No one is ever raised high without simultaneously having the rise taken out of them. Like a hall of mirrors, any proposal in this book, be it ever so humble ('Sir, Could the spring on the south door of this JCR be properly repaired?'), seems like a reflection of another reflection. And, of course, the exact point on which these little jokes once turned was lost long ago. These gentlemen, who are all, in their different ways, discovering their voice, are taking it in turns to take the piss: or, as Bennett rephrased it a few years later, the pith. In undergraduate circles, to be ridiculed is not the same as being 'abused'. The very opposite, in fact. Bennett's unlikely knack for making friends, so marked at school, has made itself felt here too.

Whitelock, the cartoonist, has the most to say: 'Craftsey hay-thatched Admiral Bennett' can also be 'Alan "Cannonball" Bennett, dynamic, goal-whamming centre forward from Leeds, describing himself as a "common, working chap" sanitary engineer'. Or: 'Meanwhile – on a grassy hill near Liversedge, a flaxen-headed ploughboy is dreaming of the poetry that will one day make him great. It is Bysshe Bennett.' This inspired description is accompanied by a picture of Bennett lying down surrounded by flowers, watched over by a cow.

Nowadays, the nearest most people get to single-sex worlds is either in prison or in a monastery. (Philip French caps this by describing the atmosphere at Oxford in the 1950s as being 'like a monastery in which all the monks have taken a vow of unchastity'.) There were women in Oxford at the time, of course, but they were still curios. You could be sent down for being caught with a woman in your room, let alone your bed, after seven o'clock at night. One could point out that women were allowed into college from noon onwards, which gave undergraduates a good seven hours – surely enough for most purposes? – but in formal terms, with access so restricted, the sexes were bound to view each other with suspicion. A survey printed in *Cherwell* on 6 June 1957 called 'Sex Wars' asked respondents: 'Do you find the opposite sex at the university attractive as a whole?' Seventy-seven per cent of men and seventy-two per cent of women replied 'No'. No wonder, then, that the gentlemen of Exeter were writing things in their Suggestions Book like 'Sir, There's a female person in Mr J-B's bed. Honest.' And 'Sir, Mr R. has gone to London on a dirty weekend. This is his third dirty weekend in ten days!'

No doubt, too, that some members of the college may have turned inward upon each other, but if they did they were too smart to let on in the book. There are no gay confessions. Instead, the suppression and repression took the form of knowingly coquettish, self-ridiculing passes, such as 'Sir, I have just asked Mr K. to go dancing with me and he accepted' and 'Dear Sir, Isn't Mr M. nice? He has got the Veronica Lake haircut and really does things for me. But unfortunately he appears most uncooperative. You, I believe, live below him. Could you not try to educate him in the behaviour appropriate to a good college man. Thank you, sir. I know you will do your best.' Wherever the truth lay, they were all having far too much fun to say.

Alan Bennett has worked as hard as anyone to preserve his buttoned-up image. It was only years later, in a glancing remark in one of his diaries, that he acknowledged that self-abuse had played as large a part in his life as in any other boy's. He has never suggested that he excited sexual interest in others: it would not be like him to say. And yet take the lock of hair, actual hair – still as blond as ever – which appears on one page of the Michaelmas 1956 JCR Suggestions Book. 'Dear Sir,' writes a college member. 'Someone has Raped a Lock of A. Bennett's hair. But the fringe is still immaculate. Yrs, D.W.G. – PS I feel it is my duty to keep you informed of what happens ON THE FRINGE.' Not a great joke, but a nice posy for destiny to scoop up.

Derek Whitelock was often in attendance: 'People are fingering Mr Bennett's hair. Mr G. is sinking fast – of such little scenes is College Life made up,' he wrote contentedly. And later: 'Do you realise, Mr President Sir, that an Unhealthy Affair is developing between Mr Bennett & Mr K. Even now they are sprawled like human spaghetti in the corner, and as the firelight glimmers among the flaxen strands of Mr Bennett's hair, Mr K.'s jaws slaver and his fearful laugh reverberates rumbustiously.'

Alan Bennett, the object of sexual attention? Bennett has for so long maintained that he was never, in today's lingo, 'sexy' that we have tended to take him at his word. But good-looking people attract attention. Bennett has referred to himself dismissively in recent years as 'the blond', usually to try to explain away his presence inside the *London Review of Books* rather than in physical terms. But at Exeter it seems he really was 'the blond'. Whitelock's last entry is: 'I say, Sir, Mr Bennett is titillating the excessively virile members of the JCR isn't he? How often these days do we hear his falsetto laughs or squawks of ecstasy mingling with hoarse, randy guffaws as he writhes in a sort of sexual scrimmage with rugger men among overturned furniture. And very nice too.'

Whitelock is choosing his words more carefully than we might imagine. It is, of course, a 'sort of' sexual scrimmage: not the real thing. Anyone who has endured life as an undergraduate will recognise that Bennett was one of the college aesthetes: an Aesthetes' XI which once even challenged the college hockey team to a match, a fixture from which the latter pulled out, and were ritually mocked in the Suggestions Book for doing so. There are, of course, no witnesses from the hockey team to make their case. Writing witty, pithy, sketchy numbers in fountain pen was not one of their strengths. One occasionally makes out, in an almost illegible scrawl, statements like 'F— B*nn*tt', and 'F—' many of his aesthete mates too, but is this the final, ragged gasp of a long night of ribaldry, or the inarticulate scrawl of a thickly haired arm? It is unclear who is writing, but it is always the drink that is talking.

There are other witnesses to Bennett's popularity. R.S. wrote, with magnificent nonchalance: 'Sir, Mr K. has just raped Mr Bennett in the JCR. Don't you think that this is off? Could we have a magazine rack in the JCR as appended below? At present they are in a nice tidy pile in the morning but someone wanting the bottom one scatters the others all over the place.'

'Sir, Mr Bennett, Mr B. and Mr G. were drunk last night,' wrote another contributor. No doubt Bennett and his friends often were: such is the prerogative of undergraduates, after all. 'The time is 9.30 p.m.,' wrote J.P.S. 'Great sounds of jubilation are issuing from the chapel. Mr Bennett has just rushed at Mr T., crying: "I must beat you." Don't you think this college has everything?'

It obviously did, for a number of people, for a while. Too much, in fact, for the college's 'character', resident Victorian and future cleric, Brian Dominick Frederick Titus Brindley. 'Sir, What has come over this college?' he wrote across two pages in shocked tones. 'When I came up its sex-life was tolerably restrained both in its extent and in its conversational importance. Now this is almost the sole topick [sic] of discussion, apparently the sole off-duty activity of members of the JCR.' So wrote the future food columnist and feature writer of the *Catholic Herald* and *Church Times*. To the politically alert undergraduate Philip French, the constant playfulness and flippancy were tedious distractions. 'Sir,' he wrote in the book, 'I would suggest that a large slate or blackboard be placed in the corner of the JCR for all the childish, banal and, frequently, obscene remarks that appear in this book. In this way they could be erased daily and no permanent record exist of this fatuity. This book itself should be rescued for bona fide suggestions such as the one that I am here making.'

Some hope. The impression one gets is of a never-ending game of literary consequences, or of a college narrative in which everyone wants to tell the story. Oxbridge teaching terms are the shortest of any university: a mere eight weeks. And yet so much is packed into those terms. Perhaps these jottings were the work of mere minutes. And yet some are in Latin or Greek. Some stretch over several pages. Others – many of them by B.D.F.T. Brindley – are of intricate and ingenious cartoons, depicting appropriate inventions like a 'Gothick [of course] fruit machine' or a piece of equipment for use in the gymnasium with a 'HIGH HORSE (for coming off)', a 'PEG (for being taken down)' and so on.

A strangely portentous sketch, for example, by Whitelock (that man again), was one of an occasional series that he produced about various college characters under the banner 'Decline and Fall of Old Exonians. 2: Bysshe Bennett.' He then writes down what, long ago in Trinity Term 1956, he laughingly imagines to be the curve of Bysshe Bennett's life. 'Brilliant First, refuses fellowship to C*RIS* CH*RCH. Outs B*V*RLY NI*HO*S in *Woman's Own*. Sensational success of publications "Sense and Sensitivity", "U", "Gold and Velvet", "My Friend Graves", "Confessions of an Aesthete", "Oh My Lord!" and "Poesy and Thoughts" (a collection of poems bound in mauve vellum). Awarded R*OSEVE*T PRIZE for letters. Hailed by Godfrey W*NN as "The lonely W*OLF". Approached by M*M. Turns back on fame at 29 and becomes shepherd in Upper Swaledale. Tells reporters "I have found Truth".' Not bad, as predictions go.

Bennett has periodic breaks from the Suggestions Book, times when he appears to be concentrating on work, or perhaps on not drinking. Occasionally his suggestions are stridently and relentlessly serious, such as his interminable requests, in Trinity Term 1956, for a more varied selection of magazines. At times like these, Bennett seems, like many of his peers, to be keen to peep out from behind Oxford's thick mesh, and to catch a glimpse of the outside world. Perhaps, having been such a regular reader of Cyril Connolly's *Horizon* magazine during the 1940s, he misses it. He may have become temporarily disenchanted, or frustrated, with the picture of whimsical, somewhat mannered, effervescence that made up so much of the Suggestions Book. He may have tired of being associated with such militant aestheticism. Or he may have become bored with its personnel, with the relentless in-jokes, the name-calling and the irony.

Perhaps all he needed was to widen his circle of friends. This he certainly did in his third year. At the start of Trinity Term 1957, two unfamiliar names signed in alongside his on the second page of the Suggestions Book. It was as if he had been out hunting and returned with a prize catch. What started all this off was a humble contribution from an unsuspecting college member, which was met with the comment 'Illiteracy will get you nowhere' and signed 'Alan Shallcross'. To this was added, underneath, 'You can talk – Alan Bennett', and under that, in handwriting larger and roly-polier than was customary in the book, 'He certainly can – Russell Harty (Exoniensis)'. Harty spirals off on the next page on a new theme: 'Sah! Who was you with last night?' – a question that, like much in this seductive but one-sided history, is never answered. At times like these, the contemporary reader feels like someone trying to gauge the success of a party by poring over a lot of empty bottles, glasses and heaped ashtrays.

Bennett and Harty befriended each other in the third year. His entrance into Bennett's life certainly seems to have galvanised Bennett, whose Suggestions Book entries are a throwback to the jauntiness of his earlier student days. This time, though, the cast of players has changed. It feels more as if Bennett and his friends are looking in, amid other activities, and finding time to give others a flavour of what they are missing. Bennett's assumption of the post of JCR secretary was a testament to his popularity, but it meant he could no longer afford to write with the old abandon. Besides, Russell Harty later noted that the Suggestions Book had a rival for Bennett's attention, in the form of an ever-present bulge in his jacket. This was caused by 'a little black book wherein are jotted remarks overheard on buses, in shops, in queues'. Keep a little black book, the theory goes, and one day it will keep you. It certainly worked for Bennett.

Aware of his own shyness, Bennett was always happy to be bowled over by someone else's forthrightness, if it was expressed with an open heart. His friendship with Russell Harty followed that pattern, just as the relationship with the most important woman in his life outside his own family would in years to come. Harty, wrote Bennett, 'was immune from embarrassment'. Whereas he bundled his own parents in and out of college 'as hastily as I could, practically with sacks over their heads, praying that we wouldn't meet anyone', Harty's parents would park their white Jaguar, 'the fruit of successful Blackburn greengrocery, smack college gate'. Myrtle, his mother, 'would emerge clad in fake coat, dizzyingly high heels and plastered in make-up' while father, 'bottle-nosed and in a loud check suit, would shuffle along in the rear, enquiring of all and sundry in his impenetrable Lancashire accent the whereabouts of 'our Russell'. It need hardly be added that whereas Russell Harty 'positively paraded' his parents, at one point even throwing a cocktail party for them to which he invited several tutors, Bennett was incapable of doing the same for his own parents. 'Your dad and me can't mix,' Lilian used to say to her son. 'We've not been educated.' Bennett knew – and Russell Harty certainly knew – that it was not education which allowed for social mobility, but embarrassment. 'What keeps us in our place is embarrassment,' he said in *Dinner at Noon*.

And yet their son found a path through his crippling shyness by acting. At first, the roles he played were written out in the Suggestions Book. And he always steered clear of OUDS, the Oxford University Dramatic Society, and the ETC, the Experimental Theatre Club. But as he became more confident with his acting abilities, he took to doing JCR smoking concerts at the end of each term. As he wrote in the Exeter College Register many years later, 'drunken and bawdy affairs they were, but unintimidating too, and the audience so friendly and appreciative that it eased me gently into the business of performing on stage'.

John Cleese used to say that Cambridge student audiences were the best audiences of all, 'because they laughed hard and then they shut up', listening eagerly for more. Bennett found his audiences similarly responsive. He says that he first performed in cabaret at the Hilary Dance in 1957, in a show partly put together by Russell Harty, and that it was here that he began to perform the cod Anglican sermon that would make his name. Another clever young undergraduate, John Wells, who remembered seeing Bennett perform in one of these smokers, wrote in the *Daily Telegraph* on 25 March 1995: 'I first saw Alan Bennett some time in the late 1950s in a lecture room somewhere in north Oxford, a shy graduate in a pale tweed sports jacket and dark horn-rims sitting at the back of a roomful of wooden chairs, most of them unoccupied . . . He sat through the other acts for most of the time with his head down, one hand to his forehead, looking, I remember, very austere.'

At the time, Wells had no idea who Bennett was. He had vaguely heard about a History graduate from Exeter College who performed in cabaret, but it didn't occur to him that the serious-looking don at the back was the same man. 'Then he got up,' recalled Wells, 'walked briskly to the front and brought the house down with two monologues, one about a scientist and involving a paper bag, the other about the mother of an unusually tall debutante. Both were meticulously constructed and on an entirely different level from the rough hit-and-miss gags on offer.' Tall women later resurfaced in a sketch for the satirical TV show *BBC-3* which also found its way into *Forty Years On*, and paper bags featured in *Beyond the Fringe* as a last resort against all-out nuclear warfare. That sketch was credited to Peter Cook, though clearly it was more of a joint effort. It was clear, too, that Oxford was seeing some other stirrings around this time. In the personal column or small ads section of *Cherwell* on 3 June 1957 was a one-line announcement for 'Teddy Hall Bar, Cabaret by Dudley Moore'.

If Bennett's sermons and other one-man sketches received a rapturous response from the Oxford students, the tutors made no less secret their admiration of his academic side, and when he was vivaed – examined orally, a trauma reserved for borderline fails or Firsts – he was awarded a First. Bennett wrote in the Exeter College Register that when the results came out he had gone down for the summer and was working at the Tetley Brewery in Leeds, but one of his friends sent him a postcard with the news. Bennett's parents, unsure what it meant, went to meet him at the brewery to ask him to explain its mysterious contents. 'I'd always done well in exams in their experience so for them this was no different,' wrote Bennett in the Exeter College Register. ' "Have you come top?" Mam asked. "Is that what it means?" '

Even in 1957 the old school had not forgotten one of its great successes of recent years. A letter to the editor of *The Owlet* from G.M.J. of Brasenose College reads: 'In these days of the Bulge I see very little of the others, for they have been banished to the outer space of Iffley. Yet I am pretty sure I saw Alan Bennett on a cloud the other day!' To be remembered, and recorded still, five years after leaving school is the sign of an extremely popular character. That summer, *The Owlet* published Bennett's final contribution, written after leaving Oxford for what he thought would be the last time. 'I find it hard to resist the temptation to be nostalgic,' he wrote, 'to write a kind of spiritual biography of the last three years.'

He goes on to mourn the construction of 'the monstrous new Woolworths building in Cornmarket', though he twins that with 'the new organic chemistry block in South Parks Road' which 'rivals it in size and dullness'. Bennett's apt comparison – 'when it comes to architecture there's not much to choose between the don and the tycoon' – is the moral precursor of his principled stand against Rupert Murdoch during the 1990s.

Nevertheless, Bennett seemed genuinely moved by all that he had seen. 'I like seeing the Rolls-Bentleys drawn up outside All Souls, the Vice-Chancellor . . . the square medieval flags out on May morning – and bells, bells all the time. I like names . . . I like being able to choose between Richard Pares on eighteenth-century politics, A.J.P. Taylor and his Ford lectures, written in part on the backs of envelopes, or C. Day Lewis on Emily Dickinson.' This was Alan Bennett, aged twenty-three. 'It is good to think, as one passes them in the Turl: "There go W.H. Auden and Robert Frost." Snobbery if you like, but it is one of the delights of Oxford.' Few undergraduates can have sounded so fully formed, even in an age when it was still fashionable for young men to try to appear older.

Having thus extended himself, Bennett reins himself in. 'But I am already talking like an old man,' he continued, 'still a little resentful that I am now thrust out into the world – though this, too, may be a myth. People have been threatening me with "the world" since before I left school. The army and Oxford both cushioned the blow. What now, I wonder?' Or when will life begin? as so many of his characters have asked.

He wasn't about to find out quite yet. With a First in his pocket, Bennett took off from Victoria Station for the Continent, still in those days a relatively romantic and remote place, with his friend Russell Harty. Arriving in Venice, they stood together in the Piazza San Marco, marvelling while a full moon shone and an orchestra played Beethoven's Eighth Symphony. It was only when they got back to their modest lodgings, Harty recalled in the *Observer* on 26 March 1973, that their problems began. 'He had dropped his styptic pencil down the washbasin, and I had fused the electric lighting with my razor.' This small comedy continued until Harty sorted the landlady out with a huge bunch of red roses, whereupon 'she . . . doubled the food and halved the price'.

Back in England, Harty went to teach at Giggleswick School –

'grey and forbidding according to the Victorian ideals of scholastic architecture', as the architectural historian Sir Nikolaus Pevsner described it – while Bennett went on to Magdalen, where he joined a very different type of college: more serious, more high-minded, more academically rigorous. For his finals, Bennett had specialised in the reign of Richard II, and in the court of the childless Richard II and Anne of Luxembourg: more formal, but with 'a zest for fashion notable in its dress', writes Gervase Mathew in his book *The Court of Richard II*. Incidentally, Richard was nearly six feet tall, with thick, dark yellow hair, and 'He remained clean-shaven later than was customary, perhaps to prolong his look of adolescence'. Inspired by his charismatic History tutor Bruce McFarlane, Bennett extended his study into Richard's retinue.

Bennett was also very struck by the differences in the dining arrangements between the two colleges. As he wrote in *Writing Home*, 'Whereas Exeter was still in the era of the proscenium arch with the dons entering stage left in single file, at Magdalen it was altogether more dramatic and fluid. There the fellows made a swift dash around the cloisters before entering in a crowd through the body of the hall, streaming through the standing assembly and up to High Table as if directed by Arianne Mnouchkine or some fashionable young man from the RSC.' He tutored there, but not very satisfactorily, recreating in his own tutorials the 'tentative, awkward affair punctuated by long silences' which he had taken part in as an undergraduate. For a shy don, the theatre was a welcome alternative, though it had a parallel in the theatricality of high table at Exeter, where Bennett compared the undergraduates with the audience and the dons with the actors as they entered – 'climbed, almost – on to the stage from the mysterious backstage of the Senior Common Room'. On the stage, at any rate, there was no doubt about who was meant to be speaking, and any pauses were – ideally – part of the script.

'The only paper I ever gave on my research was on Richard II's knights,' he told Paul Taylor of the *Independent* in April 1988, in another of his famously self-denigrating stories, 'and at the end the chairman asked for questions. Total silence. Not a single one, until an undergraduate at the front leaned forward and whispered, "Could I ask you where you bought your shoes?" '

In 1959 Bennett joined a company called the Oxford Theatre

Group, in a revue called *Better Late*, directed by Stanley Daniels – who later returned to America as one of the producers of the hit sitcom *Taxi* – which was put on at the Cranston Street Hall in Edinburgh. It was Bennett's first visit to the Fringe, and although his monologues went down well enough, Daniels did not permit him to perform any version of the sermon. Determined to play his trump card, Bennett snuck in a performance on the last night: was it ambitious of him to go against his director's wishes, or diffident of him to wait so long before giving the sketch an airing? In any event, he returned to Oxford to spend another year at high table, in the Bodleian, and biting his tongue during tutorials. But the theatre bug – what he later referred to as 'a pure streak of tinsel inside me' – had not only nipped him, but others too.

Within a few years, his tutorial students would have reason to forgive Bennett his slightly faltering teaching style, even to welcome it. The reason for that lay in the success of a show that *Cherwell*'s reviews editor, Michael Billington, now chief theatre critic of the *Guardian*, reported back on in the first issue of Michaelmas Term, 8 October 1960. Strictly speaking, his brief had been to go to Edinburgh and fill a page with reviews of the university's own shows. The headline proclaimed 'Oxford theatre keeps the Fringe on top', and Billington went on to review, in glowing terms, the Oxford Theatre Group's *Vascos*, by the Lebanese writer George Schehade, as well as the Oxford and Cambridge Stage Company's *Wallenstein* by Schiller and a university production of *The Miracles*. Confidently, the article proclaimed that Oxford's actors had borne out the truth of his introductory remarks that 'The Fringe, thriving on the inadequacy of the official Festival, prospered as ever this year'. But in his last few column inches he was forced to make an important concession.

'PS,' he wrote. 'A word about the revue in which Dudley Moore (ex-Oxford musician and Clown Prince) and Alan Bennett (currently up here researching into ten years of medieval history) took part called *Beyond the Fringe* and including two Cambridge graduates. It reduced the Lyceum Theatre audiences to near-hysteria and had them clamouring vociferously for more. Even the critics confessed they had never been so sorry to see a curtain come down.' Billington could not have known it, but he had witnessed the birth of a phenomenon.

4

What did I think I was doing?

Beyond the Fringe, 1960

In 1960 the Lord Provost of Edinburgh, J. Greig Dunbar, welcomed visitors to his city's annual pageant in his introduction to the festival brochure. The Edinburgh Festival, he wrote, 'is not a Festival for the specialist nor is it a Festival for the student in search of academic abstractions. It is an assembly for all who can assess and also believe in the influence of the Arts as a major factor in world affairs.' The opening concert, conducted by Carlo Maria Giulini on Sunday 21 August (by which time this year's festival would be into its fourth week), was Verdi's Requiem. Other star performers included Victoria de los Angeles, Gennadi Rozhdestvensky and Mstislav Rostropovich. The Glyndebourne Festival Opera and the Royal Ballet were in town. Works by Sir William Walton and Francis Poulenc were to be performed. The Edinburgh Festival is, after all, one of the biggest arts festivals in the world.

As well as all these eminent performers, one page of the brochure includes photographs of two more light-hearted events. Les Frères Jacques, who occupy the lower half of the page, are four young men, in funny hats with feathers, all wearing outsized fake moustaches. Above that is a more naturalistic photograph of the cast of a late-night revue taking place at the Lyceum Theatre. Four men, in light casual wear, are pictured through two leaves of an opened window. On the left, a tall, suavely handsome man stands, cradling his elbow in the sill. He wears a tweed jacket and tie, and is smiling, half-benignly, half-mockingly, as if a wicked thought had just crossed his mind. Next to him, eyes raised either in thought or stifling a giggle, with arms lightly crossed, stands a man a foot shorter in height. On the far side, a young, somewhat unformed face set on top of a spotted bow tie, stares boldly out, unjacketed and coltishly haughty. To his right, hands in pockets, in a three-piece suit, with black-framed glasses and a neat parting, a man stares intensely at his feet. The last is Alan Bennett, and his three colleagues are Peter Cook, Dudley Moore and Jonathan Miller: together they were the cast of *Beyond the Fringe*.

The indications are that in the early months of 1960, Alan Bennett was finding certain doors beginning to creak open, and that he was seriously exploring how far beyond Oxford's confined world his sense of humour could spread. A useful litmus test in those days was the BBC Radio programme *Monday Night at Home*, which would broadcast about a dozen humorous pieces for an hour each week. Humorists such as Arthur Marshall, René Cutforth, Bernard Braden and Ivor Cutler were frequent contributors. Bennett's debut, broadcast on 30 May, was called 'Preacher Ho' and was, of course, his very popular sermon. Bennett followed that debut, on 13 June, with another monologue, 'Catch of the Season', which has not survived.

Having established his strongest card, he was given the opportunity to play it a few months later when he was invited to make a return visit to Edinburgh, though not this time as a Fringe performer. The festival director, Rupert Ponsonby (Eton, Trinity College, Oxford), and his assistant, John Bassett (Bedales, Wadham College, Oxford), were looking for conscripts to stage a daring raid on one of the Fringe's most cherished assets: comedy. Essentially, the Fringe had so conspicuously outperformed the festival in terms of humour during the late 1950s that Ponsonby had decided to book a series of late-night revues, starting in 1958 with the musical comedienne Anna Russell. In 1959 Ponsonby scored a major hit by booking Michael Flanders and Donald Swann, with their charming and generally inoffensive revue *At the Drop of a Hat*. But for 1960 Ponsonby and Bassett decided to book three separate acts for a week at a time. The first act was to be Louis Armstrong, but the immortal Satchmo's agent decided to pull the gig. As Ponsonby told Humphrey Carpenter:

Eventually, Armstrong's agent said: 'Look, I can't find any other British dates for him, and it's not worth coming across just for that.' So at a rather late stage we were stuck. And because I'd been pretty irked by the constant theft of our thunder by clever undergraduates from Oxford and Cambridge, on the Fringe, I said to Johnny Bassett: 'Let's put on our own revue; let's beat them at their own game.'

Bennett wrote to the BBC on 16 August 1960, by which time he was already rehearsing for the new show in Edinburgh. The letter is handwritten in blue ballpoint on light blue A5 paper. The address was given as 17 Cornwall Street, Edinburgh. The addressee was 'BBC Talks Department'. 'Dear Sir,' it read, 'I would very much like to use a section of a sermon, entitled "Preacher Ho", which I recorded for *Monday Night at Home*, in a revue to be presented during the festival here. I hope this can be arranged. Yours faithfully, Alan Bennett.' The reply, dated 19 August, was from the Head of Copyright. 'Dear Sir,' it said, 'In reply to your letter of 16th August referring to your sermon PREACHER HO, the rights belong to you and the BBC would not object to your using it in any way you wish.'

The origins of this legendary show have been much discussed, and are still misunderstood to this day. Ronald Bergan, in his book *Beyond the Fringe . . . And Beyond*, isolated the main strands of myth-making in his opening sentence with the statement: 'True or false? *Beyond the Fringe* was a Cambridge revue performed by four young amateur undergraduates on the Edinburgh Festival Fringe.' He then goes on to sort fact from fiction. *Beyond the Fringe* was, essentially, a showcase for the party pieces of four prodigiously gifted individuals, with here and there an ensemble piece thrown in. All were graduates, two from Oxford and two from Cambridge, and all the happy beneficiaries of a perceived imbalance in the fortunes of the Edinburgh Festival and its raucous offspring, the Edinburgh Fringe.

In fact, the myth is part of the story. *Beyond the Fringe* might have seemed like an undergraduate show because it felt so fresh and young. If people assumed that all the performers were from Cambridge, it was probably because they acted so well together that it seemed like a top number from the Cambridge Footlights. And if it seemed like a Fringe show, well, maybe that was because it had the bite and wit that most people associated with the Fringe, rather than the more staid festival.

John Bassett is a man more generous at spotting talent in others than recognising it in himself. While at Oxford, his jazz band, the Bassett Hounds, had included the organ scholar from Magdalen College, Dudley Moore (Dagenham High and Magdalen College, Oxford), who had been making his name by performing brilliantly inventive and wildly irreverent pastiches on almost any keyboard instrument. Bassett also knew of Jonathan Miller and Peter Cook, both of whom had dazzled their fellow undergraduates at Cambridge. The wit of Jonathan Miller (St Paul's School and St John's College, Cambridge) was weirdly physical, his words diving and swooping with him. Peter Cook (Radley and Pembroke College, Cambridge) specialised in constructing tottering verbal edifices that no one could possibly match. Miller and Cook had both made names for themselves while at Cambridge. Miller had flitted into two Footlights shows: *Out of the Blue* in 1954 and *Between the Lines* in 1955, earning rave reviews from, among others, Harold Hobson of the *Sunday Times*. But whereas Miller's mind was, even then, split between the musical theatre and the operating theatre, Peter Cook had found the Footlights a home from home, and he dominated its professional and social life, featuring heavily in *The Last Laugh* in 1959 and – a show built more in his image – *Pop Goes Mrs Jessop* in 1960. Where Miller was a fairly frequent contributor to *Monday Night at Home* – the very programme on which Bennett appeared in 1960 – in the late 1950s Cook went straight for the bright lights and wrote most of two West End shows for Kenneth Williams. *Pieces of Eight* was staged at the Apollo Theatre in 1959: how many undergraduates in those days could claim that the reason they were late with their essay was because they were writing a West End show? The successor to that, *One Over the Eight*, went to the Duke of York Theatre in 1961. John Bassett had thus grouped together four of the outstanding Oxbridge performers from the last six years, and who were all able and willing to collaborate on a show for that coming August.

It is interesting to note that when Michael Billington, in his Edinburgh review for *Cherwell*, referred to Dudley it was by the appellation 'Clown Prince'. Bennett, described as 'currently up here researching' rather than by some more familiar tag, was still, to some extent, a less well-known quantity – unless you had been one of his fellow undergraduates at Exeter College. Bassett had also heard that Alan Bennett had established a reputation for 'doing funny turns' at late-night cabaret shows, which was just the sort of slot they were looking for. When he appeared on *Desert Island Discs* in 1967, Bennett told Roy Plomley that he had seen Jonathan Miller perform when the Cambridge Footlights came to Oxford and Peter Cook in the later Footlights shows. He also clarified whether he had known Moore before *Beyond the Fringe* by telling a revealing little anecdote at his own expense, that while they were both at Oxford, Bennett the postgraduate had received a note from Dudley Moore the undergraduate asking if he would like to audition for him for a cabaret evening which he was organising. 'I wrote back very high-handedly,' said Bennett in 1967, 'and said, no, I wouldn't audition, but I would perform.' There was some hint of potential internal strife, too, when Bennett turned up at the show, fully intent on performing his two pieces. He did the first and everything seemed to be going fine. Then: 'Dudley found the evening was going on rather longer than he'd imagined and tried to stop it without my having done the second piece . . . and I bustled forward and insisted on doing it.' The reason he was so keen to perform again was surely because much of his reputation as a comic performer rested on his party piece, which had already become known simply as 'the sermon'.

Alan Bennett has always said that his sermon, which was eventually retitled 'Take a Pew', 'took about half an hour to write, and was, I suppose, the most profitable half-hour's work I have ever done'. In fact, the sketch, which Russell Harty later described as '*the sermon*, which now hangs, like a leaden pectoral cross, round his neck', was constantly being rewritten and refined for different occasions until it had an all-purpose utility. Another of his more sacrilegious parodies was a version of the Queen's Christmas broadcast, of which sadly nothing survives. But as Bennett said, or rather wrote, to the comedy historian Roger Wilmut: 'I imagine various people were doing similar sketches around the same time, and it has always seemed to me that what was subsequently labelled "satire" was simply this kind of private humour going public.'

Almost every sketch was a hit with one or more of the critics, but most hailed Peter Cook's Harold Macmillan monologue, Jonathan Miller's fantasy about Lost Property on London Underground, Dudley

Moore's musical diversions, and the cast's wicked parody of William Shakespeare entitled 'So That's the Way You Like It'. The other widely praised sketch was Alan Bennett's sermon, which, as soon as it was released on LP record, was bringing in a small but tidy sum for Bennett in royalty payments.

Jonathan Miller had several spots which, schematically, exemplified his talent for saying, 'Isn't it funny that . . .?' rather than the hitherto current 'Wouldn't it be funny if . . .?' That, essentially, was what this whole *nouvelle vague* was about. If Jonathan Miller had received a pound for every comedian who has, since *Beyond the Fringe*, subjected the audience to some unusually personal thoughts, he would be living in considerably greater comfort than he now is. The sound that the audience make when they hear him talking about 'those little personal things which people sometimes do when they think they're alone in railway carriages . . . like smelling their own armpits' is of a sound rarely heard these days: it is the sound of a barrier being overturned.

Bennett's sermon was the last monologue before the show's closing sketch, the equally legendary 'End of the World'. The tone of the sermon is of a vicar whose attempts to be 'with it' are repudiated by the fact that he is very obviously *not* with it. 'As I was on my way here tonight, I arrived at the station, and by an oversight I happened to go out by the way one is supposed to come in.' A guard remonstrated with him. ' "Hey, *Jack*," he shouted. "Where do you think *you're* going?" That at any rate was the *gist* of what he said. But, you know, I was grateful to him, because, you see, he put me in mind of the kind of question I felt I ought to be asking you, here, tonight: Where do you think *you're* going?'

Perhaps the most famous remark in the whole sermon — and Bennett's earliest gift to comic posterity — is the vicar's plea that 'Life, you know, is rather like opening a tin of sardines. We're all of us looking for the key.' And, of course, 'There's always a little bit in the corner you can't get out.' It may be true that the sermon is regularly played to divinity colleges as an object lesson in how not to write a sermon. It should also be listened to regularly by would-be comedians as an object lesson in how to structure and deliver a comic monologue.

If everyone who claims to have been present on that first night had been telling the truth, the Lyceum would have been packed ten times over, but in fact when *Beyond the Fringe* opened at 10.45 on the night of 22 August 1960 the theatre was about a third full. It was a sure-fire word-of-mouth hit, though, and from the second night until the end of its short, week-long run, the show was regularly packing them in, in numbers that should have sent any theatre fireman into a state of restless unease. The national press did not all pounce on it at once, but one of the first to do so was Peter Lewis of the *Daily Mail*.

'London management are clamouring for the four young men in grey sweaters who are the theatrical hit of the Edinburgh Festival' ran the first line in an article headlined 'Everyone Wants the Four Men in Grey Sweaters'. 'They have come up with something fresh, something actually fresh in revue entertainment,' he raved on 25 August 1960. 'And their late-night show, *Beyond the Fringe*, which slays everything it touches, is convulsing festival audiences.'

The article captures perfectly the euphoria, the sense of relief, that here at last was a show that was contemporary, rather than what Bamber Gascoigne, in his preface to *From Fringe to Flying Circus*, describes as 'the tired tail end of a tradition that went back to glorious beginnings with Noël Coward in the 1920s'. As Michael Frayn, who saw the show in London a year later, put it: '*Beyond the Fringe* first fell upon London like a sweet, refreshing rain.' Describing the show as 'the official opening of the Satirical Sixties', he recognised that 'The demand must have existed, ravenous but unrecognised.'

The Edinburgh show delighted audiences and critics alike, but it certainly didn't strike all the reviewers as the harbinger of a new, sharper dramatic mood. 'Young Men's Breezy Revue: Medley of Fun and Mockery' was the *Daily Telegraph*'s headline on 27 August 1960. 'I don't remember that any Edinburgh Festival has given us a better laugh than the unpretentious late-night revue now running at the Lyceum Theatre,' wrote W.A. Darlington. He lavished praise on the 'intelligent goofiness' of 'a gloriously inconsequent [*sic*] medley including topical comment, Shakespearian parody, and imitations of types and individuals political and academic'. It was, said Mr Darlington, 'an entertainment given by four young men whose uniform get-up of dark blue pullovers and white shirts somehow makes them look younger still, so that when the curtain rises we might be in the Prefects' room at any school. But once they get to work we find they are of a more adult humour than their looks suggest.'

As a result of several other equally favourable reviews, the Edinburgh show was judged a huge success, but it had lasted only a week. When the four returned to London, they were introduced to a young would-be impresario called William Donaldson, who had inherited a fortune, lost most of it, and then reinvested most of whatever was left in a range of increasingly unsuccessful theatrical forays. Donaldson was, and still is, a split personality: a depressive, sensitive, philosophically inclined intellectual whose tastes in theatre were never going to echo those of the broad mass. He liked the show, though, and seemed keen to bring it to London. All he needed was a theatre.

While the backers bickered, Bennett returned to Oxford, and Miller to hospital. William Donaldson eventually booked the Arts Theatre, Cambridge, where Cook and Miller had performed before, and a week in Brighton. He also had a theatre owner for London: the impresario Donald Albery.

One of the harshest critics of Alan Bennett's contribution to *Beyond the Fringe* has always been Alan Bennett himself. 'I look back on those years without nostalgia, remembering chiefly the frustrations and embarrassments,' he wrote in the introduction to the collected scripts. 'The sermon apart,' he wrote, 'what did I think I was doing?'

It is typical of Bennett that he should dismiss so casually one of his most famous contributions to the stage. And yet when Donald Albery watched the rehearsals before the London transfer in April 1961, Bennett recalls: 'He was far from certain that the show would be a success but of one thing he was convinced: "The fair-haired one," as he put it, "will have to go." '

But the fair-haired one didn't go. His reserve, even his shyness, was as much a part of the show as the others' different characteristics. Back at Leeds Modern, the chronicler of *The Owlet*, no longer able to rely on first-hand accounts, had to scan the pages of the university publications to catch up with its more distant old boys. One such appeared in August 1961. 'The *Oxford University Gazette* lists A. Bennett of Exeter College among the students for the Degree of Doctor of Philosophy, and gives as the subject of his research "The Machinery of Personal Government 1394–9",' writes the editor. To this, *The Owlet* can only comment, proudly but with a truly parental shake of the head at the esoteric tastes of its former students: 'Variety is the spice of life!' In fact, variety – as far as show business was concerned – was about to be declared clinically dead.

5

A bit like Trotsky

Beyond the Fringe, 1961–1964

To warm up for London, *Beyond the Fringe* went first to Cambridge, where John Bassett says the first night lasted about three hours, with Cook either cramming in every sketch he had ever written or spinning out the existing ones into impossible lengths. Gushing reviews followed. The only other warm-up spot was Brighton, where the brief programme notes on the cast reveal Bennett's diffidence ('He is looking for a flat in Wapping'), Cook's West End triumphs ('responsible for much of the material for *One Over the Eight*'), Jonathan Miller's distractedness ('During the run of the revue, he will be continuing his work at a London hospital') and Dudley Moore's ambitious streak ('He is perpetually in demand for his orchestrations, which are extremely original in conception').

The Home Counties audience hated every minute of it. Many walked out, one man heckled the parody of the Second World War movie sketch known as 'The Aftermyth of War', and the Brighton reviews crackled with indignation. But by the time it got to London there were several new sketches. Much of the topical but ephemeral material had been discarded, and there were several quickies which were performed between lighting changes. The Edinburgh material had been shaken down, much of it rewritten, with the result that the show was tighter than ever. To herald their arrival, the four were taken to, among other places, London Zoo, where the photographer Lewis Morley made some memorable studies of them. In one shot they are all standing outside the Owl House. Peter, Dudley and Jonathan all have their hands up or eyes popping or fingers out, in imitation of an owl. Alan Bennett, one of the most distinguished former contributors to *The Owlet*, just stands there, looking more like an owl than any of them without even trying. Only in one respect – height – was Dudley Moore clearly in the minority. With Bennett topping out at six feet, and Cook and Miller taller still, Moore can be forgiven for describing his own height of five feet two inches as 'almost eccentric'.

The sketch that closed the first half, 'The Aftermyth of War', was packed with brilliant lines, many of which would take Bennett further into his career as a playwright. 'I'll always remember that weekend war broke out,' Bennett declared. 'I was at a house party at Cliveden with the Astors, and we sat around listening to the moving broadcast by Mr Churchill, or Mr Chamberlain as he then was. [Then] I got on the telephone to try and speak to Herr Hitler, who had been so kind to us on our last visit to Germany that summer. Unfortunately, the line was engaged. There was nothing I could do to avert the carnage of the next six years.'

'Civil War', the following sketch, was even more incisive, playing on the national hysteria surrounding the possibility of all-out nuclear war. When Bennett wrote to Roger Wilmut that 'I was the edgiest person on stage – the one who didn't look as if he ought to be there', he may have been thinking of his contributions to this sketch. 'I often felt the audience disliked me – "Oh, he's come on again",' he wrote. And indeed, as he quietens the house down for the second half – 'Settle down, now. Come on, settle down' – he does sound slightly patronising and remote, as if he's not expecting to be liked that much. There was also an element of coldness in his other monologue, performed in Edinburgh and London, called 'Let's Face It', which Peter Cook, whose wit could be wounding, used to call 'The Boring Old Man Sketch'.

In its way, 'Let's Face It' was the most 'satirical' item in the show. It was a plainly worded address by a bigoted old curmudgeon. Peter Cook had invented a boring man, too, much given to maundering monologues, who would evolve into E.L. Wisty. Yet whereas Wisty, or Mr Grole as he was called at the time, was such a lunatic that he became funny, Bennett's bore was too close to home to escape being rather charmless.

Mr Khrushchev is described as 'a bit of a rough diamond, but his heart's in the right place'. 'I've met and talked to the Afrikaaners, and let me tell you, they're jolly nice people.' Grole was a daft old man, whereas Bennett's character was more of an Alf Garnett prototype, whose sheer extremism is unsettling or off-putting. That having been said, even E.L. Wisty has a somewhat outdated feel nowadays: a comic character from a bygone age. Bennett's hectoring man reads rather better on the page. The piece is, at least, a cogent character creation.

Beyond the Fringe opened at the Fortune Theatre in London on 10 May 1961 and immediately received ecstatic reviews. The next morning, Bernard Levin wrote in the *Daily Express*: 'The theatre came of age last night.' He went on to wax lyrically about his 'Gratitude that there should be four men living among us today who could come together to provide for as long as memory holds, an eighth colour to the rainbow'. (No wonder Mr Levin prefers not to look back on that period.) Very few of the critics used the Satire-word. W.A. Darlington's revised review in the *Daily Telegraph* was sub-headlined 'Cascades of Happy Laughter', which again suggested that he hadn't been watching the same show as Levin, or at least hadn't viewed it from the same position. Darlington praised everyone, including 'Mr Bennett's little man's air of profundity when coming to no conclusion at all'.

Alan Brien in the *Sunday Telegraph*, on 14 May, could not have been more emphatic: 'After the first night of *Beyond the Fringe*, British revue will never be the same again. We audiences have tasted our own blood and liked it. We have been flayed alive and vastly improved in the process.' And he described Bennett's clergyman as 'the triumph of the evening'.

Kenneth Tynan's review in the *Observer*, headlined 'English Satire Advances into the Sixties' (14 May 1961), had a singular role to play in fixing it in the public's mind. He describes Alan Bennett's 'spectacles, flaxen hair and the beginnings of a lantern jaw. With his kindly, puzzled face, he resembles a plain-clothes friar, badly in need of a tonsure.' But he also notes how Bennett – 'in manner the mildest of the quartet' – is 'perhaps the most pungent in effect', praising the 'oleaginous blandness' of the sermon, but also giving an ovation to Bennett's 'wickedly accurate' analysis of the South African Prime Minister, Dr Verwoerd.

Not everyone remembers it that way. 'Can any of these earnest lecturettes have made anyone *laugh*?' asked Bennett in his postscript to the complete *Beyond the Fringe*. 'I am torn between embarrassment at their content and admiration for the gall with which I dared to go on night after night and do them.' Ever since the *Fringe*, Bennett has pointedly turned his back on the Alan Bennett who rose to fame in that show. One cause was undoubtedly the torrent of media attention that left him with 'a permanent distaste for having to explain myself or hear myself explained'. He criticised himself for his 'priggish' refusal to omit the word 'erection' from one of his monologues (which one?) when the Queen, curious as to what all the fuss was about, came to see the show one evening. (Her consort that night had seen Bennett perform before. Lord Scarborough, the Lord Chamberlain, had enjoyed Bennett's Ulysses at Leeds Modern in 1950.) If it makes him sound pompous, though, he maligns himself unjustly, or half-unjustly. Peter Cook found him 'delightfully shockable' in the early days: 'It gave me enormous pleasure to come up with some piece of smut and watch him writhe and moan in agony or amusement, stuffing his handkerchief into his mouth,' wrote Cook. Moore recalls Bennett chewing his tie when he was nervous. Cook adds that the handkerchief had a double function. Sometimes it was used 'to stifle his own [Bennett's] laughter'; at other times 'to conceal his vexation'. So it was 'quite hard to tell whether he was having a fit of the giggles or in an almost terminal state of irritation'.

No doubt Bennett was sincere when he said, many years later, that he dreaded having the next spot after one of Cook's extended, extemporised monologues, when he was 'handed an audience so weak from laughter I could do nothing with them'. He cannot have been referring to one of his own monologues, as no two single spots would have been programmed to follow each other. Still, the point remains that the older Alan Bennett has little time for the younger Alan Bennett. 'I was more of an onlooker than a participant,' he wrote. 'Looking back on it now I think of it as the work of another person.' And yet Bennett, then aged twenty-seven, must have been having a wonderful time. After each performance he was driven back to Oxford in what the newspapers claimed was a Rolls-Royce (it wasn't) lent by Donald Albery. Once back in college, he swapped the motor for his bicycle and spent the day in academic pursuit. He reported that he only had to deliver three lectures each week, so his workload was not too onerous. 'This is the first time in my life that I have been bound by routine, and it has made me appreciate what it means to people to rest on Sunday,' he told the papers. 'All I've done is wander aimlessly round Oxford, enjoying the sun.'

Bennett, plainly trying to contain his excitement, said that his plan was to wait until term ended, seven weeks after the first night of *Beyond the Fringe*, and then move into a flat in London so that he could continue his researches at the Records Office. As he went on, he appeared to make an interesting admission. 'I am not coming to London to junket around. I don't like big expense-account meals, nor the kind of people you find in expensive restaurants. *I have wanted to do satirical humour for years* [my italics], so I took the opportunity when it came. But I can't wait for the publicity to settle down and let me get back to work.'

Of course, it was never going to be that easy. As early as May 1961 the *Daily Express* was reporting: 'Quartet in a Quandary as Broadway Beckons'. The sub-headline about 'Part-time Satirists Get a Feel for Full-time Riches' looks to have caught the tone. The report is an interesting eyewitness account of the debate that was then occupying the team members about how they should handle their sudden fame. It also sheds some light on the interplay between them, allowing Alan Bennett once again to emerge as more personable and less pious than he has portrayed himself. Bennett is described as a 'spectacled, blond hybrid of Puck and Friar Tuck', who loves to sit hugging his knees and says of most things, ' "It's a myth".' (If Bennett was Puck, Moore, according to one of his peers, was an even more mythic figure. 'He secreted music like sweat . . . with a Pan-like capacity to enchant ladies,' said Jonathan Miller.)

Bennett was obviously the butt of a certain amount of good-natured ribbing. When he said, 'I don't want to do this revue-thing permanently,' the remark was met with a chorus of 'oohs' and 'aahs'. And when he said he'd rather continue with his academic studies, Miller cheeked him: 'But Alan, if we go to the States it'll make us rich for a long time . . . It'll give us such academic freedom we can even take an unpaid job for a year.' Bennett, the *Express* records, remained unimpressed. 'What happens if New York is only interested in putting us on as the original quartet?' he said. Cook's reported response to this was, 'Then we'll have to marry each other,' but Bennett, alone of all the others, seems to have been scanning the future. Was he looking forward to life after the *Fringe* or dreading the uncertainty of it? Either way, if that made him sound more anxious than the others, perhaps it was because he had more reason than them for hoping that something else was around the corner.

When the press twigged that the word 'satire' was in, it proved impossible to dislodge it from their minds. As far back as April 1963, Miller was complaining that 'Newspapers have given us the role of great satirists. An enormous broadsword has been shoved into our unwilling hands.'

Bennett picked up the theme in the same article, an interview in *Reynolds News* by John Ennis. 'We didn't start out by going steely-eyed and deciding to take modern society apart. When we began talking about the show, in 1960, we found certain things made us laugh. It just happened that things like politicians and the Church happened to figure among them.' In his introduction to the *Fringe* scripts, Bennett wrote: 'I've a dreadful feeling I may have thought I was doing some good. Oh, well.' The unease was always there. Back in 1961, he obviously wasn't sure if the show was successfully pillorying its targets or playing up to them. 'You get a great fascist roar of laughter at times,' he said. 'It's frightening to hear.'

He was also aware of the payoff between point-scoring and joke-making. 'Despite yourself, you find you want to make people laugh,' he said. 'At first we were happy if we produced a shocked silence. But after a while a shocked silence isn't enough, and to get the laughs I feel we lessen the satire to some extent.' Bennett said in *Telling Tales* that the trouble with being a writer is that you get what you invent. Inadvertently, Bennett had just predicted the fate of his 1971 play *Getting On*.

Bennett took time off from the *Fringe* to play the Archbishop of Canterbury in *Blood of the Bambergs*, which opened in 1962 at the Royal Court. His performance was described by the play's author, John Osborne, as 'magnificent'. But it was a holiday job. The revuers sailed for New York on the SS *France*, arriving on 28 September 1962. If the long voyage was intended to foster cast unity, it did not succeed. With Miller married to Rachel, and Cook not far from proposing to Wendy Snowden, both men were beginning to suffer from divided loyalties. Nor did the treatment they all received on the boat conform to what was anticipated for the four satirical sensations. 'It was nowhere near as glamorous as we expected,' Bennett told Dudley Moore's biographer Barbra Paskin. 'We weren't treated like celebrities. They couldn't fit us into the main dining-room, so we had to eat in the nursery. I remember Peter having caviar for his breakfast, but other than that we weren't treated royally at all. We didn't play for the passengers – nobody asked us.' Worst of all: 'There was even a talent contest, but we weren't asked to perform.'

The show toured Toronto, Washington and Boston before opening at the John Golden Theater, New York, West 45th Street, on 27 October 1962. The programme notes again reflect, in part, the show's four personalities. 'Alan Bennett, the oldest of the four *Fringe* authors, is a bachelor,' it tells us. 'If he seems so much sadder and wiser than his colleagues, he would put it down to two years spent in the service of Queen and Country in one of the oldest and proudest of Her Majesty's infantry regiments.' Peter Cook is right to describe himself as 'the youngest of the four author-performers', though he states in uncharacteristically serious tones, and possibly not his own: 'Never does he set out to observe people or try to reproduce them on the stage from life. He is content to start writing from a bit of conversation, without knowing where his creative imagination will lead him.' In early programme editions he 'hopes to start a New York version of the Establishment while he is in the United States'. *Private Eye*, which he now owned, had acquired a circulation of 35,000 in six months. Later versions of the programme report that the Establishment (the satirical club he had started in London) was now based at 154 East 54th Street, and that *Private Eye* had increased its circulation to 100,000 over the course of a year.

Jonathan Miller's programme entry discusses his busy writing career, as well as the birth, a few days before his departure for the USA, of a baby boy. Dudley Moore concentrates on his American connections, which were even then quite extensive, having – alone of all the others – already toured the States, with Johnny Dankworth's orchestra.

The new sketches included Bennett and, largely, Cook in 'The Great Train Robbery', which might be the funniest two-hander ever written, and Bennett's first northern monologue, entitled 'The English Way of Death'. In it, a man discusses the options facing bereaved relatives who are considering having their loved ones cremated. This was a bold, even suicidal move on Bennett's part. Transatlantic exchanges were not then what they are now. When the Beatles' first film, *A Hard Day's Night*, came out in 1964, their strong Scouse accents required subtitles in some American cities, so one has to wonder what New York audiences – albeit more sophisticated than most – made of Bennett's emphatically northern tones, of his 'Up at t' crematorium' and 'B' joves'. Bennett is not helped by having the highest-pitched voice of the four, which means he can sound shrill at times.

The humorous moments revolve around the family being unable to decide which music should go with the kindling ('Well, I think it's more hygienic') and the quick turnaround of cremations ('There's folks waiting to get in, they're that busy'). And there's a joke that Bennett reheated twice – and why not? It's a good joke – first in *On the Margin* and then in *Prick Up Your Ears,* about the bereaved not being quite sure whether they're getting the ashes of their beloved in the urn or, for all they know, 'a couple of copies of the *Yorkshire Evening Post*'. Twenty-three years later, in 1987, Bennett had Frances Barber and Vanessa Redgrave trying to scoop equal amounts of Joe Orton's and Kenneth Halliwell's ashes into an urn. 'I think I'm putting in more of Joe than I am of Kenneth,' says Joe's sister Leonie (Barber). Joe's agent, Peggy Ramsay (Redgrave), retorts, 'It's a gesture, dear, not a recipe.' Bennett later wrote of the original sketch: 'It's a pretty dreadful piece and, death not being the subject of lively interest it has since become, the Broadway audience received it in stunned silence . . . Still, I can see in it now the germ of the television plays I went on to write ten years later.'

In 1980, Bennett wrote to Roger Wilmut that 'Peter has a kind of madness on stage . . . One evening Macmillan came to see the show. Peter therefore went several steps further, remarking on the prime minister's presence in the audience. Macmillan buried his face in his programme, and the audience, out of embarrassment, gradually froze. This didn't stop Peter. On he plunged. Someone with less self-confidence would have been guided by the atmosphere.' Contrast that with Bennett's own predicament, doggedly reciting the same sketch, night after night, to little or no applause. Why? It must say something about Bennett's tough-mindedness or his self-belief as a writer that he knew there was something in that sketch which he was trying to explore. He found it many years later, but he might not have found it at all if he hadn't died, night after night, on the Broadway stage.

Public and critical reaction were as overwhelmingly favourable as they had been in Edinburgh and London. Richard Watts of the *New York Post* called it 'Immense . . . hilarious . . . a brilliant satirical revue'. Howard Taubman of the *New York Times* felt sure that New Yorkers would fall for the 'four keen-witted, riotous young Englishmen', while

Walter Kerr – 'whose reviews are generally regarded as a combination of papal bull and stock market closing report', Alistair Cooke explained to *Guardian* readers – found it 'funny on all subjects'. Cooke's encounters with a younger generation of New Yorkers left him with the impression that, in fact, the satire boom had already started in the States, in clubs like the Premise and Chicago's Second City. 'They're not too bad,' one American undergraduate told him; 'they're just too late.' To which Cooke could only reply that 'A howl of satisfied oldsters will rise to dispute him'.

President John F. Kennedy, who had seen the show in London, asked to come and see it again on 10 February 1963. Alexander Cohen, the show's producer, didn't believe it until he saw security men rigging up the famous red phone in the box office. So it was that the show which had given us the sketch 'Whose Finger on which Button?' in Edinburgh would finally receive an official response.

Kennedy didn't drop the bomb, but he did need to use the lavatory. Cohen's wife recalls guarding the door of a fairly seedy-looking 'broom closet' while JFK was in there doing his business, a labour of love for which she was thanked with a dozen red roses the following day. Ever the diarist, Bennett scrawled the words 'John F. Kennedy pee'd here' on the wall. Bennett suspected that Peter Cook might even have 'seen something' of Jackie Kennedy, though his self-abasement was running at such a height that this might have been a coded way of saying that she certainly would not have wanted to have 'seen something' of him. Certainly the First Lady became a frequent visitor to the New York version of the Establishment Club at the Strollers' Theater.

Bennett had brought his thesis with him, and he continued to work towards the completion of his Ph.D., even getting microfilms of medieval manuscripts sent over to him so that he could carry on researching into Richard II's retinue. Having seen the Kennedys' fabled 'Camelot' at such close quarters, one wonders if he felt like a somewhat surly courtier himself, forever observing the livelier antics of his three fellow performers. Still, if he needed a refuge, libraries had always been a second home to him, from Upper Armley Road and the Reference Library in Leeds to Exeter, Magdalen and the Bodleian, so he made himself at home in the Fifth Avenue public library and carried on cramming by day and hamming by night. The Ph.D. was never, in fact, completed, and, somewhat to his regret, Bennett finally admitted as much later that year, though it wasn't until 1988 that he was able to throw away all the notebooks that he had filled. From then, as he wrote in *Writing Home*, 'The rest, one normally says, is history, but in my case the reverse was true. History was not what it was at all.'

Jonathan Miller, besides having his own social circle in New York, kept up his neuropsychiatric research at the Mount Sinai Hospital. Dudley Moore, meanwhile, was steadily working his way through as many of New York's available (and sometimes unavailable) women as he could. Peter Cook was blending with ease into New York's beau monde.

If anyone had imagined that poking fun at imminent nuclear war might have hardened Bennett to the possibility of it really happening, they were wrong. The four were in New York when the Cuban missile crisis was reaching its height. John Bassett, who with Dudley Moore had occupied the musician Joan Diener's apartment on East 63rd Street, near the Queensboro Bridge, told Moore's biographer Barbra Paskin that Bennett was 'terrified that the bomb was going to be dropped, so he came and stayed with us for two nights'. While the others were living it up, Bennett was living it down. Twice, Bennett was invited to dinner by Adlai Stevenson (Governor of Illinois, 1949–53, Democratic candidate for President, 1952 and 1956) but turned him down for fear that he would be sick over his food. But he attended a party for Judy Garland at the Dakota, later the home of John Lennon, where a drunken Shelley Winters sang rude songs, and he tried nervously, and unsuccessfully, to chat to Judy Holliday, the star of *Born Yesterday*. He admitted years later that he 'couldn't wait to get back to England'.

There were more restful times, during which Dudley Moore cooked scrambled eggs for Bennett, but Bennett was clearly nervous, expecting riots one minute or a nuclear pall the next. And clearly any nervous traveller would have been forgiven for preferring to be at home rather than in the very country that might bear the full brunt of an atomic explosion. 'I don't think I really believed we would be blown up,' said Bennett, 'but it was a terribly nervous time.' The joke in the show about the four-minute warning was, of course, a reference to Roger Bannister's recent record-breaking streak: 'Now, we shall receive four minutes' warning of any impending nuclear attack. Some people have said, "Oh, my goodness me – four minutes? That's not very long." Well, I would remind those doubters that some people in this country of ours can run a mile in four minutes.' No doubt the former Exeter College athlete

Roger Bannister was flattered to be included in such an illustrious revue.

Peter Cook married Wendy Snowden on 28 October 1963, thirteen months after their arrival in the States. With two married men in the cast, Bennett and Moore took solace in each other's company. They often dined together before the show at Barbetta's, an Italian restaurant on 46th Street, and Bennett sometimes, and rather half-heartedly, went to watch Dudley playing in jazz clubs: the Bennett who had so adamantly defended Euterpe against the intrusions of this new style of music was still somewhat cool towards Moore's Errol Garner-inspired style of playing, but it was company of a sort. For about a year they had exactly the same dishes every day: gazpacho soup, fettuccine and chocolate mousse. The restaurant has made history in one sense. The Italian maître d' could never quite get his tongue around the words of his guests' show. His version sounded, to their ears, more like *Behind the Fridge*, which was to become the title of Cook and Moore's 1971 stage show.

Bennett was, as ever, aware of the seemingly endless procession of leggy women with whom Dudley surrounded himself. One of them, he recalls, 'had such big tits, she looked like her arm was in a sling'. If the observation sounds jaundiced, it could have been because, by now, cast tensions were, perhaps predictably after more than three years together, beginning to make themselves felt. Bennett, clearly tense from doing something he wasn't enjoying, can't have been an easy person to have been with. Cook seems untouched by spats, with Miller and Moore occupying the middle ground, but Bennett's name kept being mentioned in dispatches, many of them written by himself. One famous flare-up occurred in the green room when Miller aimed a tray of sandwiches at Bennett. He missed, though some point had obviously hit home.

A more significant quarrel was with Dudley Moore. As Moore said to *The Times* on 3 November 1973: 'One evening I changed some lines in a sketch we did together and . . . *we* didn't have an argument, *he* did, and I don't think we have really ever spoken much after that.' Dudley seems to have picked on a recurring theme, that Bennett was capable of finding an argument where others might not have seen one. He told Barbra Paskin: 'We had a sketch . . . where Alan was interviewed by all of us in turn, and one night I played it a little differently, to try and get something out of the audience. And it worked – or so I thought.' The sketch over – it might have been 'Home Thoughts from Abroad', a very funny cast number about the *real* America – Dudley turned to the others and said he thought it had gone pretty well. Bennett said: 'I think it's the worst performance we've ever given.' And they hardly talked again for the rest of the New York run.

'It was strange to have been going out to dinner with a guy every night and then suddenly have it stop so completely,' recalled Dudley. 'I never understood it; it was a total mystery. I guess he thought I'd tampered with his words, but I found it difficult to believe the way he reacted.' This was Bennett the perfectionist, angry at the words of his sketch being changed. It was not to be an isolated incident. More surprisingly, Dudley asked Bennett about this incident, many years later, only to be told that Bennett had no recollection of it. After a year, Jonathan Miller, itching to get back to medicine, left. The two have been neighbours and great friends for years, but Bennett said of Miller's departure: 'It was a great relief. He and I really got on each other's nerves.'

The show won a Tony award in 1963 to balance the *Evening Standard* Theatre award they had won in London, but, despite the showers of praise, the *Fringe* was beginning to fray. After the original cast finally quit the show in April 1964, there was another half-hearted attempt to get the satirically fab four to work again. This was a film proposal about a nineteenth-century German plot to undermine the monarchy with dozens of substitute Queen Victorias, but it never got beyond the treatment stage. The Fringers were, artistically speaking, finished as a creative unit.

Miller, famously, 'fiercely regretted' taking part, claiming that it had lifted him away from the thing he really wanted to do, which was first medicine, then directing, and more recently making rather striking sculptures from *objets trouvés*. 'Far better to have been a very funny undergraduate and have done with it,' he has said. For Peter Cook, *Beyond the Fringe* was one of the peaks of his career. 'I may have done some other things as good but I am sure none better,' he wrote in 1987, an admission which moved his partner Dudley Moore to tears. Moore enjoyed the lift it gave his career, and Cook admitted he had 'never had it so good'. Bennett and Miller seemed most unsentimental about it: Miller would much rather not talk about it at all.

Alan Bennett, who has made a career out of looking back wistfully, likes to tell the story of when he was invited to 10 Downing Street by the then Prime Minister, Harold Wilson. 'The Wilsons met the guests as they came in,' he wrote. 'He asked what I did, and I said I was now a playwright, but that I'd started off in a revue. "Oh dear," said Mary Wilson, "not one of those revues where there's nothing on the stage and the actors wear black sweaters?" I had to say that I meant just that. "*Beyond the Fringe*," said Mr Wilson. "But you weren't one of the original four, surely?"' Apart from casting doubt on the Wilsons' 'with-it' 1960s self-image, as well as underlining their (and many politicians') cultural myopia, this was yet another blow to his pride, which *Beyond the Fringe* seemed, more than any other show, to inflict on him. He may have retained a few fleetingly happy memories, but its success crippled him. 'I've never had notices again like that,' he told Paul Vallely of the *Yorkshire Post* in 1977. 'Afterwards I was lost for about two years. I wasn't confident of my ability to do anything by myself.'

Bamber Gascoigne once said of his modest successes with Cambridge Footlights in the 1950s that 'Like each new wave, we thought we were spearheading a revolution . . . But it wasn't a revolution that would lead anywhere. Kerensky's rather than Lenin's.' Bennett, maintaining the Soviet theme, said that the encounter with the Wilsons left him feeling 'a bit like Trotsky, eliminated from the history of the revolution'.

Bennett returned to England in 1964 to discover that another revolution had taken place. Pop culture had burst over the country from Merseyside, and suddenly it was hip to be young, rather than a carbon copy of one's parents. Girls were dressing in miniskirts, boys were whizzing around in Minis. Haircuts had suddenly exploded to a point just below the ears, and some very bizarre boutiques had begun to appear in Carnaby Street and Chelsea's King's Road. Bennett's parents, still untouched by the spirit of rebellion, were seeing out the storm at 8 Wood Lane, their last home in Leeds.

Bennett, flushed with cash, bought a primrose-yellow Mini and taught himself to drive by practising his turns in Shire Oak Street. When he switched on his TV set in January 1965, he found himself watching *Not Only . . . But Also*, a hilariously funny new show starring BBC Television's hottest new young things, Peter Cook and Dudley Moore. Every sketch, and every programme in that first series of six, was received ecstatically by the viewers and in the press, leaving Alan Bennett wondering mournfully if it was going to be Goodbyeee to all that.

Part Two

Taking The Pith

6

In a very real sense I'm a *miner* writer

On the Margin, 1967

Alan Bennett's 1975 TV play, *Sunset Across the Bay*, is about an engineer and his wife who uproot themselves from their home in Leeds and go to live in a retirement flat in Morecambe. 'Goodbye mucky Leeds,' says Mam out of the window of the minicab as it drives them past the end of their road, with ball-and-chain machines energetically thumping the old back-to-backs to smithereens. The plot, give or take the odd location, is essentially the story of how Walter and Lilian Bennett left Leeds to go and live in Clapham in 1966.

Clapham is a pleasant leafy village up a valley between Ingleton and Settle, north Yorkshire. Its buildings are of stone, and there is a busy stream running alongside the high street. It is an ideal point from which to explore the Dales, and there is a pub and several bed and breakfasts, as well as a very fine church, St James, parts of which are Perpendicular in style. For the Bennett parents, Clapham was meant to be the setting for their final years together. Walter Bennett was sixty-five when he passed his driving test in 1968. For them, private transport was a sudden and liberating experience, freeing them from the awful pressure of exchanging whispered conversations on buses or trains. 'The few years they have left together are a kind of heyday,' Bennett wrote in *Telling Tales*. He remembered them 'laughing, still silly and full of fun'.

For their son Alan, Clapham became special, too, a place where he could relax from the pressure of work. As the 1960s progressed, though, and the world moved slowly on in the wake of *Beyond the Fringe*, Bennett was finding it, if anything, too easy to get away from it all.

Bennett had returned to the Royal Court in October 1964 to play the Revd Sloley-Jones in *A Cuckoo in the Nest* by Ben Travers. But he never made a secret of the fact that he did not intend to spend the rest of his life playing small clerical parts. Having created the demand for that sort of role, having in fact defined the unmistakable stereotype, he had recognised the dangers of being lumbered with it. And the early years of the 1960s seemed to offer no escape route.

Bennett took a half-step back into the limelight when he was asked to take part in *Not so Much a Programme, More a Way of Life*. *NSMAP* was heralded as the successor to *That Was the Week that Was*, which ran from November 1962 to April 1963 and then from September to December 1963. Both programmes were the brainchild of Ned Sherrin, whose precocious talents were already being noted with some awe when he was still at Exeter College, Oxford, just ahead of Bennett. Sherrin was now producing programmes at the BBC, and *TW3* had been to TV what *Beyond the Fringe* had been to theatre. Whereas the latter killed off conventional revue, however, there was almost as much ambivalence about the emergence of *TW3*'s anchorman, David Frost, whose rise to fame was met by his colleagues with disbelief, alarm, panic and – all too rarely – scornful laughter. Alan Bennett was engaged to appear in the *NSMAP* pilot on 1 November 1964, though the contract was then rewritten to allow for a more informal arrangement. 'The producer, Ned Sherrin, hopes very much that Alan will be able to make guest appearances in some of the programmes,' the BBC wrote to Bennett's agent at London Artists. Bennett's contributions were obviously highly regarded, though his temperament was no doubt in their minds too. To some extent, then, the *rara avis* of light entertainment was being given more space in which to flap its wings. On 7 December 1964 he recorded a five-minute monologue about Virginia Woolf for the BBC's arts programme *Monitor*, which was for some time presented and edited by Huw Wheldon, and then Jonathan Miller. The subject of Virginia Woolf was one to which he would return frequently over the years.

Bennett had another spot on *NSMAP* in March 1965, appearing for a hundred guineas – a huge amount – to record an improvised sketch with John Bird. Bird, whose father was a chemist, went from a

Nottingham grammar school to King's College, Cambridge, in 1958, and was to become one of the most brilliant and incisive members of the Oxbridge comedy mafia. One of Bird's skills was in the field of improvisation, so he was teamed with Bennett. Given Bennett's unhappy memories of writing sessions with the *Fringe* cast, it was perhaps hardly surprising that his agent was informed, in a note from the producer, that 'it was then mutually agreed that the prepared sketch should not be transmitted'. However, 'The producer hopes that Mr Bennett will be appearing again in the programme very soon'. And he did. Had *NSMAP* lasted longer, Bennett's involvement with it might have been extended, but after sixty-three shows it was agreed that the format needed changing, and so the series was rested.

Sherrin's next commission was more successful. *BBC-3* went out on Saturday evenings from 2 October 1965 to 2 April 1966, with Frost replaced as front man by the drier, bluffer Robert Robinson. In October 1964 Bennett was on the point of signing a contract to make guest appearances in some of the programmes, which were to begin shooting the following month. By September 1965 the arrangement had been finalised: fifty guineas per programme for Bennett to provide up to five minutes for each date. But the writing sessions failed to fire Bennett, and it was soon realised that a better way to exploit his skills was with occasional pre-scripted material. In his memoirs, *A Small Thing – Like an Earthquake*, Ned Sherrin describes as 'whimsical' the contracts drawn up for Bennett. 'He would meet Bird or (fellow Oxford comedian John) Fortune towards the end of the week and see if the spirit moved him,' wrote Sherrin. 'If it did not, he went home, and the other two, perhaps with Doug Fisher, improvised without him.'

BBC-3 has, perhaps undeservedly, been remembered chiefly for one thing, one word in fact – 'fuck' – which was uttered, for the first time on British television, by Kenneth Tynan in a discussion on censorship with Mary McCarthy, chaired by Robert Robinson. There was much else to recommend the show but, sadly, little survives.

On 4 December 1965 Bennett was paid £31.10*s* for a three-minute item called 'Camden Town tramp'. As with much of Bennett's best work, the sketch was largely autobiographical. Bennett spent most of 1965 and 1966 living in a basement flat in Chalcot Square in Camden, NW1. Nowadays, the square is one of the most sought-after addresses in London. Its few parking spaces are fought over at weekends by crowds eager to let loose their dogs on the top of nearby Primrose Hill, before browsing in the bookshop and jostling for space among the area's cafés. When Bennett arrived, he was dimly aware that the whole area was on the verge of a sociodemographic revolution. In 1967 one house could have been split into twelve separate bedsits. Within a few years, all those residents would have moved out, to be replaced by a succession of architects, theatre directors or Labour Party activists. Bennett wrote in *Writing Home*: 'These days the process is called gentrification and involves no soul-searching . . . but we were genuinely uneasy about it [as] there was a definite sense that we were shoving the indigenous population out.' Whether today's gentrifiers feel no such unease is, of course, for them to say, but Bennett recalled an occasion in 1965 in which an old man turned up at a dinner party in one of the newly converted houses like the ghost from a past life. The last time he had been in London he had rented a room in this house; was one available now? Racked with guilt, Bennett drove the man around Camden in his car, looking for an establishment where he might be comfortable. He was also, of course, able to observe the man at close quarters. A short while later he turned the incident into a sketch for Ned Sherrin. Again, he would return to the subject very soon.

He played smaller parts, too, including an oily Victorian – a break from his normal run of parts – in *My Father Knew Lloyd George*, along with Johns Bird and Fortune and Eleanor Bron, again produced by Ned Sherrin, in May 1965. And in the same month he was offered two hundred guineas to make a programme called 'Famous Gossips'. This was to be produced by a young man called Patrick Garland.

There are signs during this period that Bennett was definitely kicking his heels. There was still money coming in, thanks to the BBC's regular use of clips from the recording of *Beyond the Fringe*. And there were occasional celebrity guest spots to prove that he wasn't forgotten, such as the twenty-five guineas he was offered for appearing on BBC Bristol's antiques programme, *Going for a Song*, in November 1965. His own career was by no means ready for such evaluation, though to a certain extent he was forced to trade on his past too. He accepted twenty guineas to take part in an interview on the subject of Oxford dons for the BBC show *Late-night Line-up* in November 1965. In May 1966 any suspicion of lingering frostiness between himself and Jonathan Miller was cast aside when Miller interrupted work on his dark, disturbing and psychologically penetrating version of *Alice in Wonderland* after receiving a telegram from Sardinia. 'TV Star Aids His Sick Pal' ran the headline in the *Daily Mirror* on 13 May, which reported that Miller had flown to Italy the previous Wednesday after hearing that Bennett was suffering from internal bleeding while on holiday. His concern for Bennett as a friend and neighbour was combined with concern for Bennett as an actor, for Miller had cast him in the role of the Mouse in *Alice,* which was broadcast on BBC1 on 28 December. Bennett played the part in his clerical voice, and is glimpsed trying to make a long speech at the Mad Hatter's tea party, during which he is drowned out by, among others, Peter Cook as the Mad Hatter. Bennett was paid £500 for the role: his duties included swimming in an indoor pool at Castle Donington near Derby. Other parts were played by John Bird, Wilfred Brambell and John Gielgud. The money was no doubt welcome to Bennett, now physically on the mend, but the activity may have felt uncomfortably close to treading water.

And yet there is no doubt that his profile was much higher. Shortly after *Alice* was televised, he told the journalist Michael Hickling: 'A woman knocked on our door and demanded I sing a song for her grandchild who was with her. So there I was in the doorway, singing, and all these hikers were passing along the street wondering what was up. I did feel a twerp.' And yet, not wanting to be awkward, he carried on singing.

On 26 January 1966 the *Daily Mail* published what appears to be the first individual interview with Alan Bennett, conducted by a young man called Barry Norman. The piece begins:

> Across the darkening room, Mr Alan Bennett shifted slightly in his chair and said: 'Would you like some more tea?' I said, 'No, thank you', not because I didn't want any but because I knew he'd have to go and get it and I didn't like to disturb him. He looked so settled, so *permanent*, lounging there in his tiny study surrounded by the comforting presence of aged books and Victorian furniture. Just glancing at him, you could see that he was driven on by a sort of fierce inertia.

Norman must have been impressed. Years later, when he got the chance to present his *Film* . . . programmes on the BBC, he seems to have been trying to create a similarly crepuscular atmosphere with the studio decor.

In this interview, Alan Bennett is framed clearly in a post-*Fringe* setting. The questioner is no longer interested in gauging Bennett's excited reaction to his overnight success: this time we are offered a picture of the whole man.

Barry Norman praised the 'splendidly prissy academic voice with which, about once a fortnight, he enlivens the sometimes tedious proceedings of *BBC-3*' but revealed that it was, 'like his legend, more or less phoney'. Bennett spoke about his perceived rootlessness. 'Really, I'm a comedian among dons and a don among comedians. It's very uncomfortable, sometimes,' he said. He told Norman that he disliked London and returned to Leeds whenever he could. 'It's a narrow furrow I'm ploughing, which is one reason why I don't do TV regularly. I'm under no illusion that I have a very broad talent to exploit, although I think it could be broader than it is . . . But I really have no hard line to follow or goal to aim at, although I'm quite an envious person. I envy Peter Cook and Dudley Moore the success they're having now, though I don't regret not being involved in it. I'd like to have that kind of success myself because if I have any driving force it's a belief that I can do things as well as other people, and if I have an ambition it's to prove to myself that I'm right.'

The piece ends with Norman saying: 'That proof could come quite soon, for he may well be getting his own TV series, based on an idea which he sold to the BBC in his usual dynamic fashion. "What were you thinking of doing?" they asked. "Well," he said, "if you gave me half an hour I think I could be quite funny."'

The BBC had already decided to put that to the test, in fact, since on 12 January 1966 their light entertainment script editor, John Law, instructed the BBC Copyright Department to commission from Bennett 'a thirty-minute revue-type script as a potential pilot for a series. Delivery date one month.' Law offered £300, and was eventually talked up to £400. The outline of the programme was still sketchy, though by April 1966 the working title was 'I Can't Help Thinking'. The head of comedy at the BBC at the time was Frank Muir, who liked the first half-hour so much that he immediately wanted to see more. He rang Bennett's agent, Michael Linnit at London Artists, and asked him how long it would take Bennett to write another five scripts. 'He's already written them,'

Linnit replied. A scribbled note makes clear the BBC's enthusiasm to work with Bennett. In blue ballpoint are the words: 'Check up whether AB is again going to be booked to take part.' By 21 April John Law was able to assure his bosses that Bennett would definitely be performing. The ingredients were coming together.

Soon a new producer was making his presence felt. Patrick Garland had been one of Oxford's most successful, and colourful, actors, making full use of the company of OUDS, the Oxford University Dramatic Society, which Bennett had so carefully shunned. Michael Linnit was offered a handcuffs deal, in which Bennett promised not to make himself available for any other television commitments during the period 1 October to 3 December 1966. The performances were to take place within that time, and Bennett was to receive a princely 490 guineas per programme. The title of the programme, in a memo dated 17 August 1966, had now been reduced to 'The Alan Bennett Series'.

The BBC clearly wanted as much of Alan Bennett as they could get, unless they were hoping that if they commissioned eight reasonable programmes they would get six good ones. A memo from Patrick Garland to the fearsome Tom Sloan, head of the Light Entertainment Group, makes clear that Bennett was now being treated as a protected species, as well as revealing how thoroughly Garland empathised with Bennett's working methods. 'Dear Mr Sloan,' he wrote on 5 September 1966, 'I spoke to Alan Bennett at the weekend about the possibility of him doing eight instead of six shows. I tried to persuade him to complete two more so that the series would run until week 52, but he really was most reluctant to commit himself to any more at the moment, because he works extremely slowly and feels quite sure that he would be spreading the material that he already has too thin on the ground. I hope this does not affect your schedules too seriously.' Sloan replied, grandly: 'This is too bad, but it was nice of you to try.' A memo to John Law, dated 8 September 1966, conveys the good news that 'scripts two and three have been accepted' and that 'the producer is Patrick Garland'. There is one further news item. Above the words 'I Can't Help Thinking', a pencilled note adds the words 'retitled *On the Margin*'.

Next, a director was required. In his memoirs, *A Kentish Lad*, Frank Muir described *On the Margin* as 'the caviar end of my menu', but at the time he was taking no chances and appointed a director, Sydney Lotterby, from light entertainment, to make a contrast with Bennett's and Garland's more arts-based leanings. 'Sydney Lotterby was got into the programme as a sort of spy by Frank Muir,' felt Garland, but in any event the relationship was pretty harmonious. Lotterby modestly says that 'all I did was point the cameras and rehearse the lines', but he did that well. Lotterby also remembers one of the first sightings of Bennett's famous little books, in which he wrote down stray overheard remarks for later inclusion. 'You'd be sitting there talking and he'd get his little book out,' says Lotterby. 'You'd think "What am I saying?" and you'd suddenly realise you'd said something that doesn't make sense. But he did it quite discreetly.'

On the Margin starred Alan Bennett with Madge Hindle, Roland McLeod, Virginia Stride, Yvonne Gillan and John Sergeant. There were also guest appearances from such performers as John Fortune – whom Bennett had met thanks to Ned Sherrin – and Jonathan Miller. Of the regulars, McLeod was an actor who had read Theology at Oxford at the same time as Bennett was there. Madge Hindle, who was later to play Renée Roberts, the wife of Alf Roberts on Coronation Street – aficionados will not need reminding that Renée achieved tele-immortality when a lorry ploughed into her car – made her TV debut in On the Margin. And John Sergeant had been one of Robert Bolt's pupils when Bolt, the author of A Man for all Seasons, was a schoolmaster at Millfield. After his success in On the Margin, Sergeant shelved his acting ambitions, partly because he had seen how Bolt's life had fallen to pieces after the demise of his marriage to Sarah Miles, and found fulfilment as a TV parliamentary correspondent.

Location shooting took place between September and October 1966, with the first show recorded on 21 October. The title hinted that Bennett's journey had taken him from the fringe to the margin, and that he was still just looking on from a distance, or from the wings. But this was a margin in which Bennett's personality was absolutely central.

The first programme of the series of six was broadcast on BBC2 on 9 November 1966. The introductory sketch, set in a doctor's surgery, was sufficiently long – about five minutes, almost unheard of by today's standards – to allow several themes to emerge. The doctor, played by Bennett, was clearly incompetent. Examining a man whose racking cough suggests that he has severe bronchitis, Bennett completely overlooks it, pausing instead to remove a bit of fluff in the man's navel. With that done, his suggestion is to 'Come and see me again in six months' time, and if it's still there and you're still here, ha-ha, we'll have a look at it under the stethoscope.'

Bennett's portrait of the doctor is not harsh, but in its willingness to highlight people's readiness to believe a man in a white coat, Bennett was simply having a go at authority. As he wrote in the collected *Beyond the Fringe* scripts: 'So it is in every situation in life: somebody must know, the doctor, the surgeon, the accountant or the Prime Minister; illness, death, bankruptcy or annihilation, somebody must know. They don't, of course. They think you do.'

In the next item, instead of a live performance, Bennett introduced rare film of some music-hall stars singing a famous contemporary song. The first week, Gus Elen, who died in 1940, sang 'It's a Great Big Shame'. Other featured artistes included Lily Morris singing 'Why Am I Always the Bridesmaid?', Wilson, Keppel and Betty doing their famous sand dance, or 'Cleopatra's Nightmare', Marie Kendall singing 'Did Your First Wife Ever Do That?' and Florrie Ford singing 'Down at the Old Bull and Bush'. Each item was prefaced with a short discussion of the song by Bennett, and then the film was run, absolutely straight. Mercifully, this was no 'ironic' or 'cheesy' gimmick. As Michael Mills wrote in a memo to the BBC's head of TV Enterprises on 6 April 1966, 'They would be presented just as they were in the original Pathé Pictorial. In other words, there will be no attempt to mock them.' The same went for the poetry slot: each week, Michael Hordern and Prunella Scales took it in turns to read a poem by Philip Larkin or John Betjeman. This slot marked a change of pace, a point of stillness, or a stone stubbornly thrown into the stream against the headlong rush for laughter.

Bennett returned to the subject of social divisions in Camden to create what became the most notorious regular element in *On the Margin*. Called 'Streets Ahead: Life and Times in NW1', it was in effect a weekly five-minute sitcom, based on the episode of the Camden Town tramp, and starring a couple called Nigel and Jane Knocker-Threw, played by Bennett and Yvonne Gillan, who were facing up to the dilemmas of being what later became known as yuppies.

'Life and Times' was one of *On the Margin*'s most significant successes. In its way it gave far more precise barometric readings of the 1960s than the escapist humour of Pete and Dud in *Not Only . . . But Also*. The range of subjects included issues such as divorce and adultery, which – though scarcely on Bennett's personal agenda – were commanding vast amounts of attention in the media at the time. There were also a number of cracking lines, all delivered with style by a very talented cast.

The final episode of 'Streets Ahead' was subtitled 'Saying Goodbye', and was about Sam and Nigel failing to say goodbye casually to each other after having a drink in a pub. Nigel, obviously stricken with guilt after his afternoon tryst with Sam's wife, adopts any number of delaying tactics, while Sam, blithely unaware, is happy to arrange to meet at any time. Sam suggests he could pop around the following Wednesday. Nigel, looking desperately in his diary, replies: 'I've just noticed it's the Feast of the Circumcision of St Paul, and I don't know that Jane isn't laying something on.' And there the mini-series ends.

The Knocker-Threws returned to life, a year later, in *The Listener*, in a cartoon strip drawn by the – if anything – even more waspish Mark Boxer. It was introduced as 'A comic strip based on some of the characters in Alan Bennett's BBC TV series *On the Margin*', and it was called 'Life and Times in NW1'. The first strip appeared on 10 August 1967, and the couples were now known as the Stringalongs and the Touch-Paceys. Problems were confronted each week. 'Simon darling,' said Joanna to her Harold Pinter lookalike husband on 7 September, 'I'm afraid you will have to speak to the children. I caught Tristram believing in God yesterday.' There was more attention paid to the rivalries of competing media couples, a problem which must have intrigued the attached Boxer more than it did the single Bennett, but there was no doubt that the original inspiration – and observation – came from Bennett.

The closing sketch in the first programme was a celebration of the opera diva 'Dame' Madge Brindley, in reality a relatively obscure character actress who had contributed some distinguished vignettes to such films as Alexander Mackendrick's *The Ladykillers* (1955). Various fake pundits offered tributes to her life, such as the 'prominent Australian coloratura Adelaide Kingsbury' who said – in a line that Roland McLeod still recalls fondly as being possibly his favourite from the whole series – 'She was the only person I think who could sing the *Liebestod* and have every person in the theatre on their feet singing it with her.' This may have been Bennett's way of waving at his old *Fringe* colleagues, since Robert Neasden featured prominently in a sketch from Cook and Moore's *Not Only . . . But Also* called 'The Making of a Movie'. The sketches were unrelated, except that Neasden and Kingsbury were three stops apart on the old Bakerloo line.

That first show was thoroughly appreciated by those on the inside, as this memo of 10 November 1966 to Patrick Garland from the controller of BBC2 demonstrates: 'I cannot tell you how entertained, amused and delighted (from all points of view) I was by last night's show. That you and Alan should have produced such a triumph as the first of a series is remarkable enough. To have done so with something which breaks new ground in several different directions is really a magnificent achievement. I congratulate you most sincerely and would be very glad if you would pass on my thanks and admiration to Alan.' The controller, otherwise known as David Attenborough, also remarks that he is 'delighted that, for once, the press have recognised it and given it its proper due'.

He was right about that. 'Until now, Alan Bennett has tended to be the poor relation of the satire set,' wrote James Thomas in the *Daily Express*, 'relegated with his whining, dry style to supporting roles in the late-night shows, playing a bumbling don or a cretin clergyman. But with one bound, as they say, Mr Bennett jumped into a very funny series of his own last night.'

There was also praise from the serious papers. 'Alan Bennett, apparently the most limited yet certainly the funniest of the famous *Beyond the Fringe* quartet, launched belatedly and brilliantly into his first television series,' wrote Sean Day-Lewis in the *Daily Telegraph*. 'The whole thing was polished and neatly framed,' wrote Mary Crozier in the *Guardian*. Similar noises were being produced from the other end of the pier: 'He is a savage imitator of those who can make nonsense sound like profundity and fumbling pauses seem like deep considered thought,' wrote Kenneth Eastaugh in the *Daily Mirror*.

Day-Lewis made an interesting comment about Bennett's recognisability at the time when he added that 'He writes dialogue of such wit that disguise is no doubt superfluous, though there is probably an even greater danger in overexposure for Mr Bennett than for his one-time colleagues, Dudley Moore and Peter Cook.'

The size of the audience for that first programme was a respectable 4 per cent of the available public, compared with 19.1 per cent for BBC1 and 18.7 per cent for ITV. The reactions of the BBC's viewing panel are also worth studying.

'Response to this first edition of *On the Margin* was cordial, if somewhat mixed,' the summary began. 'For instance, although viewers generally would agree that Alan Bennett's approach to comedy was highly original, and he himself exceptionally talented, and very likeable, many had to confess that they had enjoyed the programme only in part. They had a feeling this was the sort of comedy that "needed getting used to" to be fully appreciated, but as, in any case, the programme as it stood was quite enjoyable, they were looking forward to the next edition.

'Others, however, and in considerable numbers, had no doubts about *On the Margin*. For them, this was the wittiest, the most subtly sophisticated and original comedy show they could remember seeing.'

Bennett's versatility as a writer was again demonstrated in the second programme. The first sketch is a camp romp called simply 'Rome', in which Bennett, playing the centurion Copius Mucus, was briefly reunited with Jonathan Miller, playing the senator Umbilicus. 'But tell me, Mucus,' says Umbilicus. 'How is Gaul?' 'Oh, divided as ever,' says Mucus, and Umbilicus' wife, Hernia, is 'bound up with herself as usual'.

The final sketch in that third programme, 'The Lonely Pursuit', is one of the funniest Bennett has ever written. Parodying the sort of arts documentaries that Bennett's old mucker Jonathan Miller was shooting for *Monitor*, it is presented as a portrait of a northern writer. Bennett, as the writer, appears in various moody shots, walking through a market, walking along streets with people watching him from doorways and windows, in a graveyard and in a garden. The prerecorded script survived, thanks to the Parlophone LP of the series, and, free of audience laughter, it is wonderful, with Bennett narrating in a flat Yorkshire voice:

> I don't know whether you've ever looked into a miner's eyes for any length of time because it's the loveliest blue I've ever seen. I think that's why I live in Ibiza – the blue of the Mediterranean, you see, reminds me of the eyes of these Doncaster miners. We were all miners in our family. My father was a miner. My mother was a miner. [In later versions this was changed to 'still is'.] These are miner's hands . . . But I'm still a miner, under the skin. I suppose in a very real sense I'm a *miner* writer.

It was typical, again, of their different work practices that Peter Cook – in his famous monologue from *Beyond the Fringe* on why he became a miner instead of a judge – should have reached for an absurdist tone, while Bennett stuck closer to home, dovetailing mining and writing. The sketch ends: 'What I'm above all primarily concerned with is the Substance of Life, the pith of reality. If I had to sum up my work, I suppose that is it really. I'm taking the pith out of reality.' Which, in a sense, summarises the main flavour of Bennett's early work up to and including *Forty Years On*.

The final sketch, 'The Critics', was a gem of a very different sort. Over the years, many comedians have taken the rise out of critics, pundits, and other self-appointed assessors of the nation's cultural health. Once again, Bennett had the luxury of getting to the watering hole early enough to scoop up some of the freshest water. In the sketch, Bennett, the studio convener, introduced a panel of critics, all of whom had been to see *Yes, We Have No Pyjamas* at the National Theatre. The 'Al Alvarez' character speaks approvingly of Peter Brook's 'sterile fertility'. J.W. Lambert, played by John Fortune, applauds John Osborne's 'stale brioche'. Penelope Gilliatt suggests the phrase 'randy metaphysic'. The 'Milton Shulman' character says: 'If I say I think he's very stupid I don't say that in any derogatory sense.' Another critic says: 'I thought the biscuits had a certain Chekhovian feel to them.' The character meant to be saying those lines is Karl Miller, the future founding editor of the *London Review of Books*. Bennett would later atone for his ridicule by becoming that magazine's most prominent contributor.

The penultimate sketch in the sixth and final programme was a further instance of how Bennett's style, if not his subject matter, had developed since *Beyond the Fringe*. Bennett wrote 'The English Way of Death' specifically for the Broadway run. Uncompromisingly, almost perversely northern, given their location, it sank like a stone on the Broadway stage, night after night. Back in Britain, though, Bennett rewrote it for two performers, himself and Madge Brindle, and the result was much more successful, and certainly more easily assimilated by an English audience. Since it was basically a study of two characters, it was also the only sketch in the whole series in which the humour really springs from the characters. Madge, studying the paper in her kitchen, observes: 'See. There's a lot of deaths in tonight. Fancy, there's five columns of deaths. And there's only seven births. I think folks must be thinning out a bit, I do that.'

The subject of cremation is then brought up. 'You're lucky to see it at all, they whisk it away that quick,' says Bennett, just like on Broadway, as is the reference to not being sure whether the mourners are getting their loved one's ashes in the urn or a copy of the *Yorkshire Evening Post*, and the fact that they shouldn't shake their ashes out on the South Shore at Blackpool as it's a smokeless zone.

The final item in *On the Margin* was also the first sketch that had brought him to prominence: 'Take a Pew'. Maybe he and Garland hoped that, by recording it for television, it would finally acquire the longevity it deserved. Unfortunately, or ironically if you prefer, that recording did not survive. It is horribly cruel that a programme that was so dedicated to the theme of preservation has itself failed to be preserved on film or video.

Ever wise after the event, the media seemed happy that Bennett had bounced back. 'Now that Alan Bennett's BBC2 Wednesday series, *On the Margin*, is such a hit, knowing people are saying that of course he was always the most talented of the *Beyond the Fringe* quartet,' wrote the *Observer* diary on 20 November 1966. The diarist even claimed that the waitress in the café where they met insisted on chucking the embarrassed writer under the chin. ' "Ooh, I *gurgled* last night," she said. "You were absolutely sweet." ' Bennett, said the diarist, looked pleased but embarrassed, which was to become an expression he wore so often he might just as well have carried it around in a bag.

On the Margin is described in Mark Lewisohn's exhaustive and authoritative *Radio Times Guide to TV Comedy* as 'short-lived but well-remembered'. Lewisohn praised Bennett for '[weaving] deceptively savage satire into apparently innocuous sketches' and the show was so popular with the BBC that they repeated it on BBC2 in January and February 1967 before the more controversial transfer to BBC1 between May and July. Relations between Bennett and Frank Muir must still have remained warm, since Muir, recuperating in University College Hospital after collapsing from overwork, received a playful postcard from Bennett which read, 'Be wary of New Zealand nurses. They are so strong that when they tuck your sheets in they break your ankles.'

To coincide with the repeat on BBC1, an interview with Bennett appeared in the *Observer* on 28 May 1967. 'Looking back a few years, it's difficult to remember that Alan Bennett was an original member of the *Beyond the Fringe* team – or, indeed, that there was ever any "team" at all,' the piece began. Was it making the point that everyone had forgotten the original members of the *Fringe*? If so, Bennett's self-deprecating story about Harold and Mary Wilson could equally have been applied to his three fellow cast members. 'Peter Cook and Dudley Moore, now in marvellous partnership, have become "personalities" eagerly discussing themselves and Life in general,' it goes on. 'Jonathan Miller [is an] authority on almost everything under the sun, and wit.' The third paragraph begins: 'But what of Alan Bennett?' Thanks to *On the Margin*, Bennett 'has recently established himself as something of a national "name"'.

It also describes, in more detail than previously revealed, the walls of Bennett's NW1 pied-à-terre, 'crowded with early-Victorian glass paintings and row upon row of books: Lord Bacon's letters, Austin's philosophical papers, fourteen volumes of the English dictionary, and one on Donald McGill, of the seaside postcards'. One thinks of Peter Blake's kaleidoscope of antiquaries on the cover of the Beatles' *Sergeant Pepper* album, also from 1967: that fascination with antiquity and knick-knacks is probably the only point at which Bennett and the Beatles were pulling in the same direction in that seminal year for popular culture.

'At a pinch,' the article continued, 'we might have been in his old Oxford rooms, except there was this lumbering sideboard full of Staffordshire figures, entitled "The Death of Nelson", and blue and white pottery plates with lions on them.' It also describes the sound of a nineteenth-century clock which, it says, he brought back from Toronto. The *Observer* only described Bennett as seeming 'faintly ill at ease', the implication being that by his standards this was fairly relaxed.

One of Bennett's neighbours, George Melly, furnished the useful, and much-used, quote that, 'He is a rather complex person. And he's also a very private person. The paradox is that he finds it necessary to project his personality publicly.' The article also contained this characteristically perceptive swipe at himself, and his former *Fringe* colleagues. 'I don't think any of us were, or are, taken in by the others. Basically, we were all pretty arrogant people. Peter wouldn't be taken in by my shyness, for instance. He'd think, perhaps rightly, that deep down one was as conceited as anyone else. It just showed itself in different ways.'

Bennett told Kenneth Eastaugh in 1966 that 'I don't try to hurt now, just to entertain'. The remark may have been uttered more in hope than expectation, but Bennett can surely not have anticipated what toes he was stepping on. A sketch in programme three of *On the Margin*, for example, featured Bennett as a scoutmaster having a bit of a chat with a member of his pack, during which he has to break off every now and then to upbraid the boy. 'Don't play with your woggle, Brian . . . it's very distracting' or 'Don't suck your necker, Brian' and so on. It was an aside that Bennett would use to great (and subtler) effect in the opening speech from *Forty Years On*, two years later.

However, the sketch drew angry letters from scoutmasters when it was repeated on BBC1 on 10 June 1967, as did several other sketches. 'How much lower can the BBC stoop?' was one typical reaction. Another controversial item was a sketch about a man dictating the word N.O.R.W.I.C.H. – an acronym for 'knickers off ready when I come home' – to a telegram operator. One lady in Colwyn Bay was so angry she wrote to Bernard Delfont, who was the vice-chairman of the Grade Organisation at the time and so unlikely to be of much assistance. And a viewer from Camberley in Surrey was so enraged by the reference to Norwich that she wrote to assure the BBC that 'my television will never again be switched on except for the news until my licence expires'.

The people of Norwich do not seem to have risen up in anger at the perceived insult to their city, though a lady in nearby Ipswich found the sketch 'degrading'. A protest from veteran protester Mary Whitehouse received short shrift, but her voice was only one of many. Reading these letters over thirty years later, we cannot help but be struck, almost moved, by their injured tone. That outpouring from the angry letter-writing classes of Middle England may have led to this outburst from George Oliver, the angry Labour MP in *Getting On* (1971): 'If you ever raise your voice in public you know damn well before you've got two words out there'll be some clown stampeding for the Basildon Bond.' Bennett and Garland were not setting out to shock, but given Alan Bennett's near-sacrosanct status ever since the late 1980s, it is illuminating to see how much hostility he was capable of provoking back then.

These complaints notwithstanding, *On the Margin* was one of the best TV comedy shows of the 1960s. By the standards of later TV comedy, the pace of each show was impressively relaxed. The strength of the show is in the writing. The targets in Bennett's comedy were sacred cows: the incompetent doctor or major, the fumbling scoutmaster, the sly lawyer, the bullshitting critic; all were shown to be unreliable narrators, which led to them hanging themselves with their own rope. Pricking pomposity, in other words, was his hallmark. But what makes *On the Margin* such a delight is that it is truly, and uncompromisingly, a show created in Alan Bennett's image: lowbrow, highbrow, literary, saucy, straight and camp.

After all his years of struggle, Bennett should have been able to sit back and savour the prospect of seeing his first self-penned TV series going out. But Bennett's family cycle was running in a different, and rather more tragic, direction. It was a drama that he didn't reveal until over thirty years later, on 30 September 1999, in the twentieth-anniversary edition of the *London Review of Books*. The article, one of the most personal he had ever written, was a memoir of an evening in September 1966, when he and his father were forced to go and see the Mental Health Welfare Officer in Settle to discuss the increasingly distracted behaviour of his mother. Lilian Bennett's mental health had been in decline ever since the Bennetts had moved to Clapham. Bennett describes her fear of being spied on, overheard, watched, found out, and the time when she ran from the house in her nightgown and Walter had to persuade her to return. Six weeks after they met the welfare officer, Bennett wrote, Mrs Bennett was admitted to the psychiatric wing of Lancaster Moor Hospital, where she remained in care for eight years. Bennett records that his father never missed a visit. It is one of Alan Bennett's most simple, powerful and moving accounts of his parents' marriage.

That wasn't all. While father and son were discussing Mrs Bennett's medical history with the doctor, Walter Bennett was obliged to divulge a tragic secret, one that hitherto he had managed to keep from his son: that Lilian's father had not died a natural death, as Alan had assumed, but had thrown himself into the canal. Alan Bennett had no idea that his maternal grandfather had committed suicide. He reacted in several different ways. There was shock, obviously, and pain. But there was something else, too, which even at the time he knew was somewhat less noble. 'In 1966 I have just begun to write but have already given up on my own background because the material seems so thin. This perks things up a bit.' Eager to hear more, he remained frustrated by his father's discretion. Walter Bennett refused to throw any more light on the matter: 'he still seems to want to keep it hidden and will not be questioned about it, sensing perhaps that my interest in it is as drama and only one stage up from gossip.' He detects in his father's reactions to his questions a whiff of distaste.

On 28 August 1967 Bennett was thrown one of the BBC's weightiest garlands when he was the guest on *Desert Island Discs*. Introduced as 'the writer and humorist' by the programme's creator, Roy Plomley, Bennett chatted self-deprecatingly, with many an 'um' and an 'ah', but managing a few jokes on the way. He listened politely when Plomley praised *Beyond the Fringe*'s mixture of high and low humour, and graciously accepted that *On the Margin* had been a great success. He chose only one pop song: 'Funny How Love Can Be' by the Ivy League, which he said he had played a lot while driving from London to Leeds and back after *Beyond the Fringe* had closed in New York. His other choices included music by Brahms, Bach, Strauss, Berlioz and Walton, and he also requested the sounds of an English summer's day near a railway station, a challenge to which the BBC Sounds Unit was more than equal. His luxury item – which experience suggests he might have preferred to revise, given its faintly patronising inclusion in numerous subsequent profiles – was an unending supply of afternoon teas, and for his favourite book he chose the complete run of *Horizon*, the wartime literary magazine edited by Cyril Connolly.

Other projects around this time never came to fruition. Graham McCann, in his biography of Cary Grant, notes that Bennett was working on a screenplay between 1966 and 1967 called 'The Vicar's Wife' in which it was said that Grant might appear, but as Bennett said in a written reply to McCann: '[it] never looked like actually going into production, Cary Grant or no Cary Grant.' Had the film been made, Ned Sherrin would have been one of the producers. In his memoirs, Sherrin describes the screenplay as 'a comedy in the Ealing manner', and adds that Peter Sellers's agent Harvey Orkin thought Sellers might plump for it, but the plot revolved around a busty woman's attempts to induce a heart attack in her elderly parson husband, and since Sellers had only recently suffered a catastrophic cardiac arrest shortly after his marriage to Britt Ekland, Sherrin admits 'we ruefully realised that it had not been the most tactful text to offer'.

Bennett and Garland then made enquiries about another vicar, after taking an interest in the diaries of Francis Kilvert, the Victorian clergyman who was largely unknown when he died in 1863. The plan was to turn Kilvert's diaries into a film for the BBC, and maybe even a stage play for the Hampstead Theatre. Like the old-time films used in *On the Margin*, Garland tried to send out all the right messages when he stressed that the play would be 'straight dramatisation, without satire

'How will I ever get out of here?'
Leeds, 1930s.
(Hulton Getty)

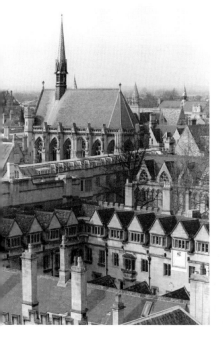

Exeter College, Oxford,
Bennett's home for eight years.
(Press Association)

Bennett (left) with his fellow stars from *Beyond the Fringe*, Peter Cook, Dudley Moore and Jonathan Miller, at the start of their advance into the sixties. (BBC)

Bennett with John Sergeant and Victoria Stride in
On the Margin, BBC2, 1966. (BBC)

Kenneth More, not getting on at all well
with Alan Bennett in *Getting On*,
Queen's Theatre, 1971.
(Donald Cooper/Photostage)

'In England we never entirely mean what we
say, do we? Do I mean that? Not entirely.'
Alec Guinness as the former spy Hilary in
The Old Country, Queen's Theatre, 1977.
(Donald Cooper/Photostage)

What was all the farce about? Joan Sanderson, Alec Guinness and John Bird in
Habeas Corpus, Lyric Theatre, 1973. (Donald Cooper/Photostage)

'Spontaneous? Then it must be stopped at once.' Bennett and John Gielgud regroup to record *Forty Years On* for Radio 4's Saturday Night Theatre in 1973.
(BBC)

A Bennett stalwart: Thora Hird in *Me, I'm Afraid of Virginia Woolf,* LWT, 1978.
(Rex Features)

Standing firm against a hostile press: the writer of *The Old Crowd* with its director and polisher Lindsay Anderson. (Snowdon/Camera Press)

The Old Crowd, LWT, 1979. The *Daily Express* splenetic reaction was: 'This was almost the living end.'
(Rex Features)

Resuscitation proved impossible. Joan Plowright, Colin Blakely and Liz Smith in *Enjoy*, Vaudeville, 1980.
(Donald Cooper/Photostage)

Must traitors sleep in the buff?' Alan Bates as Guy Burgess, freshly kitted out after Coral Browne's shopping trip in *An Englishman Abroad,* BBC, 1983.

(BBC)

The writer, plus strewn carcasses: *A Private Function,* Handmade Films, 1984.

(Snowdon/Camera Press)

Daniel Day Lewis as Dr Kafka in
The Insurance Man, BBC, 1986.
(BBC)

'Love me, dickhead.' Roger Lloyd Pack
as a different kind of Kafka, trying to
resist the advances of his father Hermann
(Jim Broadbent) in *Kafka's Dick*,
Royal Court, 1986.
(Donald Cooper/Photostage)

and in no way suggestive'. Unfortunately, Bennett sent out all the wrong messages by revealing that his enthusiasm for Kilvert was based in part on the fact that the clergyman 'was very fond of little girls without realising what it was all about', as if he were an early version of Lewis Carroll. Kilvert's stock had risen since the 1930s, when a relative discovered his diaries, and he was now seen as the cherished chronicler of a bygone age, an eyewitness of all things Victorian and every bit as significant as Trollope. Perhaps it was with that very aim in mind – to safeguard his naivety against the retrospective rereading of later generations – that the Kilvert Society was formed in 1948, and by the mid-1960s its 500 members, mindful of Bennett's fondness for impersonating clergymen, were not feeling well disposed towards Bennett's and Garland's project. 'It is so easy to put all sorts of constructions on much of what Kilvert wrote,' said Mr Oswin Prosser, the society's secretary on 24 June 1967, the day of Kilvert's annual commemoration service. 'Victorian sentimentality so lends itself to be turned into goodness knows what.'

Bennett might have had a lucky escape. In 1978 BBC2 broadcast *Kilvert's Life*, with Timothy Davies in the lead role. Although Davies was praised for his performance, F. Grice, deputy president of the Kilvert Society, complained in a letter to the *Radio Times* that the adapter, James Andrew Hall, had taken liberties with the text. 'Viewers ought to be warned that if they look through the Diary to find the episode in which Kilvert's friend Morrell dyes his hair they will be wasting their time,' he wrote. 'This incident was pure invention on the part of Mr Hall. It was not only a feeble piece of comedy, but an act of deceit.' Perhaps it was just as well that Bennett's and Garland's proposed adaptation was stillborn. With the project dead in the water, and having tried and failed to raid someone else's tuck box, Bennett returned to the cupboard to see what else was inside.

7

And don't put it in your handkerchief

Forty Years On, 1968–1970

Alan Bennett described *Forty Years On* as the happiest theatrical experience of his early life. Still remembered fondly, and frequently restaged more than thirty years after its first performance, *Forty Years On* marked the arrival of a new voice, and the return of several old ones. He had triumphed on the stage on both sides of the Atlantic, and his first TV series had been a runaway hit. The TV machine had gobbled up much of his early work, including material which had first seen the light of day when he was still at university ten years earlier. But *Forty Years On* was not just 'an elaborate life-support system for the preservation of bad jokes', as Bennett describes it in his introduction to the play.

Originally written for radio, it languished inside the drawer of an office in the BBC's Broadcasting House. While it lay there, however, Bennett rewrote it. What he had was a series of rather skilful parodies, some new, some from *On the Margin*, *NSMAP* or *BBC-3*, until he had the '(fairly obvious) idea of a school play, with the school itself a loose metaphor for England'. He also had Patrick Garland, who was extending the early promise he had shown at Oxford by going straight from making his light entertainment debut on TV to making his West End debut as a director. With such a starry team, expectations were bound to be high.

Forty Years On is an anecdotal lesson in English history from the dawn of the twentieth century to the present day, told in flashbacks, with the parts taken by staff and boys. It is also a dramatised inner portrait of the young Alan Bennett. Much of the colour of that period derives from dramatised drawing-room scenes, and Bennett gives credit in his introduction to the diaries and memoirs of Leonard Woolf and Harold Nicolson, whose bittersweet journals lend the scenes much of their elegiac beauty.

Albion House, where the action takes place, is a minor public school in southern England. It is the final day of the school year, and marks the retirement of the headmaster, during which he and the parents will watch a play, 'Speak for England, Arthur', devised by the staff and boys, which reviews some key moments in the first forty years of the last century, including the Second World War.

The role of the headmaster called for a rare combination of sympathy and comedy, both of which were found, in copious measure, in the performance of Sir John Gielgud. Much of the moulding of Gielgud's personality to the part is described in a diary Bennett kept during that period, which was first published in the *Sunday Times* on 17 November 1968 and then, years later, in *Writing Home*. With his now-familiar frankness, it charts the progress of the play from pre-casting through rehearsals at the Drury Lane Theatre until well into the run. We find Bennett listening nervously as Sir John criticises, misconstrues and eventually agrees to take the part. Bennett also sat with Patrick Garland – even then, it seems, capable of getting on Bennett's nerves with stray 'fatuous' remarks – as they auditioned over a hundred boys in two days, lamenting that they had all either been in Lionel Bart's *Oliver!* or were about to be signed up for *Goodbye Mr Chips*. (The first time Bennett arrived for auditions, he was sent to the back of the queue: a story which, had it not been true, he might well have had to invent, or at least embellish.)

It is in keeping with much in the play that Bennett, surveying the line of hopeful applicants, notes sadly how 'the other attributes of boyhood – youth, gaiety, innocence – have long since gone'. He notes their dress sense – 'matador pants, turtle-neck shirts, a few rings on each hand' – and contrasts it with how they might have dressed fifteen or twenty years before, 'in neat flannel suits with plastered-down hair'. Nevertheless, one of the boys was Anthony Andrews, the beautiful youth who would go on to play Sebastian Flyte in Granada TV's lavish adaptation of one of Bennett's favourite Oxford novels, *Brideshead Revisited*. Two others would become firm friends of his. George Fenton is a composer whose music has accompanied many of Bennett's plays, including *Talking Heads* and, most recently, *Telling Tales*. Keith McNally went to New York and became a well-known, if low-profile, restaurateur. He would become one of Bennett's fixed points in the city when Bennett bought a flat on Thompson Street in SoHo, and Bennett would become a backer in one of McNally's restaurants, Odeon, on 145 West Broadway at Thomas Street, described in the *Access New York Restaurant Guide* when it opened in 1980 as 'the hottest place downtown with the art crowd'.

There was one dire setback when, in August 1968, Bennett was flying out to Switzerland and he lost the corrected manuscript, rather as T.E. Lawrence – the subject of affectionate mockery in the play – did with the first draft of *Seven Pillars of Wisdom*. Luckily, he remembered enough of his original play not to have to include too many of Sir John Gielgud's more outlandish improvements to the text, such as the advice that they should have cardboard cutouts, not real boys, on stage. And various people, such as the literary agents A.P. Watt, the executors of the Sapper estate, objected to the parodies of Sapper, Buchan and Dornford Yates, though very often the families themselves thought it was all great fun. Mrs Vinogradoff, the daughter of Lady Ottoline Morrell, was less amused when she 'got wind of' the sketch about her mother, and asked Patrick Garland for it to be removed. Garland was clearly panicking but Bennett, the man who had once refused not to say 'erection' in front of the Queen, was in no mood to allow the end of the first act to be bowdlerised.

The casting of Gielgud was a masterstroke. For one thing, Gielgud knew many of the people referred to in the play: Nijinsky, Diaghilev, T.E. Lawrence (again) and Ottoline Morrell. The Alan Bennett who had been so impressed to meet an old Exonian friend of Scott and Zelda Fitzgerald was getting more accustomed to that kind of literary fraternity.

And if Gielgud had known them, Lady Diana Cooper, who came to see the play in London, had gone one step further. When she came backstage to chat to Sir John, she revealed she had been in tears during the headmaster's beautiful speech at the end of Act One in which he describes a visit to a country house, called Kimber, on the eve of the First World War, with friends such as Edward Horner, Julian and Billy Grenfell, and Patrick Shaw-Stewart. 'How did you know to choose all those names?' she said to Bennett. 'They were all my lovers.'

The play previewed in Manchester, where the management for Stoll Theatres tried to coax Bennett into doing some pre-publicity interviews. He wrote in his diary that he refused to cooperate on 'gossipy, taste-whetting pieces, all the silly paraphernalia of show biz which I loathe'. By September, his opinion of the press was further diminished when one reporter told him baldly that it would make better copy if he and Garland claimed they had auditioned seven hundred boys (rather than a hundred and seventy), and when another described him as looking young for forty-three. Bennett was, by now, thirty-four.

During the Manchester run, Bennett joined Peter Cook and Jonathan Miller at the 69 Theatre for a discussion forum called 'This England'. Bennett noted that 'the seven years since *Beyond the Fringe* have hardly altered the relationship between us'. Miller was still 'voluble and lucid', Cook 'seizes opportunities for laughs' while as for himself 'I make occasional heartfelt but dull remarks'. The difference, said Bennett (apart from the fact that Dudley Moore was not present), was that he no longer wished he could be as funny as Peter Cook or as dazzling as Miller. Once again Bennett seems to be doing himself down. He would no sooner have agreed to stand in front of a live audience and be dull than take his clothes off in front of them. He still wanted to be funny, but in his own way and on his own terms, and he was finding out how to do that. Bennett took the part of Tempest in the play, a junior master who is responsible for much of the shenanigans that so baffle and enrage the headmaster.

Gielgud was the first theatrical knight with whom Bennett worked closely, and Bennett was clearly awe-struck – as were most who came across Gielgud. Apart from his wonderful skills as a raconteur, and despite being, at times, 'maddeningly changeable', Bennett is full of praise for Gielgud's manners, his composure, his lack of malice, and above all his modesty, even humility. As the play progressed, and Gielgud abandoned his earlier caution and began to address the audience as if he were picking out old friends, Bennett observed how the chorus of boys – whom he praises as 'imaginative and articulate' – was becoming one of the best things about the play, and how they confounded his earlier, rather pessimistic assumptions about the youth of Britain.

On 4 October Walter and Lilian Bennett – temporarily herself again, one assumes – came to see the play in Manchester. Bennett does not record the full range of their reactions, except that they mistook Mac, Gielgud's dresser, for Gielgud, and thought he was ignoring them. But other personalities, more widely known, were starting to come and see the play, vindicating Bennett's belief that it would succeed by word of mouth, rather than by the fanfare of media hype. One day it was Cyril Connolly, the former editor of the journal *Horizon*, a full set of which Bennett had asked for on his desert island. Another day it was Noël Coward, who was 'brimming with enthusiasm and saying all the right things'. Is it modesty that prevents Bennett from detailing Coward's reaction, or is he beginning to get used to his success?

But, as Bennett noted, by the time the run was properly under way, it had become more like just another job for the cast, and that feeling of togetherness, of forging something new – often in the face of cash-conscious management or sniping local reporters – was gone. Appropriately, since the play was so markedly about looking back with sadness, even the fact that the show was such a hit struck Bennett with less force than the memory that it had once been so much fun. As he said later, the moment when he and some of the boys went for a canter on horseback along the Downs during the Brighton run was liberating for him simply because he knew that he would never have done such a thing when he was in *Beyond the Fringe*.

Refusing to play to the media's preconceived notions about him, Bennett had not written a play about the Church, or Oxford dons. However, the area he chose was not so very far away, and the subject was England, or Englishness.

This, then, is old England, represented by the headmaster, whose opening speech, despite being drowned out at times by a remembrance of time present, the drone of a jet aeroplane, very soon became a classic comedy monologue that was every bit as popular in comedy request programmes as the sermon in *Beyond the Fringe*. The headmaster clearly wishes he were delivering a closing oration like Moses bidding his people farewell at the end of Deuteronomy. But Moses did not have to deal with the boys of Albion House: 'I think it was Baden-Powell who said that a public schoolboy must be acceptable at a dance and invaluable in a shipwreck. But I don't think you'd be much use in either, Skinner, if you were playing with the hair of the boy in front. See me afterwards.'

Repeatedly urging his audience to attend 'a silent prayer', the headmaster tries hard to attain the higher ground. 'The more observant ones among you will have noticed that one of Bombardier Tiffin's legs was not his own. The other one, God bless him, was lost in the Great War.' (Bennett has been pursued by false or missing legs, whether in the classic 'One Leg Too Few' sketch by Cook and Moore from *Beyond the Fringe*, or the false leg of Donald Albery, the man who brought *Beyond the Fringe* to London.) He continues: 'Some people lost other things, less tangible perhaps than legs but no less worthwhile – they lost illusions, they lost hope, they lost faith. That is why . . . chewing, Charteris. That is why the twenties and thirties were such a muddled and grubby time, for lack of all the hopes and ideals that perished on the fields of France. And don't put it in your handkerchief.'

What intensifies the humour is the deep emotion the headmaster feels as he tries to make his point. 'Thirty years ago today, Tupper, the Germans marched into Poland and you're picking your nose. See me afterwards.' No wonder the T.E. Lawrence monologue, which first appeared in *On the Margin*, is repeated here. 'Tee Hee Lawrence' was never made to look funnier, even if the television viewer from Northwood who complained about it was probably not in the audience.

At the heart of *Forty Years On* is a debate about the value of modernity. We are witnessing a farewell ceremony, not just for the headmaster but for the world that reared him. In the last words of the play: 'To let. A valuable site at the crossroads of the world. At present on offer to European clients. Outlying portions of the estate already disposed of to sitting tenants. Of some historical and period interest. Some alterations and improvements necessary.' The death sentence has been passed: Bennett's lament is that so little of England's past will be preserved during the transition into the new world. Streets and shops could, in theory at least, be saved from the bulldozer. Memories, though, and lives, were more nebulous. Amid the chaotic summer of 1968, with rioting students in Paris being sent reeling by water cannon, and Vietnamese villagers set alight by napalm, as Americans buried yet another Kennedy amid more scenes of national mourning and outrage, there was no such blood-letting over the struggle for power in Bennett's world. Just a tinge of sadness in a community as hermetic and self-contained as the most inward-looking of Oxford colleges.

What debate there is is between the new king and the old king. 'Have you ever thought, Headmaster, that your standards might perhaps be a little out of date?' snaps Franklin, the incoming head played by Paul Eddington, when he finally loses his temper. The headmaster responds: 'Of course they're out of date. Standards always are out of date. That is what makes them standards.'

Retiring king and succeeding king circle each other warily throughout the play, with most of the best lines going to the former. 'The trouble with you, Franklin,' says the headmaster, 'is that you have this unfortunate tendency to put ideas into the boys' heads.' The headmaster also suspects that he, or his generation, is being ridiculed, rather like what might have happened if the old footage of Gus Elen or Florrie Ford had fallen into the wrong hands, instead of Garland's and Bennett's in On the Margin. 'There's an element of mockery here which I don't like,' he chides Franklin. 'I don't mind your tongue being in your cheek, but I suspect your heart is there with it.'

Ever the parodist – from the revised, updated Cinderella to his gallery of rambling vicars – Bennett had an entire slate of styles across which to spread himself this time, given the historical arc of the play within a play. Critics purred with delight at his Wildean wit: 'I see the Dean of Windsor has been consecrated Bishop of Bombay,' says Lady Dundown, an Edwardian dowager in a wheelchair, played by Bennett. Withers, the butler, played by Gielgud, says: 'Bombay. Hmm. If I may say so, ma'am, that seems to me to be taking Christianity a little too far.' The tone is maintained in Lady Dundown's best-known remark: 'But then all women dress like their mothers, that is their tragedy. No man ever does. That is his.'

Some conversations, such as that between Bertrand Russell and Lady Ottoline Morrell, recall the Biggin Hill reverie in 'The Aftermyth of War' from Beyond the Fringe, though Bennett has allowed himself some more fruit and a lot more sauce. Lady Ottoline Morrell says to 'Bertie': 'I had an accident yesterday. One of my breasts popped out of my frock.' 'Oh?' says Bertie. 'Which one?' which prompts an angry rumble from the headmaster, offstage, and a further encounter between Franklin and the headmaster.

In Act Two, the headmaster grows ever more anxious, and in the process makes more and more of an obstacle of himself on stage. The boys try to prepare for the next scene while he worries aloud to Matron about Franklin's plans for the school:

> The first thing he will do is abolish corporal punishment, the second thing he'll do is abolish compulsory games. And the third thing he'll do is abolish the cadet corps. Those are the three things liberal schoolmasters always do, Matron, the first opportunity they get. They think it makes the sensitive boys happy. In my experience sensitive boys are never happy anyway, so what is the point?

The headmaster's loyalties are with the hearty singing of the rugby club rather than the vivid re-enactment of a literary soirée in which 'There by the window talking to Leonard and Virginia were the Berlins, Irving and Isaiah', a joke that resurfaced in the celestial cocktail party that closed *Kafka's Dick* in 1986. The monologue also reheated some of the material he had used in one of his *Monitor* appearances in 1964: 'Of all the honours that fell upon Virginia's head, none, I think, pleased her more than the *Evening Standard* Award for the Tallest Woman Writer of 1927, an award she took by a neck from Elizabeth Bowen. Dylan Thomas, for instance, a man of great literary stature, only came up to her waist. And sometimes not even to there.' If the collision of Dylan Thomas and Virginia Woolf sounds unlikely, that is because it was meant to be Cyril Connolly. When Connolly came to see the play, Bennett thought, perhaps oversensitively, that he was unhappy at being part of the anecdote, and replaced him, a move he later regretted, since inside almost every shy, self-conscious man there is an outgoing, confident man trying to get out. With *Forty Years On*, everyone wanted to get in. Bennett had created the literary equivalent to Peter Cook's Establishment Club, with famous names hammering on the door and clamouring to be admitted. For a while it was the only party to be seen at.

Headmasters, of course, are irrevocably associated with the Establishment themselves, something which the headmaster understands but which Franklin does not. To the boys, Franklin is no longer on their side. As the headmaster says: 'However daring and outspoken you are, to the boys you are a master, and all your swearing and your smut, your silk handkerchiefs and your suede shoes can't alter that. We're in the same boat, Franklin, you and I.'

As the act unfolds, Hugh, a Conservative MP, delivers a fiery outburst against 'the mulberry-faced men with carnations in their buttonholes' whom he thought the war would see off, but who are still there by the end. 'Ranged behind Churchill now are the very men who kept him out of office all through the thirties . . . And they will destroy him yet because it is their England he is fighting for . . . The England of Halifax who went hunting with Göring.' Bennett's sentimentality is not to praise figures of the past simply for having lived in the past. His heroes – as he said in *Telling Tales* – were George Guest, W. Vane Morland and R.A.H. Livett. These three men were, respectively, the directors of Education, Transport and Housing throughout his childhood and adolescence in Leeds, and their names were 'as constant and unchanging as Tyrrell of Avon, the film censor whose certificate preceded every film one ever saw; or H.O. Peppiatt, the Secretary of the Bank of England, whose signature authenticated every note'. He described them as 'the municipal pillars of my youthful Leeds', who did much to make public education and a civilised life available to him and his fellow students. Anything less than that, and they were fodder for the satirist in him too.

The play ends with a trial scene, as, too, does *Kafka's Dick*. The stage is transformed into a courtroom, with Neville Chamberlain, suddenly the villain of the play, brought back from death to play the defendant. Franklin is Neville Chamberlain, Tempest is counsel for the defence, and the headmaster is the judge. In this kangaroo court, Chamberlain is sentenced to perpetual ignominy, despite the extenuating circumstances that he was born in Birmingham. We flit within seconds from the invasion of Poland to Churchill's victory speech, from the darkness and anger of 1939 to the brilliance of 1945, and with it comes the play's closing moments. The cast are seen picking up their belongings, and the headmaster, having discarded his gown, returns to the stage, the play within a play almost forgotten. Just as he predicted, the headmaster and Franklin seem to be coming closer in spirit as the headmaster derides 'our crass-builded, glass-bloated, green-belted world [in which] Sunday is for washing the car, tinned peaches and Carnation milk'. Franklin follows on in the same vein, a near-literary cousin of Evelyn Waugh's Hooper in *Brideshead Revisited*. 'A sergeant's world it is now, the world of the lay-by and the civic improvement scheme.' It can only have been a coincidence, but Peter Cook, playing the devil in his 1967 film *Bedazzled*, uttered a similar curse when he vowed: 'I'll cover the world in Wimpy burgers . . . I'll fill it full of concrete runways, motorways, aircraft, television and automobiles, advertising, plastic flowers, frozen food and supersonic bangs.' Both predictions, however differently expressed, have come horribly true.

The headmaster's final, saddest tirade continues the unashamedly anti-populist theme. 'The crowd has found the door into the garden. Now they will tear up the flowers.' There is a part of Bennett which wholeheartedly preferred a world of Edwardian exclusivity.

Then the headmaster shakes hands with Franklin, takes one last look at the boys, and leaves as Franklin leads the choir in 'All Creatures That on Earth Do Dwell' – a strange, sad, sentimental ending to a play overflowing with sentiment and a lament for a lost England, a lost Eden. Bennett was completing his introduction to the play on Armistice Day, and as he wrote he heard the guns rumbling across Hyde Park for the start of the two-minute silence. 'I find the ceremony ridiculous and hypocritical, and yet it brings a lump to my throat,' he noticed. 'Why? I suppose that is what the play is trying to resolve.'

'Brilliant, if rather too self-indulgent,' wrote John Stevenson of the Manchester preview at the Palace Theatre, describing it as 'A sort of "Get Lost Mr Chips"'. Then it went to Brighton, where Sydney Edwards, writing in the *Evening Standard* on 25 October, concluded from that town's praise that 'Mr Bennett appears to have a hit on his hands'. Edwards, a Brighton old hand, was in the audience on one of the famous occasions in the seaside town when the audience delivered its verdict on *Beyond the Fringe* by getting up and leaving. When they talked, Bennett was in forgiving mood. 'I'd like to do something all together again,' he said, referring to Cook, Miller and Moore. Miller, he said, he saw almost every day (since they were now neighbours). He saw less of Peter and Dudley. 'I think we still have a good effect on each other,' he appears to have said in unusually positive tones. 'We restrain each other from our worse excesses. We had something then and I think we've still got it.'

Bennett referred approvingly to the quartet's 'certain distrust of each other', and to their being 'all anxious to get our own bits in'. He also admitted that there had been a small tiff during rehearsals that very day. 'I have got a bit of a temper and it's been a bit of a trying morning,' he told Edwards. There seems no doubt that the young Bennett could be quite peppery during rehearsals.

Bennett thinks of Brighton as 'a dangerous place'. In part this was because the cast of *Beyond the Fringe* had faced such a hostile reception there. 'The seats were going up like pistol shots there,' he recalled. But they were in a more conciliatory mood for *Forty Years On*, and it was from this point on, when Gielgud got what Bennett describes as 'his second wind', that the mood among the cast began to improve.

It opened at the Apollo Theatre in London on 31 October 1968. The critical verdict was overwhelmingly positive. Writing in the *Guardian*, Philip Hope-Wallace, or Willis Hope-Wallet as he had been renamed in the critics' sketch from *On the Margin*, described it as 'a wry, irreverent and often wildly hilarious kind of *Cavalcade* in reverse'. He was sure that some people would find it 'in bad taste, cruel, not to say blasphemous'. He felt that T.E. Lawrence and Neville Chamberlain had been subjected to 'rough justice'. But as for Sir John Gielgud, 'I have never seen him funnier', and, more important still, 'I found myself laughing helplessly, more often than at any such time this year so far'.

Peter Lewis of the *Daily Mail* described the play as 'a crazy history lesson' and that 'Underneath the ridicule, a feeling of great affection persists'. In the *Evening Standard*, young Alexander Walker called it 'the most light-hearted, and certainly most literate, entertainment I've seen and heard in months'. Gielgud, who after a triumphant run gave way to Emlyn Williams in 1969, was praised as 'deftly comic'. Walker also praised the large chorus of schoolboys and its 'earlier versions of rugby club ballads which the stage censor would not have permitted even on Saturday nights'.

In the *Sunday Telegraph*, Frank Marcus called it 'a string of extremely funny revue sketches', which he meant as a compliment. He also heaped praise on Tempest, played by Bennett, whom he called 'Waspish, ribald and always deflationary'. 'At last,' he wrote, in tones which modern readers of the *Sunday Telegraph* might not recognise immediately, 'suffused with Edwardian nostalgia but still hearteningly and un-ashamedly socialist in tone, the past is buried.'

The nearest to disaffection came from Irving Wardle in *The Times*, who began by calling it 'an invertebrate and ill-argued mess. The school never expands into its metaphorical identity and . . . it is hard to select any consistent attitude of breadth of interest commensurate with a theme.' Wardle tries to praise the play but cannot hold back the opinion that what he has been seeing is 'the ultimate fifth-form show'. He had praise for Patrick Garland's production, which he called 'a model of controlled anarchy', but concluded: 'As a playwright Mr Bennett has no voice of his own but, as we know from his revue work, he has a deadly ear for other men's styles.'

Forty Years On is sumptuous: a marvellous, complex bouquet of tones and accents, nodding its head in many different directions and housing numerous wickedly accurate parodies. But it is a young man's play, and it is, surely, a loosely woven skein of revue sketches. Ronald W. Strang, in the *International Directory of Theatre*, wrote: 'The conceit is by no means novel, and in the hands of [Howard] Brenton or [David] Hare has been more abrasively pursued, but Bennett has the courage to play it for all it is worth, granting equal weight to nostalgic evocation and to ridicule.'

If England, in the form of Albion House, existed as a sort of fragile, threatened ecosystem, Alan Bennett discovered a real ecosystem in the area around Clapham, scene of his parents' relocation. And if the writer of *Forty Years On* was looking for a hobbyhorse, a prime case fell into his lap when the owner of the electrical shop in Settle decided to remove an old mounting block in the same year that *Forty Years On* was first performed.

A mounting block is a set of stone steps usually built against a wall and near a pub, which enables the more portly type of horse-rider to mount their steed with some dignity. There was one such block outside Settle's electrical shop, close to a former inn, but by 1968, when horse traffic was markedly down on the preceding century, the block was seen as an irrelevance and – sin of all sins – an encumbrance to drivers wishing to get to and from their cars easily. Without any further consultation, the block was removed, and the march of the twentieth century took another step forward.

Riding to the rescue came Alan Bennett, who could see, almost before anyone else, that this was the thin edge of the wedge. As anyone who has walked down Skipton High Street since then will know, it was just as well that he did. In 1968, he became president of the Settle and District Civic Society, a post he has held ever since. As unwilling as he was to talk up his own plays, he was always more forthcoming when it came to talking to local journalists such as Peter Cooke (with an 'e') of the *Yorkshire Post* about his campaigns. At first, he told Cooke, the Yorkshire folk felt that the society was not campaigning in their interests, but 'Now they realise the society is not a collection of interfering busybodies, who merely want to see the place tarted up in a spurious manner.'

Forty Years On won a Special Award at the 1968 *Evening Standard* Drama Awards in January 1969. In stepping forward to receive it, Bennett had to endure a mock tirade from Frankie Howerd, who said that it was one of the few plays he had seen during 1968. He cursed Bennett for being 'not only talented but young with it'. Bennett reminded his audience that the last time he had held such a trophy was in 1962. 'I haven't seen the award from that day to this,' he said, referring to *Beyond the Fringe*. 'I think Dudley left it in someone's car.' Knowing what Dudley liked doing (or, more accurately, liked to have done to him) in cars, it seems quite likely that the preservation of a gong was very, very far from his mind at the time. At the 1968 Variety Awards, Alan Bennett shared a Special Award with Sir John Gielgud for *Forty Years On*. The tortoise was drawing level with the hares.

One flare-up spoiled an otherwise exceptional year. After a filmed extract from *Forty Years On* (made for *Release*, and shown in November 1968) was played to the assembled winners, losers and other guests at the 1969 Variety Club Awards, Bennett was sent a cutting from the *Yorkshire Post* reporting that a TV viewer in north-west Leeds was so incensed by the sketch that he had complained to his MP, Sir Donald Kaberry. Kaberry wrote to the BBC director-general, Sir Charles Curran, to report the offending item. Curran's conciliatory reply infuriated Bennett, and on 23 April 1969 he fired off a long and rather indignant letter to Curran (addressing him frostily as 'Dear Sir'). 'If the BBC decides to . . . illustrate the awards with extracts from the material on which the awards were based, it seems to me not in its province to apologise for the nature of that material.' Bennett's final (and third) paragraph is practically peevish, a tone he very rarely adopts in public. 'You were not entitled to apologise for the nature of this material . . . to apologise at all seems an absurd inconsistency.'

The same day, he drafted a more sober letter, for the attention of the great Huw Wheldon, to whom by now he was sufficiently close to address as 'Huw'. (The danger of being lightly rapped on the wrist, as happened at Exeter when he forgot himself and dared to refer to the chaplain by his Christian name could, if he had been a different sort of person, have been safely confined to the past.) He told Wheldon that he had received only one letter of complaint about the extract, 'accusing me of presenting the British public with a basin of shit in a bowl of piss: I should imagine it was much the same sort of person who wrote to Kaberry, and whose opinion now seems to carry such weight at Broadcasting House'.

This was more typical Bennett, a man who let others dig a hole for themselves. 'Unless the BBC is prepared to back up its writers and declare its faith in them, and not kowtow to this sort of complaint, we are nowhere,' he concluded. Curran's reply is a model of diplomacy, his defence resting on the claim that the *Yorkshire Post* had told only half the story and had coupled that with a misleading headline to boot. The BBC, he said, had not apologised for the nature of the material. 'As you rightly imply, it would have been impertinent to have done so,' wrote Curran, more succinctly than Bennett's intemperate but sincere outburst.

An interview by Sydney Edwards in the *Evening Standard* in October 1968 was topped with an interesting stand-first or sub-headline. Too long for any modern newspaper, it reveals how the press, or at least the elders – 'back bench', in some quarters – who composed such stand-firsts, viewed Bennett. 'Alan Bennett once said he felt like a drummer who had left the Beatles before they became famous,' it read. 'A couple of years ago when Messrs Miller, Cook and Moore were flourishing, enlarging their empires in all directions, his output consisted of the occasional professor or clergyman on Saturday-night satire. But the poor relation has caught up.' Bennett had not just left the group; he had formed his own band. And *Forty Years On* had been such a happy experience that it was natural to want the old team to stick together, so he and Patrick Garland, as well as the designer Julia Trevelyan Oman, started out on a new play with the same spirit of optimism and enthusiasm. It was even arranged for rehearsals to start at the same stage, Drury Lane, and on the same day, August Bank Holiday 1971, as in

1968. 'In some cultures they would have slit the throat of a chicken,' wrote Bennett. 'In view of what was to happen it would have been just as effective.'

8

When does life begin?

Getting On, 1971–1972

Gloucester Crescent, where Bennett moved in 1969, lies in the middle of what HMQ in *A Question of Attribution* would have called 'one of my All Walks of Life' areas. Although its Italianate houses are built on what were originally the fields of Camden Town in the 1840s, it is only a stone's – or a beer can's – throw from Arlington House, which for many years has offered shelter to homeless men. Their mumbled disagreements frequently disturb the equanimity of the fruit and veg market stallholders in nearby Inverness Street. Regent's Park is a short stroll away, as is the canal at the end of Oval Road. Meanwhile, each morning, hundreds of well-paid, well-dressed men and women leave their fashionable homes to travel to their newspapers, TV or radio stations, theatres, production companies, publishing houses or advertising agencies. Jonathan and Rachel Miller had already been there three years when Bennett arrived. Bennett's next-door neighbours were the journalist and novelist Alice Thomas Ellis and her husband Colin Haycraft, the gentleman publisher. His firm, Gerald Duckworth, occupied part of the old piano factory at number 43, a building in its own way as remarkable as that other circular Camden gem, the Roundhouse. Over time, other residents would include the Labour MP Giles Radice, the artist David Gentleman, the writer Deborah Moggach, the journalist Fiona MacCarthy, the indefinable

George Melly, the *Woman's Hour* presenter Jenny Murray, the editor of the *London Review of Books* Mary Kay Wilmers, the writer Claire Tomalin and, a few years later, her second husband, Bennett's old army friend Michael Frayn. The house Bennett moved into, and for which he paid a not exorbitant £11,000, was on the corner, though the side windows were blocked out. It had four floors, each floor only going back one room, which seemed to enhance its doll's house appearance. This, then, was to be Bennett's permanent London home from now on. There was no longer much point in pretending that he had not become an integral part of the life and times of NW1.

Gloucester Crescent had its own atmosphere, its own rhythm and its own rituals. It also had its own homeless eccentric: a woman who turned up from time to time and parked a series of increasingly dilapidated vans in the street. She first came to Bennett's attention in around 1969: it was as if she were part of the furniture of the street. Something in Bennett's mind must have marked her down for future exploration. Then again, Miss Shepherd was quite a striking presence – quite a pongy one, too, by all accounts – and to a writer like Bennett who was keen to draw the marrow of eccentricity from the bone of everyday life, here was a ready supply. Miss Shepherd tended to come back to the Crescent: something in it triggered an association, as random streets often do to homeless people. By 1971, accounts of Miss Shepherd's eccentric behaviour were becoming a daily occurrence. During this time, Bennett suggested she spend her nights in a lean-to at the side of his house. By about 1974, Miss Shepherd had parked her van in Bennett's drive, where it remained until it was replaced by another in 1983. Her electricity was supplied through a wire thrown out of one of Bennett's windows, and references to her crop up throughout his *London Review of Books* annual diary. Such was Bennett's generosity that she even appeared on the electoral roll alongside Bennett between 1977 and 1989. This unlikely pairing of the writer and the derelict lasted fifteen years. 'I was never under any illusion that the impulse was purely charitable,' he wrote in what was eventually published under the title *The Lady in the Van*.

Miss Shepherd's sense of privacy made Bennett seem like a chattering parakeet. She barely ever crossed his threshold, and even the mildest enquiries about her origins were almost invariably thrown back in his face, a reaction not unlike Walter Bennett's response to his son's conjectures about William Peel's suicide. So throughout the 1970s and 1980s, Bennett and Miss Shepherd were neighbourly strangers to each other, and the other residents of the street merely sighed and laughed: which of the two was being the more eccentric was, presumably, a matter for conjecture.

Miss Shepherd's entrance into Bennett's life suggested a curious parallel with one of his former collaborators: Peter Cook. As a schoolboy, Cook had become fascinated with a Mr Boylett, whom he claimed served at high table at Radley. Cook delighted in impersonating the poor man, whose obsessions with inanimate objects were the very incarnation of the obsessive interest in trivia which Cook found so funny. One of Mr Boylett's most famous sayings, according to Cook, was that he thought he had seen a stone move, and one of Miss Shepherd's earliest pronouncements – always spoken with absolute conviction – was that 'I ran into a snake this afternoon. It was coming up Parkway. It was a long, grey snake – a boa constrictor possibly. It looked poisonous.' The statement could easily have come from the lips of Mr Boylett, who was adapted into Arthur Grole for the stage, and finally E.L. Wisty. A good deal of Peter Cook's creative life was a sort of elaboration on Wisty's thoughts. From Miss Shepherd's sighting of a snake in Camden, one has the feeling that Bennett had found his very own E.L. Wisty, not sitting on a bench, as Cook's droning man so often was, but in a van on his doorstep.

As well as settling into life in Camden, Alan Bennett was carving out a useful niche for himself by appearing with reasonable frequency on a number of favourite national mainstream TV programmes. Each of the *Fringe* four went according to their personal tastes, it appears, so while Peter Cook and Dudley Moore were popping up on *Juke Box Jury*, between 1965 and 1970 Bennett made six appearances on the genial panel game *Call My Bluff*. He was remunerated with £50 for each appearance. He also began his fruitful career as a children's storyteller, recording four stories for *Jackanory* between 1968 and 1970 – there tended to be five programmes per book – for £50 per programme. Mercifully, his splenetic letter to the BBC director-general did not explode in his face, since the producer Iain Johnstone booked him three times to present *Points of View*, between July 1969 and June 1971, at £40 per programme, by which time all payments for the services of Alan Bennett were to be paid to Forelake Ltd.

In 1969 Ned Sherrin briefly employed Bennett as a script doctor for a new show he was writing with Caryl Brahms. *Sing a Rude Song* was about the life of Marie Lloyd, one of the music-hall legends, whose footage would have gone down well in *On the Margin*. Sherrin says that Bennett contributed 'a couple of important comedy scenes with which we were having difficulty', and the show transferred in 1969 from the newly opened Greenwich Theatre to the Garrick. Maurice Gibb of the Bee Gees starred in it. When Bennett later revealed a lifelong partiality to the Bee Gees' music, it may have stemmed from this period.

As the 1960s drew to a close, Bennett seemed to be taking stock, perhaps wondering in which direction to head next. Besides *Points of View*, Bennett also hosted one in the series *An Evening With . . .* on 9 May 1969. With readings by himself and Judi Dench, they began with an extract from Evelyn Waugh's *Put Out More Flags* and continued with more of what the *Telegraph*'s TV reviewer Sean Day-Lewis described favourably as 'comfortable literature': Vita Sackville-West, John Betjeman, Virginia Woolf and, what Bennett said was his favourite book, *The Pursuit of Love* by Nancy Mitford. Bennett's commentary confirmed to Day-Lewis that 'He remains unspoilt, unsmart, unpretentious and funny'.

In 1970 Bernard Levin's book *The Pendulum Years* was published, in which the 1960s were put under the microscope of the famously astringent columnist. Bennett, described by Levin as 'the least extrovert and most individual' member of *Beyond the Fringe*, received the lavish praise that he was 'the only man who seemed to have taken the measure of the decade, and indeed, infant though he was, of half a dozen previous decades too'. In February, Bennett chose to reveal another string to his bow – Alan Bennett, art lover. From 16 to 18 February 1970, he was paid 120 guineas to present the BBC2 arts programme *Canvas*, which was broadcast on 20 May. The talk he presented, lasting twenty minutes, was based on the trips he had made to Leeds Art Gallery as a boy. Between filming and transmission, on 10 May, he found himself on the edge of a precipice with two of his most famous collaborators, Peter Cook and Dudley Moore. For fifty guineas, Bennett had agreed to suffer one of the most sought-after indignities then available to any celebrity, that of being catapulted into a pool of foam for the entertainment of a studio audience. This ritual humiliation took place during the notorious, but unforgivably erased, item known as 'Poets Cornered', one of the highlights of the third series of Cook and Moore's *Not Only . . . But Also*, which was produced by Jimmy Gilbert. (The foam bath was the penalty for hesitating while improvising a poem. Everyone, eventually, got dunked.) Such a penalty would not have appealed to Sir Roy Strong, the former head of the Victoria & Albert Museum, who famously eloped with Julia Trevelyan Oman, the set designer of *Forty Years On* and *Getting On*. Bennett struck Strong during this time as resembling 'a gawky, overgrown schoolboy'.

These distractions aside, by November 1970 Bennett had finished writing his second play. The germ of the idea had arisen during rehearsals for *Forty Years On*, when he had detected, in talking to the young cast, a sense of futility about all the examinations that they were meant to be trying so hard to pass. Where was it all leading? As he told one interviewer: 'Over eighteen they could not go back to school. No one ever told them that this was the last bus and if they missed it they would have to walk. They do have to walk.'

The play he wrote, *Getting On*, could be described as the midlife crisis of a man who doesn't realise he is having one, or who knows what is going on around him, but not what is happening *to* him. The man in question is George Oliver, a Labour MP described as 'about forty, rather glamorous once, now a bit florid, worn, running to fat'. But the play is more to do with domestic politics than the corridors of the House of Commons. George is finding the challenges of modern life – from hiring a minicab to the new digit-only telephone exchange system – rather a trial. It is all, he feels, a stumbling block placed there to trip him. No wonder Geoff, the good-looking nineteen-year-old handyman who spends most of the play hanging around their home, assumed he was a Tory when he first met him.

George is 'a former northerner, and deeply misanthropic' who wishes his suits were like those worn by Sir Kenneth Clark or the head of an Oxford college. Or, for that matter, his friend Brian Lowther MP (played originally by Brian Cox), public school-educated but sitting on the same side of the House as him. George's wife, Polly, is 'thirtyish, attractive, perceptibly younger than George, harassed, scatterbrained, or deliberately giving that impression, but not stupid', an impression confirmed by her being played by Gemma Jones, the actress with possibly the most sparkling eyes of her generation. The only woman George really gets on well with is Polly's formidable mother Enid, played by Mona

Washbourne, a big-hearted, motherly woman who, unknown to and unenquired into by George, thinks she has a terminal disease. George and Polly chat and argue about class, and the banter between them never stops, but there must be something missing from the relationship, as it soon becomes apparent to us – though not to George – that Polly is having an affair with Geoff.

While the younger cast members like Polly and Geoff have found a provisional remedy in illicit sex, another route to the same end threatens to be Brian's undoing, since he is being threatened, anonymously, with exposure in connection with a bungled gay pick-up which took place a long time ago.

By the beginning of Act Two, Geoff is such a fixture, and one, furthermore, to whose darker purpose George is so blind, that he can be called on to read bedtime stories to the Olivers' two small and heard but not seen children. George gets glimpses of himself in the mirror – protuberant stomach or yellowing teeth – and bemoans his senescence. But every emotion unleashes another torrent of angry, over-fluent words. It is left to his eldest son, the angry young teenager Andy, to get to the core of the play: 'I get my A-levels, say. I don't care. I get a degree, maybe, say . . . I don't care. I get a job. I don't care. I mean, George. When does it happen? When do I start to come into it?' It is a question that has run like a thread through much of Bennett's writing, right up to *Telling Tales*: 'When does life begin?'

Eventually, Geoff departs for Torremolinos – in those days just beginning its tourist ascent – to set up a restaurant with a friend. And when George conveniently leaves the stage long enough for Brian and Polly to have a proper chat, Polly challenges him to admit what she has intuited, that he, too, has had a fling with the decent but peripatetic Geoff – all safely offstage, of course. Brian confesses, and the two rejected lovers, jointly, if not entirely convincingly, bemoan their fate. 'That was what I wanted, really,' says Polly, 'a good boring man. George is so interesting all the time, it gets boring . . . Now I've got to go back to being just what I was.'

In his own blustering way, George sounds at times as elegiac as the headmaster in *Forty Years On* who still pined for a time when distances were measured in cycle rides. But whereas the headmaster heaps elegy after elegy on the beautiful people of the 1920s and 1930s, George Oliver's most furious outburst – addressed to the unflappable, uninterested Andy – is about the birth of the National Health Service, how it was put together 'at the desks of little men with bad teeth and terrible haircuts, runtish little civil servants . . . smoking too much in their cold government green offices in Nissen huts on bomb sites shivering through that winter of 1947 that went on until June'. He ends by saying: 'And I glory in that. Snobbish, sceptical, sneering socialist that I am, I glory in it.' The headmaster's arcadia looked back to a clean world built around a privileged few; the Labour MP looks back to a time designed to liberate the grubby majority.

On 24 September 1971 Bennett again opened his doors to the *Evening Standard*. This time, the intruder found in Alan Bennett 'a compulsive collector of old photographs at two bob a time from a barrow down the road in Camden Town'. The barrow was owned by a man called Reg, whose death in 1987 drew a page of tribute from Bennett. Reg's stall evoked a strange empathy in Bennett. He told the *Radio Times* in November 1982 that he felt a little like these pavement vendors. 'That's what I feel my writing's like, the contents of a drawer. I wish it wasn't, but it is.'

The encounter included what was, for a while, a mini-rite in Bennett interviews: ' "Tea or coffee?" he asks, sounding rather like a don in the darkish kitchen downstairs. And up it comes in china mugs, stirred vigorously.'

This time, the kitchen is scoured for clues. 'In contrast to the jungle upstairs, the long kitchen is a neatly organised bachelor's home. A grandfather clock ticks beside the white scrubbed table. The Welsh dresser contains a set of china plates, there is a small rug on the stone floor beside the black grate and at the far end of the room is his desk, covered with papers. All around the walls are more framed Victorian photographs . . . He giggles. Then he points out a faded cricket team which has a monkey on the knee of one of the gentlemen and a large cat on the knee of another. "What do you think of that, eh?" ' Reading these interviews years later, Bennett's warmth and candour make a striking contrast with the reticence and chilliness of recent years. It is easy to forget how accessible to the press he once was.

To a modern ear, trained to a greater heterogeneity of accents, it is also surprising how taken aback Londoners were by alien accents. Bennett, soon to become the most familiar northern voice on radio or television since Wilfred Pickles, is studied with anthropological detail.

'He talks about his holiday at a villa and stretches out the word *veela* to make it sound somehow wicked and grand. He complains about that "sticky stoof" that falls from the elms in the front garden.'

The casting of *Getting On* proved sticky too. Bennett and Garland could not agree on the right actor to play the lead role, so it was only after considerable searching, and about half a dozen rejections, that the part was offered to Kenneth More. More was a great British actor, and would probably not have appreciated Bennett's parody of the stiff-limbed walk that he had learned in order to play the part of Douglas Bader in *Reach for the Sky* (1957). Bennett said that he and Garland both felt that the part could rejuvenate More's career, in the same way that Olivier's career had enjoyed a late blossom when he played Archie Rice in John Osborne's *The Entertainer*.

The play, which was dedicated to Keith McNally, one of the chorus of disillusioned boys from *Forty Years On*, opened at the Queen's Theatre on 14 October 1971. Peter Lewis in the *Daily Mail*, one of the first pressmen to trumpet the virtues of *Beyond the Fringe* in 1960, found it 'amusing and at the same time acutely depressing'. He described it as having 'a plot of sorts', though in the end he felt that 'the piece really consists of a series of grumbles for Mr More'. John Barber in the *Daily Telegraph* made the point, the first part of which has been repeated many times since, that 'the jokes that hold up the action are good ones. But the play does dawdle.'

It is hard to disagree with that view. Whereas *Forty Years On* was a more or less straight revue, and gloried in that, *Getting On* feels like a series of essays in which the conclusions have already been reached before the start. There is not much room for development, and as a result the play feels stifling. It must have touched a nerve in the public, though, as it ran for nine months, and that success obviously impressed the *Evening Standard* Theatre Awards judging panel. The critics, who included Bernard Levin, Robert Robinson, Antonia Fraser and Milton Shulman, declared that Bennett's play had 'surface wit combined with its deeper examination of the complex problems of ambition, idealism, disillusionment and the private life of a public man', and *Getting On* was judged the Best Comedy the following January, thus handing Bennett a remarkable *Evening Standard* Theatre Awards hat-trick, which had started with *Beyond the Fringe* (Best Musical, oddly enough, in 1961) and *Forty Years On* (a Special Award in 1968).

From the outset, Bennett seemed, at best, ambivalent about this latest triumph. Peering at the award, he said, 'Yes, it's a useful, solid object, but actually it's not quite as heavy as the ones I won before. I don't think it would fetch as much if I had to flog it some time.' If that sounded dismissive, he felt he had good reason. At the awards ceremony he made his audience laugh by saying he felt like a gardener who, having lovingly reared a marrow, found at the local horticultural show that he had been awarded the prize for the best cucumber. Again, the audience laughed, though few could have known the serious message behind those disarming words. For the fact was that the play which those critics were watching, on its opening night in the West End in October 1971, was not the play he had originally written.

Speaking to the *Evening Standard* back in September, Bennett revealed his own surprise on reading an interview in which Kenneth More said the part was the best he had ever played. Crucially, Bennett only *saw* the remark. More didn't address it to his face, because by the time the play arrived in London, More and Bennett were not on speaking terms.

The play previewed at Brighton, where Bennett was surprised at how nervous More was: 'Nothing in his debonair and easy-going exterior prepared one for the vulnerable actor he became that night. It was plain he had been expecting the audience to love him, and when they didn't he felt lost.' That first week, wrote Bennett, 'the Brighton audience lapped up the jokes but yawned at the bits in between'. More, feeling under pressure to give his public what it wanted, felt that the play worked best as a comedy and so started weeding out those lines which, in his opinion, did not work.

After the first week, according to Bennett, More called a rehearsal to make more cuts, and instructed the management to prevent Bennett from entering the theatre. 'The following day,' Bennett writes, 'I found myself barred from the theatre altogether and in fact never saw the play in its entirety from that day until it closed in the West End eight months later.' Patrick Garland, forced into the unbearable position of having to choose between his playwright and his leading actor, felt he had no choice but to stay with More, who was, after all, providing most of the box-office pulling power. The result was that, with More sometimes adding his own lines to make the play more palatable, Bennett felt like a mother whose baby had been taken away at birth. That, at any rate, is a slightly longer explanation for the Author's Note, at the front of the collected plays, that 'The text here . . . had been clumsily cut without my presence or permission and some small additions made: the jokes were largely left intact while the serious content of the play suffered.'

More's version of events, recorded in his chatty memoirs *More or Less* (1978), is, not surprisingly, different. He remarks that he and Bennett were 'polite' to each other, and that he admired his ability, and continued to do so, but 'somehow we just did not hit it off'. The reason for that, he says, stemmed from 'an incident' that took place in Brighton. More says he went into Mona Washbourne's dressing room in Brighton an hour before the play was due to open, and found her in tears. 'Alan's just been in and reduced me to nothing,' she told More. 'He said I am playing the part all wrong. Now I feel completely lost.'

'To me,' wrote More, 'this was the most disgraceful thing to do to any artiste when he or she is about to appear on stage.' More went to see Patrick Garland straight away.

' "Pat," I said, "you have got to get Alan Bennett out of this theatre tonight, otherwise I'm not going on." '

' "I can't do that, Kenny," he said. "He's an old chum. We were at Cambridge together." '

Wrongly allocating Bennett's and Garland's university should not substantially damage More's case, though it is evident, reading between the somewhat stilted lines of his memoirs, that More and Washbourne had formed an anti-Bennett alliance by now. Bennett could obviously be prickly when he felt his lines were being tampered with. He had demonstrated that when he exploded at Dudley Moore during the run of *Beyond the Fringe*, and his letter to Sir Charles Curran also showed how he could turn a seemingly small incident into something much hotter. By now, though, relations between More and Bennett seemed irretrievable. As More wrote: 'I was furious and overreacted, I suppose, but I was protecting my cast. Patrick Garland realised I meant what I said, and told his old friend. I have never really forgiven Alan Bennett, and I don't think he has ever forgiven me.' More, who spends just under a page on the incident, compared with Bennett's six, describes the incident as 'one of those unfortunate things that can happen in the theatre when everyone is strung up, the author no less than the cast'.

Writing after More's death, which he describes as 'courageous [and] very much in the mould of the parts he liked playing', Bennett regretted that More did not seize on the part to deepen his scope as an actor, since 'He wasn't the simple, straightforward, good-natured guy he played: he was more complicated than that.' Bennett, who knows more about concealment than most, wrote that 'Acting is . . . to do with exposure, not concealment.' His verdict on Kenneth More is that 'because he wanted so much to be liked he left a large tract of his character undeveloped'.

Bennett's doubts about the rewritten play are vindicated to some extent in the critic Peter Lewis's remark in the *Daily Mail* that 'Mr More never took the risk of showing what was sad about getting old, or, for that matter, what was good about it.' But if it had been so impoverished, would the *Evening Standard* Theatre Awards judges really have drawn comparisons with Chekhov? Not bad for a play which its author claimed had been intellectually disembowelled.

At the time, the press and public had no idea that a palace coup had taken place, but it was years before relations between Bennett and Garland were restored. During this time, one interviewer remembers Bennett refusing even to acknowledge Garland in the radio studio where they were meant to be promoting the play. Still, the rift was eventually healed, and many years later, in 1998, they joined forces to work on one of the second series of *Talking Heads*. The blood-letting of *Getting On* remains an unfathomably turbulent incident, and another indication of the ferocious possessiveness Bennett felt about his own writing. If that ferocity has cooled in recent years, it may be because Bennett now has the stature and the recognition to know that his word is not going to be so easily contradicted.

When he spoke to the *Standard*, Bennett said that he wished he were offered more speaking parts, since 'I'm not reconciled to settling down with a typewriter. But that looks as though it's going to be my fate. I wish people would ask me to act more so I could get away from it.' One job he did get was to read the Saki short story 'Tobermory', about a cat that sees more than it should, on BBC2 in its *Storyteller* series on 8 May 1971. There were other odd jobs around this time. In 1971 he wrote and performed a sketch on BBC2's *Review* show in early March in which he claimed to recall an 'informal visit' undertaken with Bertrand Russell to the Tuscan villa of Bernard Berenson, the American-born Italian art lover with one of the all-time great addresses – 'I Tatti, Florence' – in 1939. Essentially, it was another party piece: for Bennett, the coincident surnames of the two Berlins, songwriter Irving and philosopher Isaiah, were too good a joke to let slip, and both men were mentioned in the sketch. It was rare, in those days, for a year to slip by without the joke recurring.

With Garland unavailable, Bennett needed to find another director to interpret his work, and he had the luck to team up with a man who was to become one of his most important creative partners. Stephen Frears was born in Leicester, ninety-three miles south of Leeds and midway between Leeds and London, in 1941. He went to Gresham's and Trinity College, Cambridge, and before he started working with Bennett he had two credits to his name: *The Burning*, which he directed for the stage in 1967, and his first film, *Gumshoe*, in 1971. Frears had been a directorial assistant to the great Lindsay Anderson at the Royal Court, where he had met Bennett during the run of *A Cuckoo in the Nest*. He had also worked on Anderson's 1968 masterpiece *If* . . . The script that Bennett wrote was a television play, and a rapidly back-pedalling departure from contemporary life. The initial title, for which the BBC had paid £400 to acquire the rights in May 1970, was *There and Back to See How Far It Is*. Wisely, some time in August 1971 the title was changed to *A Day Out*. The man chosen to produce it, who would also become a firm friend and supporter of Bennett, was Innes Lloyd. The film was originally commissioned under the *Thirty Minute Theatre* banner, but was shelved because it was felt to require too large a budget. The duration was obviously also a problem. In recent years Bennett has talked about his attempts to make his drafts or screenplays shorter, but in August 1971 it was felt that the film would work better over fifty minutes, not thirty, and that it should be shot not on videotape but on the more visually appealing – and expensive – cellulose, and in black and white to give it more period feel.

A Day Out is the simple tale of a bicycling outing from Halifax to Fountains Abbey made in 1911 by an all-male cycling group. The lyrical atmosphere is undercut by the knowledge that all the cyclists are perched unwittingly on the edge of an abyss. To emphasise this point, at the start of the play the cyclists gather at the memorial to the victims of the Boer War, while at the end of the play the party – their numbers sharply reduced – will meet again, years later, round a hugely expanded memorial to an even greater loss of life.

There is always, of course, nostalgia. 'I can remember when all that were fields,' says Mr Shuttleworth, looking out over Hebden Bridge. 'Ay, but there's all this,' says Boothroyd, contentedly. 'It'll be a long time before they build up England.' Other serious issues are touched on briefly, such as Boothroyd's pro-temperance feelings and support for Methodism. The distant rumble of gunshot which Gibson hears, an ominous foreshadowing of the trenches, is from a gamekeeper shooting rooks. Class warfare is hinted at, too, though it's hardly bellicose when Cross interrupts a game of croquet being played by some upper-class girls. *A Day Out* is pretty slow going compared with the unseemly scramble of later TV plays – but its main achievement is in the subtle layering of atmosphere, and the unsettling knowledge that this world is doomed, and that the characters are, as Bennett said about his own parents in one of the most ominous phrases in *Telling Tales*, 'driving towards the dark'.

Bennett kept a diary of the filming, spanning 1 to 25 May, which was reprinted in *The Listener*. Like first love, the events he describes are fleeting but deeply felt. Bennett records the throwaway witticisms of cast members, and delights in noting the film-set catechism before a shot, from 'Quiet. Going for a take' to 'Action'. For most of the time, most people are sitting around, waiting for short, sharp bursts of frenetic activity, just like the film world always is, and like war, too, in a way. The trouble was that although Bennett had specified what weather he wanted, he couldn't provide it. So instead of 'The sun casts long shadows across the path, trees are alive with birds, midges flickering in the sun' to suggest a gentle Edwardian idyll, it was so bitterly cold that the butterflies which were let out of their box one day dropped dead immediately from hypothermia. Knowing with hindsight how bitterly cold it was makes it harder to enjoy the pastoral beauty of the film.

As well as creating bucolic melodrama, Bennett was still deeply attached to the real thing, as he revealed on 29 March 1972 when he spoke to Peter Cooke (with an 'e', again) of the *Yorkshire Post*. Cooke records the fact that Bennett travels once a month from Camden to Leeds so as to discharge his duties properly as president of the Settle Civic Society. On a crisp spring day, in weather evidently better than any they had encountered during the filming of *A Day Out*, the two men stood at the top of Castleberg Hill, with Settle, 'dappled in warm spring sunshine', a hundred feet below them. The reporter describes how 'Grey stone buildings threw the green of field and valley into sharp relief. In the distance the limestone fells beckoned and an air of tranquillity lay over everything.' Within five minutes, says Cooke, Bennett's enthusiasm was impossible to contain as 'he threw out his arm and exclaimed: "Can you wonder I don't want to see this spoiled?" ' Leeds, says Bennett, he can do without 'apart from the galleries, the parks and the precinct'. It is in the Dales that he feels at home. 'Within hours of arriving the tension disappears.' And he himself drew attention to his accent. 'After a day or so my accent broadens and I'm more like my real self.'

Bennett had known Settle for only six years, but he says he was very quickly welcomed into the community, a community that he said was very much alive. 'Nobody could call Settle a pretty place – not like some Wolds villages. But it has lots of character. And we don't want it spoiling,' he said, in Yorkshire tones that must have delighted the journalist. Having restored the Shambles, the town's 300-year-old market hall, Bennett was hoping to transfer the society's energies to Upper Settle, the oldest part of the town. 'If people can see what can be done with grants, skill and loving care, then the battle is halfway won,' he said, sounding as if the 450-mile journey from London really did make a different man of him.

Getting On was not a directly political play, but, read against the light of the downfall of Harold Wilson's government, it does seem to reflect a disillusionment with the Labour Party. As Brian Lowther says to George Oliver: 'Some essential part of our humanity has been removed. It's not honesty or straightforwardness, or the usual things politicians are supposed to lack. It's a sense of the ridiculous, the bloody pointlessness of it all, that's what they've lost.' It would be another twenty years before Alan Bennett wrote a play that involved politicians. For now, Bennett's response to the incumbent Heath government was to write a play that positively wallowed in the ridiculous.

9

You can't be branching out into yoghurt
at our age: *Habeas Corpus,*
The Old Country, A Visit from Miss Prothero,
1973–1978

The January 1973 newsletter of the Settle Civic Society had a special message from its president for anyone intending to make improvements to their home. 'Modern semis are fine, thatched cottages are fine – but not in Upper Settle,' he wrote. 'Don't put in a glass door, which is fine in suburbia . . . Don't make doors look rustic. Rustic signs, wrought-iron nameplates both stem from wanting houses to look "quaint". Settle houses don't look quaint and never will.' Picture windows were out too; they were too suburban. And bow windows don't exist in houses 'except on Christmas cards'. The formidable taste monitor was, of course, Alan Bennett, and few local residents can have tried harder to banish the encroachment of alien suburban tastes into their neighbourhood. Rarely, too, can the child have been so clearly the father of the man. The Alan Bennett who railed against the desecration of inner Leeds in *The Owlet* had already built his house then, and it was one in which picture windows were definitely not welcome.

Bennett's dim view of suburban architecture didn't prevent him writing about it, or at least using it as a setting. *Habeas Corpus* is an energetic romp about Arthur Wicksteed, aged fifty-three, a general practitioner resident in 'Brighton's plush, silk socking district of Hove'. He is, as the critic John Walker said in the *International Herald Tribune*, 'a doctor who longs for contact with young flesh while shrinking from his frustrated, libidinous wife'. Or, to put it another way, he and his entire household are sex-mad. This is Bennett's *Oh! Calcutta*, a play that commemorates the demise of the Lord Chamberlain and his blue pencil, and dances a prolonged conga on his grave.

The characters occasionally lapse into doggerel, none more so than Mrs Swabb, the Greek chorus. 'I am Fate. I cut the string. I know all goings out and comings in. Naught escapes me in a month of Sundays. I know if they change their undies.' The text contains the bare minimum of stage directions, all of which adds to the sense of scurry, and the slightly hysterical atmosphere. Plot descriptions are necessarily spindly and to some extent irrelevant. The ensuing scenes include a false breast fitter called Shanks (played to great acclaim by Andrew Sachs), some Polaroid snaps, and a threatened suicide. Sir Percy loses his trousers, the spotlight is briefly hogged by a large hypodermic, and Dr Wicksteed is caught red-handed – and some – with Felicity by Sir Percy, who threatens to strike him off the general register. 'What more does he want?' asks Mrs Wicksteed. 'Not more. Different,' says Wicksteed.

Bennett, now thirty-nine, spoke to D.A.N. Jones of the *Observer* on 13 May 1973. He told him a little about his life, saying that his lifestyle was that of 'a bachelor uncle. I supper out with married couples five nights a week.' He also said that he had only voted Tory once, when Labour seemed committed to further development of the motorway system, a scheme against which Bennett had long-held prejudices. He said that when he died he wanted to be buried in a churchyard, and that the revised prayer book had made him feel distanced from the Anglican fold. 'I don't think this is superficial,' he insisted. 'The prayer book is attached to a period in my life. Hymns make me weep. People seemed to go through a religious phase in their teens more than they do now.' D.A.N. Jones described the humour in Bennett's latest play as 'getting pretty desperate . . . as if he's becoming something of a tragic comedian'.

The part of Wicksteed was played by Sir Alec Guinness, in whom Bennett found a lifelong friend. Guinness was already a legendary actor, and also, like Kenneth More, to some extent a target for the Fringers' humour. He was also, though, a man after Bennett's heart or soul, being scrupulously private, deeply modest and, latterly, very religious. Bennett was to become a regular visitor to the home of Guinness and his wife Merula, and his name often crops up in Guinness's volumes of diaries, always bicycling away bravely into the late-night traffic after dinner in town, and chatting about national issues, or gossiping. In *Habeas Corpus*, Sir Alec Guinness sent theatre-goers away with a shiver in their spine when he asked Bennett and the play's director Ronald Eyre if he might perform a solo dance at the end, 'depicting rapid decline, stiffening joints, decrepitude and the fear of old age and death', as he described it. The dance was choreographed by Eleanor 'Phiz' Fazan, who had been responsible for sprucing up *Beyond the Fringe* in preparation for its London run in 1961.

Habeas Corpus opened at the Lyric Theatre on 10 May 1973 where it was warmly received by Jack Tinker, the *Daily Mail*'s new theatre critic. His review began, 'To say simply that this is the funniest new play to shake the West End out of its present abysmal lethargy is to do it and its outrageously talented author the disservice of understatement', and he placed Bennett alongside Congreve, Wilde and Coward for 'his ability to look life's cruellest absurdities full in the face and spin its eternal foolishness into elegant farce'. At the *Daily Telegraph*, John Barber concluded: 'Their antics raised hysterical laughter in an audience who did not seem to mind their repetitiousness or the latent spleen.'

Speaking to John Higgins of *The Times* on 19 May 1973, Bennett's frustration with the press seemed to be bubbling ever closer to the surface. 'Why is there so much categorisation? Critics assume that you have to earn the right to be serious. They are always anxious to pin you down, to stick labels on you.' He also complained that 'Now the play is on I feel bereft and out of the family . . . Perhaps I should have taken one of the parts myself.' In the end, the temptation was too great, so on 11 February 1974, when Guinness stepped down from playing the lead role and was replaced by Robert Hardy, Bennett returned to the family – as Mrs Swabb the cleaning lady. When he met Ian Jack of the *Sunday Times* a week before curtain up, Bennett's Camden home was described as 'the kind of rich street that has taken to buying bicycles and sepia Victorian photographs – usually of people who aren't relatives – to hang on the living-room wall'.

Jack, too, had a good look around. 'The photographs on Bennett's walls are of schools, regiments and works' annual dinners, where lines of factory foremen and senior clerks have twisted around on their chairs from long linen-covered tables to face the camera . . . Bennett said he could not have pictures of his own family on the wall because they were just snaps and would require very small frames.' They might also, of course, tell visiting journalists more about his background than he would like to reveal. Jack says that Bennett acknowledges that this 'cult of old objects' was now shared by a good number of (middle-class) people and that it was a trend which Bennett himself had gone some way towards encouraging, thanks to his plays 'which often look backwards, but mainly because of a winsome lack of ability to take himself seriously'. The junk people put in their homes these days, Bennett said with a shake of the head. 'George Melly [then a Gloucester Crescent resident] has got an old petrol pump on his living-room table. It's hideous.'

A photograph taken to accompany an interview with Alex Hamilton in the *Guardian* shows Bennett at his most dapper. His top button seems to be undone, and he is lying, back to the wall, hands clasped on his thighs, legs stretched out towards us, pointy shoes poking up in the air. The relaxed look contrasts with Bennett's initial uncertainty, in which he had asked if he could see a list of questions in advance 'because he wasn't a man for ready answers'. Hamilton reassured him that he wouldn't leave any gaps where Bennett paused to think, and then added, for our benefit: 'Actually, I can't recall any pauses.'

Hamilton described the basement walls: 'festooned with ancient photographs of groups – schools, regiments, weddings, teams and so forth. A myriad tiny faces, for the most part surmounting Sunday best, stared sternly out of the sepia age of photography.' Hamilton wondered if any of the faces were of Bennett's family, and Bennett at first demurred, saying his family wasn't grand enough, but then he picked the smallest photograph off the wall, which showed four Bennetts, two parents behind and Alan and his brother Gordon in front, the evacuation photograph taken in Wilsill during the phoney war of 1940 when they went to stay with Mr Weatherhead at Byril Farm ('which is now, alas, not a farm and has carriage lamps', wrote Bennett in *Telling Tales*). The boys are in shorts, long socks, short-sleeved shirts and ties. Alan, then aged six, with his gleaming fair hair, is looking down, half-smiling.

To Alex Hamilton, Bennett expressed relief for having come out of a very 'bigoted and hidebound' period in the last ten years. No longer 'an awful Christian Tory', he had ceased to feel scornful towards socialists and jazz fans (hence the warm feelings towards Melly). The main obstacle at the moment, he said, with the recast play coming at the tail end of the three-day week and Edward Heath's disastrous showdown with the National Union of Miners, was whether there would be enough electricity to keep the theatre lit. But, said Bennett, that wasn't the only reason he cycled into the West End each night: it was speedier. And he was quick to point out that his bike was no boneshaker: it had ten gears, which made it 'trendy', a concept about which he was, at best, ambivalent.

Sunset Across the Bay, directed by Stephen Frears, was completed a few days before he stepped into Mrs Swabb's shoes in *Habeas Corpus*. It was Bennett's most forthright statement yet about the damage that retirement swiftly wreaks on the human body, which is paralleled with the enormous ball-and-chain thump that brings down whole terraces, simultaneously tearing down the communities which they once bred. Those back-to-backs were lifelines, though – as in *Forty Years On* – the people in them did not realise what they had lost until it was too late. Without the routine of work, the couple, fondly played by Harry Markham and Gabrielle Day, find their lives meandering and aimless, like the worst kind of holiday. They try hard to love their new house, but it is precisely its newness, and the lack of association with their past, which makes it so difficult to appreciate. The milkman comes round and offers her yoghurt. 'You can't be branching out into yoghurt at our age,' she says, sounding faintly shocked. Often the refrain 'They do in Leeds' comes to her lips. Dad potters around town, trying to fit in with the new pace of life and not quite managing. He chats to people, but he seems condemned to be an observer, uprooted from the community that he knew, peering in from on the margin as people go about their daily lives, regardless of whether he is there or not, much as Bennett's own father must have felt for a while when he and Lilian Bennett left Leeds for Clapham. Feeling poorly during one of their strolls along the promenade, he stops at a lavatory, and we know what is going to happen. His act of departure is, in its way, heroic, though Mam is left on the beach, wondering what has happened to him, her gentility preventing her from entering the Gents' herself. Like *A Day Out*, which also dealt with death, the precise moment of death is not dwelt on, but built up to and then crept away from. There would be dozens more deaths in the years to come, and without doubt this death is a pinprick in the fabric of the world, and yet the note of tragedy it strikes is terribly resonant. Mam and Dad were the sort of people whom Bennett described in *Telling Tales* as having names 'already weighted in the direction of the grave'. As with so many of his plays, a daring change in lifestyle is presented as a risky venture upon which tragedy or death invariably attends.

'On paper it sounds gloomy,' wrote Shaun Usher, the TV critic of the *Daily Mail*. 'The quality filling this play, however, was subtler, gentle sadness – entwined with wry humour.' He praised it as 'a mixture of the heartfelt and the banal, delicate and precise yet never sounding invented'. Those final moments were tragically prophetic too. A few months later, when his parents were out walking on the beach at Morecambe, Walter Bennett complained to his wife that he felt 'jiggered'. The walk was abandoned, and he and Lilian returned home.

Ten days later, and a few months after *Sunset Across the Bay* was transmitted, at six o'clock one August morning, while *Habeas Corpus* was still playing in London's West End, Walter Bennett suffered a heart attack in Clapham. The local doctor, who was at the scene promptly, summoned an ambulance. When the ambulance left, with Walter on board, it was escorted by two police cars, one in front, one behind, to ensure that it made as quick a progress as possible to the nearby hospital. The doctors at Airedale Hospital in Keighley did everything they could, but Walter Bennett died on 3 August 1974. His son Alan was forty.

Walter was buried towards the back of the little cemetery that stands on the tiny road between Clapham village and its railway station. Bennett's old Oxford friend Russell Harty came to the funeral at the churchyard in Clapham. Lilian, says Harty, 'was distanced by shock and a pill'. They left her with family and friends as they had to get a train back to London. The trouble was, by the time their car arrived at Lancaster, the 7.30 train had left. Immediately, Harty swung into action. 'I found the stationmaster and began to explain the sorrowful circumstances of our journey.' Looking round, he saw Bennett hanging well back behind a luggage trolley, looking acutely embarrassed. The stationmaster was duly impressed. 'Who is your friend?' he asked. 'It's Alan Bennett, the playwright,' said Harty. 'In that case,' said the stationmaster, 'we'll have to see what we can do.' He returned after two minutes. 'I've had a word with the Royal Scot. Not scheduled to stop here. When Mr Bennett – grand lad, isn't he? – comes back, you two stand at that end of the platform. I'll bring her in for you. You two jump on. Don't say nothing to nobody.' No witnesses who were on board that train that night have ever come forward, so one must only conclude that the two men's entry on to the train was as unobtrusive as it was intended to be.

To cope with the shock of his father's death, and to keep an eye on his mother, Bennett moved back to Yorkshire for eighteen months. Lilian Bennett's deteriorating mental and physical state was to be one of his chief worries for the rest of his life, and, to judge from references to ailing mothers in his plays and journals, he was guilt-stricken that he could not spend more time looking after her, as well as feeling that there was little in the way of practical help that he could offer. In the meantime, he left the private health company BUPA, so impressed was he by the care with which the NHS had fought to keep his father alive. Bennett said in 1977 that his father's death stopped him writing for a while, and that he was only able to ease himself back in by writing for TV. It was the most traumatic experience of his life, little eased by the staging of *Habeas Corpus* in New York in 1975. 'I can't explain why,' he said later, as if he needed to. 'But the joy went out of life then.' It was only years later, once the initial blow of losing his father had lessened somewhat, that he realised it had been oddly liberating, because until then he had never dared write freely about sex. All that was about to change.

A school reunion of sorts took place when *A Poke in the Eye with a Sharp Stick* was recorded on 1, 2 and 3 April 1976 at Her Majesty's Theatre. Like its bigger, flashier brother, *The Secret Policeman's Ball* (1979), the show brought together the leading lights from several generations of comedians. To increase the slightly incestuous feeling, there was widespread collaboration, with performers turning up to do each other's sketches. It thus amounted to both an acknowledgement of the past and an initiation of newer talents, with John Cleese, say, replacing and also picking up the mantle of Kenneth Williams. There were several conspicuous absences. Just as in *A Day Out*, where the living regroup at the end to remember the dead, Dudley Moore and Eric Idle sent apologies for their absence. They were not dead but living in America, which, to the cast, amounted to the same thing.

Bennett performed 'T.E. Lawrence' and his telegram monologue, both of which were received like old friends and with none of the hostility or controversy that had surrounded their first airing in *On the Margin*. It was a chamber show, where you brought along your favourite sketch, or the one you could remember with least effort. It was a very English project: throwing a bunch of people into a room in order to talk about something completely different from the original purpose for which they had been brought there. The show was directed by Jonathan Miller and filmed by Roger Graef for the BBC's *Omnibus*, and it was transmitted on 29 December 1976, eight months after the original recording.

A month after this event, Bennett was again getting his teeth stuck into local Yorkshire concerns with the attempt by the Settle and District Civic Society, now also known as the North Craven Heritage Trust, to block the proposed sale of part of the garden of Giggleswick vicarage. The vicarage is a listed building, with stables and a parish room dating from the early seventeenth century and the main house from 1820. With its large walled garden, it was, the society told the *Yorkshire Post*, an 'integral part of the village', the whole of which was designated a conservation area. Bennett's suggestion was that the diocese should let the planning permission lapse, and then sell the vicarage and garden as one unit rather than splitting them up. The diocese decided to retain the stables and the servants' rooms, which became the parish hall. They then built a new vicarage in the grounds and sold off the rest. An amicable settlement seemed to have been reached.

On 20 October 1977, as part of its *Premiere* season, BBC2 screened a new Alan Bennett play. *A Little Outing* was directed by Brian Tufano, who later did the camerawork on BBC2's acclaimed 1994 production of *Middlemarch* and, more recently, the justly praised film *Billy Elliot*. It is a quietly humorous tale about a family trip to see Mam in the Oak Dene Residential Home. Much time is taken up preparing to go out, get in the car, get inside and get home. Mam is found in the conservatory 'just having five minutes'. Dad is nervous that he will end up in the same place, a fear which is greatly intensified when he accidentally wets himself. Mam needs gentle reminding about who everyone is, but the atmosphere in the home, with its high Victorian ceiling, is quite happy, even though one of the old boys periodically tries to escape, and an old lady passes the time by asking, 'Are you my taxi?', both recurring themes in Bennett's future work.

Bennett's Yorkshire roots were saluted by the *Yorkshire Post*'s Paul Vallely on 7 May 1977. 'Normally writers work out their autobiographical preoccupations early in their career and then turn to broader subjects. With Alan Bennett, the reverse is true,' he wrote. At one point in their conversation, Vallely says, the telephone rang. It was Bennett's neighbour, Jonathan Miller, ringing, so Vallely claimed, as part of a prearranged escape route, to invite him across the road for tea if Bennett needed saving.

After his success in *Habeas Corpus*, Alec Guinness starred in Alan Bennett's next play, too. *The Old Country* opened on 7 September 1977, and Guinness was joined on stage by Rachel Kempson. Hilary and Bron seem, for all the world, like any middle-aged couple having an argument over their favourite composer or the names of vegetables. Hilary says he might write to *The Times*, though he's not sure what to write. Bron finds a Garrick tie for him. They are forced to entertain two people: Eric, who is from Portsmouth, and Olga, who has a foreign accent. Hilary's diatribes are straight out of the Alan Bennett/George Oliver little red book. 'I imagine when it comes to the next prayer book . . . God will be written in the lower case to banish any lurking sense of inferiority his worshippers might feel.' When Eric has gone, Hilary tells Bron that he can't stand him. 'We have nothing in common at all,' Hilary says. 'Except the one thing,' says Bron without emotion. 'You're all traitors.'

It is only when Bron's sister Veronica arrives with her stout husband, Duff, that we realise where we are. Not in the Home Counties. Not even England. Duff and Veronica have come to visit Hilary and Bron because Duff is lecturing, on Forster, in Moscow. And Hilary and Bron are in Moscow because Hilary was a spy, a sort of fictional counterpart to the double agent Kim Philby, and Moscow is the city to which he fled with Bron fourteen years earlier, and in which he has now pasted together his favourite bits of the country he left behind. It was Bennett's most spectacular *coup de théâtre*.

Duff, it seems, has come with a message. 'Come home,' he says. 'How can I come home?' says Hilary. 'I am home. I am a Soviet citizen.' It is Eric's wife Olga who supplies the dynamic spark that this mostly static play needs. It turns out that Hilary is needed for a swap, as part of 'a gesture. A tidying up.' As Olga says, 'We have no one they [the British] especially want. But you will do.' Hilary shows no remorse, for anything, it seems. 'The best disguise of all is to be exactly what you say you are. Nobody ever believes that.' It is one of the great epigrams of the play, and perfectly suited to the mouth of Alec Guinness, who would go on to play Smiley in the TV adaptations of John Le Carré's Cold War spy novels. And then the cars are ready, and Hilary, unlike Philby (and Eric), leaves the USSR. 'This time on Tuesday we shall be in Wiltshire,' says Duff. 'Poop poop,' says Hilary.

Around this time, Tom Sutcliffe of the *Guardian* wrote to Bennett requesting an interview – and was turned down. 'What I can't really get over is my reluctance to explain myself or have myself explained (away),' Bennett wrote. 'I don't want to be interviewed . . . because I feel less afterwards.' It was Bennett's way of saying that his work explained itself, or revealed as much of himself as he wished to show.

As if the journey to Moscow were sufficient foreign temptation for a while, the BBC chose to initiate 1978 with a single-episode drama by Alan Bennett which was one of the most enclosed, confined and restricted pieces of writing one could imagine. *A Visit from Miss Prothero* was performed by Hugh Lloyd and a woman who was to become one of Bennett's best-known interpreters, Patricia Routledge. It was first transmitted by BBC2 on 1 January 1978.

Directed by Stephen Frears, *A Visit from Miss Prothero* is a mini-revenge play. Miss Prothero's role as a baddie is even enshrined in stage directions, such as: 'Miss Prothero doesn't laugh. She vaguely flinches. Miss Prothero is one of those people who only see jokes by appointment.' She has turned up on the doorstep of her former boss, Mr Dodsworth, a widower now retired from Warburtons and hoping to eke out the rest of his days with nothing more demanding than a pet budgie for company and a little exercise across the bowling green, 'Cookery classes, pottery, cordon bleu' and the occasional chat with a fellow Rotarian. Into this staid arcadia strides Miss Prothero, an embittered virgin hungry for male victims to assuage her sexual inertia. Instead of showing him the error of his ways, Miss Prothero, with feigned reluctance, tells poor Mr Dodsworth how completely the entire docketing system which he put in place has been revamped and improved by the new broom, Mr Skinner. Miss Prothero says she didn't want to tell him because 'It would have broken your heart'. But that is precisely why she has come to see him.

If any viewers failed to make contact with the play's emotional core, it could only be because the play's comedy failed to make one empathise with Mr Dodsworth's dilemma. Could that aspect of his job really have mattered that much to him? If one half-hour visit from an interfering old bore had really succeeded in pulling the carpet from under his feet, it didn't say much about the small victories that he had seen through.

But who is the real villain of all this revisionism? It is the computer, the effects of whose growing influence Bennett was one of the first English playwrights to highlight. The computer has made many of Mr Dodsworth's innovations redundant. It has made Mr Dodsworth redundant, too, though he had the sense to jump before he was pushed. One year before Mrs Thatcher came to power, when the government of James Callaghan was sinking to its knees under pressure from an overanimated trades union movement, *A Visit from Miss Prothero* hit on several very topical themes, not least because the cultureless, heartless, monstrous, interfering Miss P with her handbag and shrill voice bore an eerie resemblance to the nation's First Lady in waiting, Mrs T.

'Is there any television playwright who can touch Alan Bennett?' asked Stanley Reynolds in *The Times*, reviewing *A Visit from Miss Prothero*. 'Is there anyone else who can take the most humdrum, indeed the most boring-looking subject, and make them both funny and touching in such an easy-going manner?' Bennett must have wondered when this honeymoon with the critics would end. The answer was sooner rather than later.

10

This is anti-television

The Writer in Disguise, 1978–1979

Back in the days of purely terrestrial TV, when there was more parity between the two main broadcasters' entertainment output than there is nowadays, both the BBC and ITV aspired to commission significant chunks of televised drama, and both were proud of their successes. The independent companies, unfettered by the paternalistic Reithian tradition, were still the young pretenders, and they took a justifiable delight in their victories. Nevertheless, there was no denying that more importance was usually attached to the Beeb's output. Alan Bennett had grown up under the influence of BBC radio and television, and when he thought he had become one of its principal dramatists he had reason to feel part of a charmed circle. 'I have a great affection for the BBC, one which is almost sentimental,' he wrote to Huw Wheldon in 1967. 'I enjoy working for it; the atmosphere is always sane, liberal, and fruitful. But one of the chief factors in this is loyalty.' That loyalty was tested to the limit in 1978, when Bennett approached the BBC with three completed TV films and the promise of more to come. Despite his well-known capacity to undersell himself, he must have been feeling more prolific than at any time since he had submitted the six half-hour scripts that became *On the Margin* in 1966. What he wanted from the BBC was a commitment to produce a series under his name. It was to be the most serious endorsement of his writing so far. And, to his disgust, that commitment was not forthcoming.

'At the moment the BBC seems to favour plays that make very direct statements,' he told Nicholas Wapshott of *The Times*. 'Mine don't. They wander, they joke and they don't reach many conclusions.' When the answer came back from the BBC that they could only commit themselves to producing one Alan Bennett play a year, it was like a slap in the face. Enraged at what seemed like this act of betrayal, Bennett must have felt as if he had been thrown out of the garden. Luckily, he didn't have to look far. The director of programmes at London Weekend Television was a young man on his way up, who had little regard for the corporate hesitancy that seemed to prevail in the BBC at the time. His name was Michael Grade, and he backed Bennett all the way. The result was that 'Six Plays by Alan Bennett', later published – minus one – as *The Writer in Disguise*, was slated for release beginning in December 1978. The ensuing plays were to provide Grade with some of his sweetest memories, as well as landing him with one of the biggest headaches – not to say bills – of his life.

The team that gathered around Bennett ranged from the talented to the formidable. Stephen Frears, who had directed three Bennett films so far, now tried his hand at producing, but also found time to direct four of them. The other directing duties were handed out to the young Giles Foster, and to a man who had stamped his mark on 1950s theatre and 1960s films, Lindsay Anderson. The first play, *Me, I'm Afraid of Virginia Woolf*, was transmitted by LWT on 2 December 1978, with Bennett as the narrator, a small part for the young Julie Walters, and the part of Trevor Hopkins's mother played by Thora Hird, the first time this great Bennett interpreter had appeared in one of his plays. Hopkins, played by Neville Smith, is thirty-five and a literature lecturer at the local adult education centre. The first scene finds him in his doctor's surgery, where, as in *Intensive Care*, he is obliged to register the presence of a junior trainee. The doctor makes it clear that Hopkins has been attending his clinic far too much for a man of his age, and he turns to his young assistant for an instant diagnosis. The young man, in a whisper, wonders if his problem is sexual. The doctor, with all the wisdom of experience, adds: 'But I'm afraid he scores no points there, does he, Mr Hopkins? Mr Hopkins and I went into all that pretty thoroughly, and it appears that while he is not married, wise man, Mr Hopkins has a lady friend.'

And so the discussion continues, with any anxiety over Mr Hopkins's hormonal preferences temporarily allayed.

The doctor sends him away with some more antidepressants, but drugs are not the key to his recovery. Hopkins's personal relationships are unsatisfactory. First, there is his mother, who drops in on him in the canteen. The dialogue between them is some of the best, and truest, Bennett ever wrote:

Hopkins: What've you come down here for? What do you want to see me about?

Mrs Hopkins: What do I want to see you about? Do I have to want to see you about something? I want to see you about having brought you up single-handed. I want to see you about having put you in for a scholarship. I want to see you about being my son.

Hopkins is never short of charges with which to berate his mother. His name, he tells her, is especially painful to him. 'You're in the outside lane before even the pistol goes. It's not Trevor Proust, is it? Trevor Strachey. Trevor Sibelius. Lenin, Stalin, where would they be if they'd been called Trevor?'

Hopkins has a girlfriend, a yoga teacher called Wendy (played as a suitably damp piece of cheesecloth by Carol Macready), though their relationship is transparently unhappy – to Trevor, at least. For one thing, she calls him Trevor all the time, which he can't stand. (Bennett has written several times that his parents never referred to each other by name except in a dire emergency.) She yearns, verbally, to be able to sit quietly with him without the need to talk. According to Wendy, 'As I see it . . . the body is the basic syntax in the grammar of humanism.' To which the narrator – Bennett in voice-over – retorts: 'Why did they have to wade through this every time? Other people got foreplay. All he got was *The Joys of Yoga*.'

So far, the outlook seems fairly gloomy, but the really transforming element in *Me, I'm Afraid of Virginia Woolf* is that, for the first time in Bennett's work, a saviour is at hand. The saviour is Skinner, the only male member of Hopkins's Bloomsbury Group study class, and the only true representative of the younger generation. (This is the third time Bennett has deployed the name of Skinner, the first two being in *Forty*

Years On and *A Visit from Miss Prothero*.) Skinner is married with a child, but he has energy and wit, and a sense of mischief that Hopkins finds captivating. His offence is to scribble graffiti on two poster-sized study aids, drawing a moustache, a small beard and a large cigar on E.M. Forster, and a large pair of breasts on Virginia Woolf. Hopkins is taken aback, but, once he realises it is Skinner's work, he is intrigued. Bennett returned to the theme of the smart literary vandal eight years later with his screenplay about the lives of the two most infamous municipal property assailants in lending library history: Joe Orton and Kenneth Halliwell, who were jailed for six months for defacing the library books of Islington Council. In a fortunate twist, Skinner runs into Hopkins just after Hopkins has been punched on the nose and is on his way to hospital. In the final scene, after a long evening together in Casualty, Bennett the narrator intones: 'Without believing in corners, that night he had turned one . . . Something had happened.'

The final moments are touchingly erotic. The screen directions are: 'In the final credits sequence, Hopkins shares the frozen frame with Skinner, who is also smiling. But it is Hopkins whose smile is wicked. Skinner looks rather fond.' The film plays out to 'A Wonderful Guy' from *South Pacific*: 'I'm as corny as Kansas in August, I'm as normal as blueberry pie/No more a smart little girl with no heart, I have found me a wonderful guy!' It is the first happy ending in Bennett's work, and one of the only ones.

After the first film was broadcast, Bennett submitted himself to an interview with Thompson Prentice of the *Daily Mail*, whom he met in a room in the South Bank Tower, the home of LWT. The interview was published on 9 December 1978 and contained the extraordinary multiple gaffe that Bennett was 'an undergraduate at Cambridge University when the brilliant *Beyond the Fringe* first brought him to national prominence'. Bennett also denied to Prentice that he still wrote in little black books, though given Prentice's uneasy grasp of details, we should be cautious about accepting his word for it. Bennett told another reporter, James Murray of the *Daily Express*, that 'I take notes in my chequebook of what friends and relatives say', which gave rise to the gratuitously unpleasant headline 'Laughing All the Way to the Bank'.

The South Bank Tower may have sufficed for Thompson Prentice, but for Nicholas Wapshott of *The Times* only NW1 would do. In the interview, which appeared on 27 November 1978, the journalist found himself in the downstairs room where Bennett worked, which was also his sitting room. 'It is a subdued, almost gloomy room with green stippled walls, overladen with pictures like a Victorian parlour,' Wapshott began. Then he spots something new: real art on the walls. Perhaps Bennett had been on a spending spree. 'The central painting is by Vanessa Bell, a beach scene with Virginia Woolf [her breasts free of graffiti] sprawled horizontally across the sand. In the background is Quentin. To the right of the fireplace is a small self-portrait of the young Alan Bennett, a round-faced, sandy-haired boy, made owl-looking by a pair of steel-framed glasses. He looks much the same today.'

Perhaps reassured by being at home, as well as safe in the knowledge that Wapshott wouldn't put him down for the wrong university, Bennett said a great many things which he hadn't said to Thompson Prentice. The little black book had by now become one of the Bennett shuttle-cocks, alternately accepted and denied by Bennett. In Wapshott's version, the little black books were still very much alive. Wapshott dwelt for some time on Bennett's modesty, on the fact that he seemed 'genuinely untouched' by his successes. But Bennett seems to have been bothered by the feeling that he hadn't *impinged*, a feeling which – God knows – has plagued a fair share of writers over the years. Not for the last time, he was keeping a careful eye on his peers. 'I'm never mentioned in books about the contemporary theatre,' he said. 'Oleg Kerensky wrote a book not long since interviewing 417 contemporary playwrights and I didn't even manage to get into that. I do have a definite sensation of not existing.' If the book Bennett was thinking of was *The New British Drama*, published in 1977, Bennett was exaggerating slightly, since Kerensky's study was of 'fourteen playwrights since Osborne and Pinter'. Then again, if you're going to be excluded from a club of 14, you might as well be excluded from a club of 417. (Feeling overlooked was part of Bennett's condition, or his art. On 2 January 1990 he wrote in his diary, about Václav Havel: 'I seem to be the only Western playwright not personally acquainted with the new President of Czechoslovakia.')

Wapshott also raises for the first time – at least in print – a topic that would come to be repeated many times over: the question of whether 'this clever aping of others' innocent remarks' was patronising. Bennett felt that, on the contrary, if you were laughing at someone you could be celebrating them, and that many writers attempting to convey northern English made the mistake of just writing 'roughened up' standard

English. He also indulged himself in a little diatribe about his adopted city, comparing it unfavourably with New York. 'These days I rejoice in New York,' he said. 'Americans are a graver, fairer and more honest people than we are. They lack irony but we have an overdose of it. It's got into our bones.' At the height, or the depth, of James Callaghan's Winter of Discontent, London life seemed to Bennett 'churlish, avaricious and grudging. Whereas New York is vigorous, generous and witty.' He liked it so much that he was even thinking of using the city as the basis for his next play, though this has yet to emerge. Another forestalled project was his attempt to adapt Waugh's *Brideshead Revisited* for John Schlesinger. (John Mortimer eventually achieved this in 1981.) Bennett said that his own plays 'quite often make me wince', which was a way of saying that 'I like writing, but don't like what I've written'. He never, he said, watched his own plays on TV.

Doris and Doreen, directed by Frears, was broadcast on 16 December 1978. Here, too, the spectre of new work patterns threatens the old structures, as surely as the new headmaster at Albion House threatens the old headmaster, and the distant prospect of war hangs over the cycling party in *A Day Out*. Bennett cannot hide his fear of industrialisation, of a work practice that would become known, in years to come, by that blissful euphemism 'rationalisation'. Miss Doris Rutter and Mrs Doreen Bidmead have been ploughing their furrow in Precepts and Invoices for longer than they care to remember. Like Mr Dodsworth in *A Visit from Miss Prothero*, their whole world is built around an in-depth knowledge of a rigid structure, though unlike him they have had no hand in creating it but merely cleave to it, fearful of what might replace it. Their world is made up of Costing, Personnel, and divisional battles between different departments in Newcastle and Newport Pagnell. To them, a statement like 'One PS104. Two PS104s. Three PS104s' is the stuff of life. And yet, it very slowly emerges, something is out to get them.

Viewed from the unfair vantage point of hindsight, *Doris and Doreen* is a pretty long play. The clues take for ever to untangle, and by the end one cares very little whether they live or die, only that they should yield to the inevitable scythe of progress. And yet the themes it introduced were tremendously important, and would be fleshed out with ever greater intensity in Bennett's next plays. The old ways, represented by the pre-computerised green forms, are the green fields. What will remain of England? The female office gossip and self-important bore would soon be seen by everyone but herself as a woman of no importance, before eventually mutating into a fully formed talking head.

Given Lindsay Anderson's attitude towards television – he told Dan Farson that he regarded it as 'the greatest disaster in the history of mankind' – one may well wonder why the acclaimed but controversial director of *This Sporting Life* (1962), *If . . .* (1968) and *O Lucky Man!* (1972), as well as numerous classic productions for the Royal Court, should have consented to work in the medium. The answer was twofold: first, Anderson was a fan of Bennett; second, he insisted that it should be a collaborative process between himself and the writer. He always, he told friends, regarded *The Old Crowd* as a film, not a play.

The controversy surrounding this play, the third in the series, has become a legend, and one discussed at length in *Lindsay Anderson: Maverick Film-maker* by Erik Hedling. In the chapter he devotes to *The Old Crowd*, Hedling's enthusiasm for the play, as well as his use of the word 'diegetic' (*OED*: 'Diegesis: Narration, narrative; in a speech, the statement of the case'), is eye-opening. Bennett had encountered controversy before, with *Beyond the Fringe*. He had rowed with actors before, as with Kenneth More in *Getting On*, but until then the critics' attitude to his work had ranged from pretty favourable to wildly favourable. All that was about to change.

The Old Crowd was first transmitted on 27 January 1979. It is set in a large, roomy, Edwardian London house, where an affluent, middle-class couple called George and Betty have invited some friends to a house-warming party. As the lights go up, a crack appears in the corner of the wall near the ceiling, followed by the sound of plaster crumbling. It is a minatory detail in James Weatherup's set design. The first people to arrive are Harold and Glyn, who have been specifically hired for the party as wine waiters, or actors impersonating wine waiters. To them, George explains that 'we have a slight problem. Typical story. Workmen here going on six months – floors up, ceilings down. Nightmare. Job completed. Workmen depart. We come to use the toilet and it doesn't work. Four toilets and three don't work.' Not only that. Although George and Betty moved into their new house ten days earlier, none of their furniture has arrived. It has been mysteriously diverted to Carlisle. Still,

George and Betty decide to have their party all the same, and the background against which the guests – all of whom know each other – is conducted is this dramatised *tabula rasa*. Readers of *The Clothes They Stood Up In*, several years later, might think they are in similar territory, but this is far darker. They sit, dwarfed by the table, in the echoey house and feed on a tension, of which they seem unaware, just as much as on the dinner.

People do not speak so much as declaim, and if one didn't already know that Lindsay Anderson had had some hand in redrafting the script, it would have suggested itself very strongly from the dialogue. A big, hearty man called Rufus makes the longest and most passionate speech in the film, savagely echoing George Oliver from *Getting On* or Duff from *The Old Country*.

'This piss-stained ammoniacal little island,' he says in what is also a biting parody of John of Gaunt's monologue from *Richard II*, 'where you can't wipe your bottom without filling in a form first.' Another Anderson contribution comes in the form of Glyn the waiter's sexual predatoriness. When he takes off Stella's coat, say the stage directions, 'his hand rests momentarily but purposely on her breast', inducing the fabulously ambiguous response, 'Oh, thank you very much' from Stella, whose dull husband Dickie spends most of his time following everyone around.

In Act Two, Glyn becomes even bolder when Stella, played by the achingly sexy Jill Bennett – recently divorced from John Osborne and joint holder with Bennett of a 1968 Variety award – quite deliberately drops her napkin. Glyn falls to his knees and crawls under the table to her foot. Having handed the napkin to her, he takes off one of her shoes, then cuts a hole in her stocking with a pair of scissors and starts to suck her big toe, a reference – in a film packed with references to Buñuel – to the woman sucking the toe of the statue in *L'Age d'Or* (1930). It is one of the most erotic toe-in-mouth under-the-table moments ever captured on film. Once again, the hand of Anderson is evident in the toe of Jill Bennett, though more so when he quite literally tears down the fourth wall, allowing us, the viewers, to eavesdrop on the camera crew filming the action. This shuffling of the cards in the pack of voyeurism and artifice is a little stilted, but it quickens the pulse.

Anderson's way of shooting made no concessions to TV. Through his insistence on doing full-face close-ups rather than conventional TV three-quarter close-ups, he pushed production costs up to about £250,000 – a sum sanctioned by the visionary Michael Grade, wrote Tom Sutcliffe on 27 January 1979 in a long and nakedly enthusiastic behind-the-scenes article for the *Guardian*. As if to emphasise the cracks in the characters lives, as well as underlining the artificiality of televised drama, much use was made of cutaway shots in which the camera, panning round, casually picked up the outer stage around the actors, including cameramen and other members of the production crew. This was literally behind-the-scenes drama.

At intervals throughout the evening, the guests bemoan the absence of their friend Totty, but towards the end of Act Two she makes a dramatic entrance, joining the others for a showing of some of George's favourite slides. As the slide show comes to a close, Totty slips painlessly away. Her death does not greatly disturb the guests, though there is some debate about what to do with her body. The final shot is of the static on the television screen which George's mother has been watching, alone, upstairs and unattended – a visual pun on the mad Mrs Rochester in *Jane Eyre*, or Norman Bates's mother in *Psycho*. It is, to be sure, a puzzling film.

After the shooting was over, Anderson wrote to Tom Sutcliffe: 'It really is extremely sophisticated for a television play, and I can hear the sets being switched off, or over to the other channel, all over our benighted island.' Bennett kept a diary of the production period, which clearly shows him falling very much under Anderson's spell, an experience he had in common with many who came within shouting distance of one of the last, great, independent, radical, liberal, traditionally socialist voices in British drama. He described the experience of showing a script to Anderson as being 'like having your homework marked', and repeated Anderson's observation that the script 'had epic qualities' before admitting that he himself wasn't sure what those qualities were. 'The play's greatest virtue is that it doesn't seem like mine,' he wrote. That was certainly true. Anderson, added Bennett, 'believes in talking to the press at length about what he does, preparing the public for it. I've always thought that a recipe for disaster.'

One of the reasons why *The Old Crowd* generated so much antipathy was because it had been anticipated so keenly, which was in turn because the whole production process had felt so exhilarating. 'The atmosphere at about one a.m. on the last day of shooting when I went to the studio was unlike anything I've ever felt there,' Tony Wharmby, LWT's head of drama and executive producer of the Bennett series, told Sutcliffe. 'This is anti-television,' announced Anderson. 'We're going to destroy the myth of the television play.' In the event, the TV critics made sure that Anderson would never work on TV again.

The *Sun* reviewer, Margaret Forwood, who sounded as if she was not yet into her teens, derided *The Old Crowd* as 'unintelligible'. (This, at least, was in the days when the *Sun* reviewed TV plays and not just quiz or chat shows.) 'If this is a good play, I am the next director-general of the BBC,' she wrote, adding helpfully that she wasn't.

Richard Gott of the *Guardian*, who had earlier sent Tom Sutcliffe down to the studios to report back, earned Lindsay Anderson's undying hatred by being so 'angry at having to sit through such drivel' that 'only two days later have I simmered down sufficiently to put pen to paper'. Gott put the play down to arrested development, claiming that Bennett was more comfortable in – and had never escaped from – the world of public school humour. This ignored the fact that Bennett himself had not attended, still less escaped from, public school. Fifteen years earlier, said Gott, 'it might have seemed daring and avant-garde. In 1979 it seemed trite and irrelevant – and intensely unfunny.'

Julian Barnes, writing in the *New Statesman*, showed little of his Francophile love of radicalism when he wrote: 'I can't remember a more raucous travesty of a play, or a more wasteful misuse of talented and expensive actors.' Writing in the *Spectator*, Richard Ingrams, whose suspicion of the radical tradition in film-making was entirely predictable, wrote mockingly that 'The director, the tiny, conceited Lindsay Anderson, explained that it was he who had helped shift Bennett "towards a kind of surreal or poetic non-realism", which is a long-winded way of saying "rubbish".'

The only critic to mount a defence of the play was Herbert Kretzmer in, of all papers, the *Daily Mail*. Describing it as unsettling, he felt it 'said more about the state of Britain than a dozen hectoring *Panorama*s'. He concluded: 'That a commercial channel should have mounted such unnerving matter on what is traditionally the safest night of the week is, despite the doomwatch warnings of the play, an occasion for hope.' On the other hand, Richard Last in the *Daily Telegraph* derided Bennett for 'attempting the move into Pinter country. If the intention was black comedy, it came out as a rather inconsequential off-grey,' he wrote.

Most of the criticism seems to have been aimed at Anderson, as if, had Bennett not exposed the script to such an obvious oddball, the viewers would have had another gentle comedy to enjoy. In fact, far from Anderson's 'dangerous' left-wing views being responsible for mucking up the text, Bennett's and Anderson's *jeu d'esprit* at the expense of bourgeois values reveals the British press's Stalinist view of an artist as having to operate within a strictly defined pattern. Any attempt to step outside those boundaries would be slapped down hard.

Anderson made his own typically trenchant apologia in his introduction to the text. One conclusion he had drawn from the affair was that 'television is the most conformist of the media, a powerful and pernicious stifler of originality, a bastion of the status quo'. He blamed the Establishment, in other words the press, for not rising to the challenge he had set them.

On 25 February 1979 London Weekend Television broadcast an edition of the *South Bank Show* introduced, then as now, by the broadcaster and novelist Melvyn Bragg. More of a magazine programme in those days, the first half took a look at the recently released film *The Deer Hunter*, before moving on to Bennett's most controversial TV series. Bennett, in a jacket, V-neck jumper and tie, and Stephen Frears, in a baseball jacket, looked slightly bemused by the fuss but in no mood to back down. Bennett began the strand by reading out some of the many letters that had been sent in, stressing such phrases as 'An insult to the public intelligence' and 'This is not entertainment', and reading out the writers' names, such as 'Mr Dolby of Bolton', as he would have done when presenting *Points of View* between 1969 and 1971. It's easy to see why Bennett agreed to this: the phrase 'Angry of Tunbridge Wells' has a special resonance in the minds of the British public, being a signifier for 'nit-picking busybody'.

Had he been upset by the criticism, asked Bragg. 'I was taken aback that it was so viperish and vitriolic,' said Bennett. He repeated Anderson's humorously doom-laden prediction to Bennett that it would be 'a small hiccup' in his career. Bragg challenged them: wasn't this what junior film-makers get out of their system at film school? Bennett disagreed. 'If it is old hat, why were LWT deluged with calls?'

The united front never faltered against Bragg's tactful but tenacious probing. 'If that's a failure I'd like a great many of them,' said Bennett. Frears added: 'This doesn't preclude the possibility that Alan might want to develop it.' Bennett took the point further: 'What Stephen is saying is that I can maybe write some of the other things I do which people like off the top of my head. Well, off the top of your head is not the place to write from.'

Seen years later, *The Old Crowd* is dark, exhilarating and riddled with dramatic moments. Its radicalism is primitive but still has the power to stir. The exposed camerawork may no longer be dauntingly experimental, but nor is it irritating. The cast, which also included John Moffat, Isabel Dean, Rachel Roberts and Valentine Dyall, give performances that are highly theatrical, and in some cases almost overpoweringly sensual. It is perhaps even good enough to merit Erik Hedling's description of it as 'one of the most original, refined and aesthetically courageous expressions of a symbiosis between theatre, film and television'. When, a few years later, in *The Singing Detective*, Dennis Potter and his director Kenneth Trodd started to play very similar games with the camera and the form as Bennett and Anderson had done, the TV critics could not get enough of it. For once, Bennett had got to the watering hole too early.

The fourth play in the series of six, broadcast on 3 February, did not cause the LWT switchboard to light up, though it, too, dealt with some controversial issues. *Afternoon Off* was about the efforts of a lonely hotel waiter to locate the whereabouts of a girl who, he has been told, might be interested in him. Lee, the waiter, played by Henry Man, is described as Cambodian or North Vietnamese. The girl he is chasing is called Iris, a name which he consistently mispronounces as 'Eilis', even while holding the box of chocolates which he hopes to give her when he tracks her down. Instead, he sets out on a wild-goose chase that exposes him to Scarborough on early closing day. As marginal as Dad in *Sunset Across the Bay*, he wanders into a chamber music recital by mistake and eventually gives his precious Dairy Box to an elderly patient in a hospital who happens to be called Iris.

When he has the luck, or bad luck, to stumble on Iris's father in a factory, we get to understand rather more about Iris than he does. It appears that she is 'a woman of easy virtue', an impression that is rudely corroborated in the penultimate scene when he finally finds her, in bed with Bernard, his fellow waiter from the hotel dining-room, played by Phil Jackson. Back in his room, Lee takes comfort in the only sexual option left open to him: a hand-job.

Afternoon Off was a pretty one-handed affair, in fact. A search for love that barely allowed its protagonists to meet, it was a love story that was doomed before it had even begun. Typically for Bennett, he chose to concentrate on the most marginal figure in the story, and to put every possible obstacle in his path, which, despite Henry Man's warm, handsome, smiling face, makes the play feel pretty lifeless and long-winded at times until it totters towards its inevitable climax.

The fifth play, *One Fine Day*, was broadcast on 17 February 1979. The play was set in the office of Frobisher, Rendell & Ross, a firm of estate agents, and the central character, George Phillips, was played by the Irish 'sit-down' comedian and professional Catholic, Dave Allen, who was one of the most familiar and popular stars of mainstream TV. Working with a 'straight' playwright was a new departure for Allen, who played a contradiction in terms: an unambitious and ungregarious estate agent who takes the terms of his job description too far and falls in love with a building.

The broadly comic plot outline is misleading, since *One Fine Day* is not 'funny' at all, but it has some claim to be the best of the series, and one of Bennett's best-ever works. The chairman of Frobisher, Rendell & Ross, played by the late, great Robert Stephens, is a bully with a broad smile. The agents, who are all men, speak in the peculiar argot of corporate types parading a false and herd-like individuality – wickedly parodied by David Nobbs in *The Fall and Rise of Reginald Perrin* – in which four-thirty in the afternoon is described as 'the witching hour', people ask, 'Where's Arthur at this crucial juncture?' and colleagues mutter, 'Sorry, no understand problem.'

The main problem is Sunley House, a tall, modern, unattractive north London office block with impressive views of Alexandra Palace, which has lain empty and unoccupied for over a year. It is Phillips's 'baby', but the young and ambitious Rycroft, played by Dominic Guard, is on his tail, and is keen to make a name for himself by selling the property and thereby cutting Phillips out of any future deals.

Phillips feels distanced from his home. There, his main ethical dilemma is whether to object to his son's girlfriend staying over. His wife has embarked on a series of adult education classes as a means of external distraction, and she also has to take off to Colchester to nurse her ailing father. A few years later, in *Intensive Care*, Midgley would discover that separation from one's spouse frees one to pursue other interests, but in

One Fine Day Phillips is not looking for extramarital reassurance. Just as his son's girlfriend stays over at his home, so Phillips stays over in Sunley House, though here, too, there are obstacles, not least when he finds himself locked out one morning and has to crash through a lower window to escape.

But slowly, and rather touchingly, Phillips develops an affinity for the unloved Sunley House, unvisited except by a commissionaire and occasionally an Alsatian-holding security guard. It's an unusual step for Bennett, who so famously championed the merits of pre-Victorian buildings against the ravages of 1960s architecture, but what he does is to turn Sunley House into a refuge. Its featurelessness is its most appealing feature. High up, protected from the rush of the street, Phillips can be alone with his music and headphones, and a copy of the Bible that is perhaps a discreet nod in the direction of Allen's comic persona. Here, he can eavesdrop on the couple visible from a nearby rooftop (and whose shifting relations reflect his own moods) and he can relax. Blessed by blue skies, *One Fine Day* is, in a way, the bucolic idyll that *A Day Out* never quite managed to be. When he was discussing *Sunset Across the Bay*, Bennett recalled the shock with which he heard that one of his aunts was perfectly happy at being transplanted from her back-to-back to the fourteenth floor of Wortley Heights. Perhaps *One Fine Day* is a belated recognition and celebration of that spirit.

In a rather neat parallel to Phillips's dilemma with the 'sleeping over' issue at home, Phillips finds himself sleeping over at Sunley House, an arrangement which seems to suit both man and house. The weaselly Rycroft, finding a broken window, determines to sniff out whoever the intruder is, and ends up camping out in the building himself, a base stratagem which explodes messily in his face, or trousers, when Welby, the boss, turns up early to show a party of visiting Japanese businessmen round, only to find Rycroft dozing in a deck-chair in decidedly non-working clothes. Welby sacks Rycroft forthwith, and Phillips, having cleared his desk in anticipation of his odd, midlife-crisis behaviour being discovered, is restored to his boss's favours. It is a profoundly sympathetic and affecting film, and Dave Allen's performance is magnificent, showing the unspoken sadness and pain of his life in tiny giveaway sighs of the soul and his downcast eyes.

The sixth and final play, *All Day on the Sands*, was broadcast on 24 February 1979. It was a return to the leaner territory of *Sunset Across the*

Bay, though this time there was a clear generation gap between Mam and Dad and their children, Jennifer and Colin. In the middle, portrayed as innocents, are a honeymoon couple who, simply by staying in bed longer than most, earn the undying hatred of Mrs Cattley, played by Jane Freeman, proprietress with her husband of the Miramar boarding house in Morecambe. Mr Cattley, played by Ken Jones, is a marvellous, Pooterish caricature, broadcasting with 'that Riviera feel' over his Tannoy in his little cubbyhole under the stairs that 'The service of breakfast will shortly be commencing in the Portofino Room.' Mam and Dad are trying to make the best of their annual holiday, though Dad is trying to conceal the fact that he has been made redundant from his job. The main focus of the drama is one of Jennifer's sandals, which Colin accidentally drops on to the roof outside the honeymooners' window, and then retrieves by stealing a fishing rod from another boy on the promenade.

Themes of imprisonment and lack of sexual fulfilment run rife across the six plays. Seeing *Afternoon Off*, one might wonder if Bennett felt, like Lee, that some people are simply never going to find love, or are looking for it in the wrong place. If you saw the world through the eyes of Phillips in *One Fine Day*, you might conclude that you were only really safe in your own company. After watching *All Day on the Sands*, you might think that the honeymooners were such an external presence that Bennett felt he was never going to be in that situation himself. But, like Trevor in *Me, I'm Afraid of Virginia Woolf*, there was a saviour round the corner.

Part Three

Racing Tortoise

11

Critics killed my play

Enjoy, Objects of Affection, 1980–1982

Some time around 1979, Alan Bennett must have felt that he needed someone to dust or clean the accumulated scripts, books and other possessions that were cluttering his shelves and mantelpiece. The woman who came into his home, and eventually his life, was Anne Davies, a divorcée ten years younger than him. She had three sons from her marriage to a plumber called Roy Davies, and she may have been good at house-tidying but she was even better at listening, which Bennett evidently needed. Bennett was intrigued by this attractive, dark-haired, brown-eyed woman. She didn't seem to inhabit any of his orbits, being neither a chatterbox northern woman nor a figure on the fringe of London's theatre world. Her very strangeness was attractive to him, and he evidently felt he could talk to her.

Anne was the daughter of Hungarian, non-English-speaking refugees, one of whom – her father – had been in a concentration camp during the Second World War. She ran away from home aged twelve and was taken in by what newspaper reports later called 'a theatrical family'. She was entertaining, impulsive, scatty, fresh with her language, and nothing like his mother. And one day, Alan Bennett, lifelong homosexual though he thought he was, found himself in bed with her. After it was over, they must have agreed that the house might need cleaning again, fairly soon. Anne returned. It was one of the most impulsive things he had ever done, and – most satisfying – it was completely private. Neighbours thought she was spending a lot of time there, but said nothing, just imagining that the house must need a lot of tidying, which, given the amount of writing Alan Bennett was doing at the time, it probably did.

In the early 1980s Alan Bennett lent his voice to radio commercials for McVitie and Tefal. So, from an advertising point of view, Alan Bennett was associated by the nation with wholemeal biscuits and non-stick frying pans. For those people who preferred not to have their listening punctuated by commercials, Bennett made regular appearances during the 1970s on one of BBC Radio 4's most popular panel shows, *Quote . . . Unquote*. Devised by Nigel Rees, this was, if ever there was one, the programme that Alan Bennett was born to appear on. Guests were asked to identify famous historical quotations, or favourite remarks from the twentieth century. Whether as a historian or as a lover of gossip, much of it passed on to him by some of the biggest names in the arts, Bennett was well placed to answer such questions. But there were also rounds in which guests were invited to throw in comments made by family members, or friends, or simply stray remarks overheard in the street. Not surprisingly, Bennett was the perfect panellist, and his contributions were received with rapture. He was also one of the few team members whose own lines might end up on the show, quoted by others. When he dropped out, it was because he had guessed, shrewdly, that 'it was just a way of stripping you of all your best stories, and to very little profit'. One could see in this the stirrings of an annual published diary, and, in time, *Writing Home*.

In September 1980 Bennett told the *Evening Standard*'s Michael Owen that his new play 'is all about family, really', adding: 'I'm not sure what else it is about. It's quite funny, though. At least, I think it is.' His new play was called *Enjoy*, although '*Endure* would probably have been better', he wrote later. It opens in the living-room of the last back-to-back in the north of England. The main characters, Mam, played by Joan Plowright, and Dad, played by Colin Blakely, are chatting about their daughter Linda, of whose whereabouts Mam keeps needing to be reminded. Bennett's real mother was herself well on the way towards such forgetfulness by now. On 23 March 1980 Bennett recorded in his diary that 'Mam is convinced there are people outside the house and that they are waiting to take me [Alan] away'.

In what amounts almost to Bennett's first foray into science fiction, or at least futurist drama, he has conjured a nightmare world in which the locale of his childhood has become the subject matter of a council edict. Mam has no idea what Linda gets up to. Dad is convinced she's a personal secretary. 'Sweden boasts some fine modern architecture plus a freewheeling attitude towards personal morality,' he says proudly. 'But our Linda's a sensible girl. She won't be bowled over by that.' There is also an allusion to a missing person, about whom Dad has firm views. 'I do not want his name mentioned. You will never see him again. He is dead. He does not exist.'

Then comes a knock on the door. A piece of paper is inserted through the letterbox. It is from a qualified sociologist sent by the town council, informing them that their neighbourhood is shortly to be demolished, and that 'in the past, redevelopment has often ignored many valuable elements in the social structure of traditional com-munities . . . Your council is anxious to avoid the mistakes of the past and preserve those qualities.' Mam opens the door and, with no hesitation at all, Ms Craig walks in, plants her handbag down, occupies a chair, removes a pad and waits. Bennett's next set of stage directions is fairly clear. 'Ms Craig is a man. Not a man in outrageous drag, a man who is a woman perhaps but nevertheless a man.' The next stage direction is 'Silence'. There may have been silence in the theatre too.

The unsympathetic portrayal of Ms Craig bears witness to two schools of thought that were currently doing the rounds. Arising out of the women's liberation movement of the 1960s, the title 'Ms' was still viewed with suspicion in more conservative circles. Ms Craig's somewhat woolly job title, with its overtones of do-gooding and interfering – the nanny state, as it came to be called – was also regarded with hostility, so Bennett's satire on Ms Craig and her profession falls accidentally into a category marked out for ridicule in the columns of the *Daily Mail* or *Spectator*. But Bennett, though socially conservative, was never in sympathy with those publications, and it is more useful to read Ms Craig's character as a satire on Bennett himself, observing from the margin, silently taking notes when he hears something meaningful or significant. Alan Bennett has described himself scribbling down notes wherever people congregate, even on buses. But Ms Craig is sitting in

Mam and Dad's front room, directly observing them and commenting on it to her notebook. Unlike *The Old Country*, where Bennett carefully built up a sense of unreality, here he dares to present us with something that we know, immediately, is not what it pretends to be.

Mam and Dad try to carry on chatting as if she wasn't there, which is of course impossible. As Mam says: 'I'd offer you a cup of tea, but if we're meant to behave as if you're not here I can't, can I?' Ms Craig does not, of course, respond. Dad idolises Linda. 'You won't find girls like Linda stood on every street corner,' he says with horrible irony.

One could also see *Enjoy* as a fantastical commentary on Bennett's attitude to the press. When Mam goes off to make the tea, Dad starts by defending himself and manages to turn his guns on to himself. 'And don't think you're going to pick up any information about me and her either . . . Our so-called sexual relations . . . I don't want to give you the idea I'm trying to hide something, or that anything unorthodox goes on between my wife and me. It doesn't. Nothing goes on. Nothing at all. I don't know whether that's unorthodox. Judging from all these magazines it probably is. No foreplay. No afterplay. And fuck all in between. But don't expect me to expand on that.' It parodies the dilemma faced by anyone caught in the media's spotlight, with the subject damned by their own silence, and damned if they speak too. It also reflects the foibles of many characters in Bennett's plays and films, each of whom is given just enough rope to ensure the noose fits tightly around their neck.

There is some jostling between Mam and Dad as to who is behaving more naturally, or naturalistically. Mam plays up by getting out the best cups. Dad plays down by belching openly, and so forth. Then Dad decides he could do with the company. 'It's a change from suffering in silence.' Mam is getting forgetful: 'Why am I sitting on this chair? I never sit on this chair,' she says. She has a mania for domestic hygiene – 'I wage a constant battle against dust.' She is also obsessed with lavatories. As Dad says: 'My wife is the world authority on toilets. She has an encyclopedic knowledge.' These three characteristics were, more or less verbatim, shared with Lilian Bennett. Mam and Dad turn on Ms Craig and are about to insist she leave when Linda walks in.

Linda is, as the stage directions state, 'quite plainly a tart'. It turns out that she had gone not to Sweden but to Swindon. Linda swears and moans about the whole street, and both Dad and Mam seem to revel in it. 'Our Linda comes home to unwind,' says Dad. Linda goes upstairs to pack. She is leaving, to live in Saudi Arabia, to get away from what she calls 'this . . . pigsty'. 'We love you,' says Mam. 'I don't want love,' says Linda. 'I want consumer goods.' Try as she might to wound them, the Craven parents, taking after Alan Bennett's specially endorsed non-stick pans, are deaf to her jibes. Bennett-knockers sniffed misogyny, but Bennett was just making the point, not very subtly, that all children abuse their parents.

Linda, who admits she has 'sat on' a typewriter though 'never behind one', tells her parents she is going to marry a prince, whom she's not yet seen but who has seen pictures of her. As ever, Mam remains positive. 'Oh well. It may ripen into love,' she says. When Mam and Dad run out to see the Rolls-Royce that is coming to take Linda away – Bennett and the other Fringers had, in 1961, tumbled over each other in the course of a press interview to witness the arrival of the Rolls-Royce hired for them by the theatre management – Ms Craig walks round the room, speaking for the first time, picking up objects of whose history she is very well aware.

When, in Act Two, Dad comes across a girlie magazine with photos of Linda, he collapses and is assumed dead. Mam is tapped in the familiar dilemma of how to seem. 'Should I be showing grief? Do I mourn or not?' There is much discussion of what to do with the body, with slightly more genuine concern than was shown over Totty's corpse in *The Old Crowd*, but this climaxes in a very Ortonesque hurdle to overcome, which Mam comes across when she removes his trousers. Dad has acquired a sizeable posthumous hard-on.

Finally, Mam tells Ms Craig about her lost son Terry, whom she adored. They both start to dance, and at the end, almost nonchalantly, Ms Craig says, 'Mam', and her disguise is redundant. Mam's response is: 'About bloody time!' And so it emerges that we have been watching a scene from the Joseph story, or *Twelfth Night*, with the outcast family member hiding among the bosom of his family before identifying himself to them.

The atmosphere has now turned into a sort of pantomime, with everyone determined to live happily ever after. Dad, who has made a miraculous recovery, can even relish the prospect of his beloved daughter appearing in dirty magazines. 'Magazines like that . . . They go into thousands of homes,' he says, a brilliant parody of the delighted father.

The play ends with large sections of the stage being dismantled – a progression from *The Old Crowd* where they merely crumbled. 'I don't know where we're going but I'm looking forward to it,' says Mam. Dad gets taken off to hospital, Mam is happy in her new/old house, and Ms Craig gets the last speech: 'Home for me at the moment is a little place on the edge of the moors, a farmhouse . . . Leeds . . . it's just a glow in the sky. I feel I'm ready to start now.' We have been in that territory before, of course, with *Sunset Across the Bay*, though not with such a farcical backdrop of family intrigue. Once again, Bennett is showing us characters resolving to make a brand-new start.

Bennett seemed happy with the first few weeks of the play's run in Richmond – 'I begin to wonder whether it might amount to something' – though four days later this hesitant optimism had evaporated. '[I] find it has turned into *A Girl in My Soup*, with the actors hopping from laugh to laugh with no thought for what's in between.' If Bennett was dreading that he was about to witness another *Getting On*, at least he seems to have patched up relations between himself and the cast. Directed once again by Ronald Eyre, *Enjoy* opened at the Vaudeville Theatre on 15 October 1980, in the same week that an even more controversial play, Howard Brenton's *The Romans in Britain*, opened at the National.

Swallowing his disagreement with Richard Gott over *The Old Crowd*, Bennett agreed to be interviewed by Tom Sutcliffe in the *Guardian*, and the piece appeared the day before the first night. It was, still, a tortuous process. Sutcliffe wrote that Bennett – still in pole position to win the title of World's Most Reluctant Interviewee – first postponed, then cancelled, then said: 'You'd better come quickly, at once, before I change my mind again.' In response to a question about whether the writing process was self-dramatising therapy, he said: 'If I could see the sort of questions you ask so clearly, I probably wouldn't write.' And he repeated Bron's line from *The Old Country* about not being happy, 'but not unhappy about it'. That, he said, 'is more or less my situation. But I also don't believe that's anything to do with anybody except me.'

As usual, Bennett made the tea. In his teacups, he said he would like to move to New York, but that 'family commitments' ruled this out, since his failing mother was currently living with his brother Gordon. He didn't mention the new Prime Minister, Margaret Thatcher, by name, but insisted that 'I'm not like a rat deserting the sinking ship'. He did, however, pin the blame for his disaffection with England on one target, and it was not political. 'I also don't like the *Private Eye* thing here,' he said, referring to his old colleague Peter Cook's satirical organ: 'soon as anyone raises their nose above the horizon they should be slapped down.' He, however, had been spared. 'The most they've ever said of me was "sentimental northern playwright".' Of course, as Bennett knew from his college days, to be written about mockingly can also be a sign of affection.

Satire and nostalgia, Sutcliffe wrote, were words that Bennett loathed. Bennett said that although most people might see *Enjoy* as 'just a comedy, I would see it as some kind of a metaphor about writing. Although it's about social issues, it's also about treating one's background and one's parents as material, using them for some purpose or other.' Sutcliffe had obviously spotted the 'material' right there, having noted, in passing, 'a degenerating Dormobile' parked in the front of Bennett's house, though he said nothing more about it.

Sutcliffe liked *Enjoy*, calling it 'surreal' and 'poetic', but most critics hated it. Milton Shulman in the *Evening Standard* wrote that 'I'm afraid the mixture of derision and banter tends to be more confusing than amusing'. Even a letter from Joan Plowright's husband, Laurence Olivier, to *The Times*, did not help, nor did a plea from playwright Arnold Wesker, in a letter to the *Guardian*, that the play was 'lyrical, resonant of truths and enormously funny', and his query that critics 'may be intelligent people but are *only* people . . . They could, just could, be wrong!' It didn't help, though, and by 19 October, with the Sunday newspapers even more damning than the dailies, it was announced that *Enjoy* would close on 6 December, just two months after it opened.

Bennett was furious, and blamed the critics. 'Critics Killed My Play' ran the headline in the *Daily Mail* on 13 November 1980. 'Critics don't want to laugh as well as cry at the same time and that resulted in very disappointing reviews,' he said, under a self-explanatory photo-caption that ran 'Bennett – angry'. 'Bennett claims that critics have rejected his writing style,' wrote the *Daily Mail*. He spoke again, candidly, to Michael Owen of the *Evening Standard*. 'I do feel one or two of the critics were very vindictive and I do object to being lectured by them,' he said. The *Evening Standard* headline – 'Alan Bennett's Flop' – seemed, in the circumstances, inappropriately gleeful. *Enjoy* was obviously intended to be a funny, fast, furious play, and it should have been enjoyed as such. There are dozens of very funny lines, and its very slenderness masks a deeper complexity about identity and our attitude to the past. Its failure suggests that not only were the critics unwilling to change their preset ideas about Alan Bennett, but – more dangerously – nor was his public. The job of critics is to deliver a verdict. If they like what they have seen, author, cast and producer may be happy for a few months, though critical approval does not guarantee full houses. If, conversely, enough of them don't like it, the play might fail. If a writer objects to a critical mauling, an additional charge of sour grapes can usually be made. Two years later, Bennett was still feeling sore about *Enjoy*, telling Rosemary Say in the *Sunday Telegraph* that he was happiest writing TV plays at the moment, as people couldn't get at him so easily. This drew a letter from the playwright William Douglas-Home, on 4 November 1982, in which he expressed the view that 'to lose a playwright of his calibre would be a loss the theatre can ill afford'. Douglas-Home offered the view that 'the climate of rejection invariably changes for the better every six or seven years'. Bennett should just buckle up and see it out, in other words.

Enjoy is definitely one of Bennett's 'problem' plays, and not just because – together with *The Old Crowd* – it breaks the rule that his TV plays were set among working-class people in the north, and his stage plays among middle-class people in the south. Bennett said in an interview that the play was 'about children wishing to preserve their parents exactly as they were and not giving them a life of their own'. In fact, his mother's deteriorating mental state was not giving Bennett much of a life at the time, although in May 1981 he was the patient, being treated at University College Hospital for a mysterious stomach condition. By November, Bennett writes that his mother was having difficulty putting names to objects, which is the classic symptom of Alzheimer's disease. 'It's one of those things with things going round,' she said, staring at a clock. 'And then when they've got there, they've had it for a bit.'

Bennett was always keeping an eye out for his peers. 'An article on playwrights in the *Daily Mail*, listed according to Hard Left, Soft Left, Hard Right, Soft Right and Centre. I am not listed,' he wrote in his diary on 11 November 1981. 'I should probably come under Soft Centre.' When, in April of the following year, Roy Hattersley mistakenly referred to him as Alan Brien, Bennett was indignant at being mistaken for the journalist who had praised *Beyond the Fringe* to the skies. He had, after all, been reading some of Hattersley's selection of Larkin poems with Judi Dench at the Riverside Studios in *An Evening With . . .*, a show he had himself hosted a few years earlier. Within a few years, Bennett's fame would absolve him from reading for other people.

In his 2000 diary, Bennett recalled an appearance he made with John Fortune in the Amnesty show *The Secret Policeman's Other Ball*, recorded between 9 and 12 September 1981, which he remembers with relief as 'my last satirical fling'. He and Fortune performed a sketch in which two men, one gay and one straight, talk about their sexual encounters. As Bennett remembered it, the audience came expecting reruns of old *Python* numbers, and so did not laugh at the sketch he was in. He wrote: 'That was the end of satire for me, and also, I'm happy to say, the end of appearing in those mammoth charity shows which always turn out over-long, slyly competitive and never the least bit heart-warming.'

In the spring of 1982, with Michael Grade no longer at LWT, relations with the BBC Television Drama Unit were restored, and have not been seriously challenged since. It was a crucial period in British broadcasting, as the three main stations were preparing for the advent of a new player, and one that would gradually become a serious rival to the other terrestrial channels. Channel 4 was launched on 2 November 1982. What better way for the BBC to atone for its churlish behaviour towards Bennett than by championing him as their secret weapon against the worst that the new interloper could bring? The worst that Channel 4 could offer in its first week was, in fact, *Countdown*, the letter-based quiz show that made *Quote . . . Unquote* look like a doctoral thesis, but the BBC was taking no chances. ITV could only look on as Bennett was restored to the centre of the BBC's affections with his own series of offbeat dramas, which were published as *Objects of Affection*.

As a first-strike tactic, a one-off play, *Intensive Care*, went out on 9 November under the *Play for Today* banner. It told the story of a thirty-nine-year-old schoolteacher, Denis Midgley, and his hospital vigil at the bedside of his dying father. Gavin Millar, who was directing it, cast Bennett as the teacher, a role for which he had to audition. Midgley is called away from a parents' meeting, full of inarticulate children and angry, badly dressed parents, to the hospital where his father has been taken after suffering a stroke at home.

Keighley Hospital, where *Intensive Care* was filmed, was, of course, the hospital where his own father died, though Bennett later did his utmost to deny that the play was autobiographical. When Midgley arrives, his auntie Kitty has already been there some time. Auntie Kitty is vocationally bent on attending the bedsides of dying relatives and friends. 'She said nothing, kissing him wordlessly, her eyes closed to indicate her grief lay temporarily beyond speech,' Bennett wrote in 'Father! Father! Burning Bright', a short story he wrote at the time to try to extend his grasp of the characters and themes he had created. Gradually, other relatives join him. Midgley cannot leave the hospital. Feeling guilty at not having visited his father the previous weekend, and worried that he will not be there when his father dies, he makes his bed in the ward. The doctors and nurses tell him he will not have long to wait.

Like Phillips in *One Fine Day*, Midgley is wearily married, to Joyce, whom he phones from time to time for an earbashing. She has an elderly mother to look after, and complains that 'I am married to the cupboard under the sink'. But she does care about him, and about his father. As he goes off to the hospital, she says, 'He is dying, Denis. Will you exist now? Will that satisfy you?' She can see that this might be his last chance to begin his life afresh. Joyce is one of the very few characters in any of Bennett's plays or films who expresses a genuine concern on someone else's behalf, not just their own.

Midgley panics whenever he is too far away from the ward, and on one occasion scrambles through a flower bed in an effort to find the entrance to the anonymous modern hospital. But his father seems to be hanging on. Long enough, in fact, for Midgley to become increasingly attracted to Valery Lightfoot, the night nurse, played by Julie Walters. Midgley goes back to Valery's room with her and asks if he can go to bed with her. Valery doesn't seem against the idea, but says she has to work tonight: perhaps he could come back tomorrow, so long as his father doesn't die in the meantime. Midgley goes back to the ward. He sits by his father's bed and watches the dot skipping on the screen. 'Hold on, Dad,' he mutters. 'Hold on.' His urges – and urgings – at this point are clearly little to do with filial love.

His father's hold on life is now intimately tied up with Midgley's hopes for some kind of sexual follow-through with Valery. But he is still stricken with guilt at the prospect. Bennett, however, provides Midgley with a *deus ex machina*. The following day, he meets a woman in the ward, Alice Dugdale, of whose existence he had been unaware. She turns out to have had an affair with his father, and she still remembers him fondly. It is as if Denis has received a sign from his father that he may pursue this adulterous one-night stand. Midgley returns to Valery's room, she takes the phone off the hook, 'Midgley takes off his glasses and the scene fades out'. It is a very Alan Bennett sex scene. The lights come up, Valery puts the phone back on the hook, it rings, and, of course, during the few moments in the whole film that Midgley has taken his eyes off his father, the patient has died. 'What were you doing?' says his aunt Kitty to him when he runs back. 'Living,' says Midgley, and then, more to himself, 'He's won. He's scored. In the last minute of extra time.' Directed by Stephen Frears and with superb performances from Thora Hird as Auntie Kitty and the author himself, *Intensive Care* is one of Bennett's best and most celebrated plays, ablaze with tender moments relayed through pursed lips. It is also, perhaps inevitably, the most father-fixated of all Bennett's plays, though Bennett made clear to Michael Hickling of the *Yorkshire Post* that 'I never felt I let my dad down'. *Intensive Care* is about how one person's death can, in some circumstances, release another individual, no matter how hollow that victory may feel. It was considered a triumph for TV drama at the time, and it still is.

Bennett bunked off the press launch in London by doing something more pleasurable: going to the dentist. When he returned, the *Yorkshire Post*'s Michael Hickling observed him trying to drift to the edge of a group of journalists, who then regathered around him, with Bennett back in the centre. Bennett would then try again to creep towards the margin. 'This curious social process – a group persistently re-forming around an unwilling centre of attention,' wrote Hickling, 'went on for about half an hour.'

Another interview from around this time, on 3 October 1982, comes from the *Mail on Sunday*, to where Paul Vallely had now drifted. Bennett talked about his father, and northernness, but he also gave voice to one of the sentiments that crops up most freely in his own plays. Looking back at *Beyond the Fringe*, he said: 'Now all that seems another life, a prelude to real life. Today I feel more relaxed with myself. I've stopped trying to improve my character.' He also said that he had begun to think of himself as a playwright, rather than the person who told

Nicholas Wapshott in 1978: 'I never wanted to be a playwright, nor do I feel like one now.' The article also made out that he was returning increasingly to Yorkshire, and that he had sublet his New York flat. Not that Bennett wished to be portrayed as a northern writer returning to his roots, but there was no denying that he was very happy up there, away from it all.

All the plays in that series – broadcast under the overall title *Objects of Affection* – were set in the north, and Bennett got to work with some of the best young directors of the day. In the first, *Our Winnie*, directed by Malcolm Mowbray, Sheila Kelley played a mentally retarded girl on a visit to her father's grave: a play with a vague sort of happy ending, though not particularly profound. *Rolling Home*, directed by Piers Haggard, was a more complex work set in a geriatric ward (and, incidentally, in which Bennett's Rule of Hospitals applies yet again, namely that on no occasion may a hospital be mentioned without someone adding that a royal personage, Princess Anne on this occasion, opened one of its wards). The key relationship is between Mr Wyman, an elderly man played by John Barrett, and a male nurse called Donald, played by David Threlfall. Mr Wyman's dreams of escape are fed by Donald, who constructs a utopian dream world of a happy couple living in a lovely house on the other side of the hospital's forbidding wall. One night, when Donald and his girlfriend are grabbing a rare opportunity to have sex in the orderlies' room, Mr Wyman takes advantage of some building work being done to the wall, and discovers what is really on the other side – namely his own death. It is a tragicomic little family tableau, and its blame-free culture (no one thinks of suing the hospital for negligence) would be unthinkable in the litigious post-Thatcher period. And once again, the rare snatching of sex is punished with death.

In *Marks*, which has a more monolinear storyline, Ian Targett plays a jobless teenager called Les whose somewhat unlikely idea of a present to his mother, played by Marjorie Yates, is to have the word MOTHER tattooed on his arm. This backfires badly as it reminds her of her abusive, tattooed ex-husband and so shatters the fragile bond between mother and son. 'You were perfect. You didn't have to do anything for me . . . Now you're not perfect,' she shouts at him angrily. It is one of Bennett's most impassioned studies of the fraught relations between generations, though in a rather contrived coda we discover someone who appreciates the tattoo, when Les turns out to be gay. Bennett always presents the coming-out process as a final tableau, rather than as a dramatic process. Once again the theme of homosexuality is explored, or hinted at, with Bennett seemingly still not quite sure how best to express it. Instead of sex, a more oblique attempt at intimacy is rewarded not with death but distancing.

Say Something Happened, directed by Giles Foster, is a vehicle for three great Bennett interpreters, Thora Hird, Hugh Lloyd and Julie Walters. Once again, in a pattern recognisable from *Enjoy*, it is the turn of Social Services to suffer light ridicule when a retired couple open their door to a young woman from the Social Services Department who has come to fill in a register of senior citizens within the council area in an effort to prevent 'mishaps' involving 'old people who have become isolated within the community'. Mam and Dad are fiercely independent, and refer dotingly to their daughter Margaret, who seems to have a glamorous life as a personal secretary to a Mr Brunskill. Again, no young woman is safe in a Bennett play without her older, married boss making a pass at her. Work romances generally take place across and in defiance of generation gaps, office hierarchies and conjugal troths. As so often in Bennett's plays, the parents are sedentary, receiving news about their peripatetic daughter via postcards. As Dad says: 'She had a passion for geography. It was always: "Get out the atlas, Dad. Show me Perth. Rio de Janeiro." ' Dad in *Enjoy* feels the same way: 'She was a wanderer, right from being a kiddy. It was always: "Get out the atlas, Dad. Let me sit on your knee. Show me Las Vegas, Dad. Rio de Janeiro." ' In the end, and struggling at times in a new job in which she doesn't yet feel confident, the social worker hands the couple a big HELP sticker, in case they should suffer a fall in the home. Thora Hird survived perfectly well without it until the last in the first series of *Talking Heads*, 'A Cream Cracker under the Settee' (1987).

He could not have known, but the play that was to make the greatest impact was also the only monologue. *A Woman of No Importance*, its title borrowed from Oscar Wilde's 1893 play, was also the only three-act play of the series. It starred Patricia Routledge as a middle-aged woman and all-round bore who delivered a commentary on what turned out to be her approaching death. Peggy Schofield owed much to two earlier characters played by Routledge, Peggy Prothero in *A Visit from Miss Prothero* and Doreen Bidmead in *Doris and Doreen*. As before, Peggy's balance of mind is dependent on the status quo at work. But once this has been disrupted, her physical health packs up too.

With only one character and two cameras to worry about, Bennett originally intended to direct this himself, though in the end, because he was working on one of the other plays, Giles Foster took over the direction. Bennett had conceived it as 'a series of midshots with the camera tracking in very slowly to a close-up, holding the close-up for a while then, just as slowly, coming out'. He didn't want any cuts between scenes, and was glad when Ms Routledge said she would not need the autocue. The design was meant to stress the play's 'directness and simplicity', though Bennett says Foster found the restrictions it imposed 'irksome and unnerving' at first. The worry was that the 'fairly relentless nature of the piece' might be seen as an example of 'talking heads', which was at the time taken to be 'a synonym for boredom', and only one grade up from dead air.

Office worker Peggy's daily routine is numbingly repetitive. She has her friends – Miss Brunskill, Mr Cresswell, Mr Rudyard, Pauline Lucas, Trish Trotter and Joy Pedley. Then there are her (mostly female) enemies like Miss Hayman and her (male) idols like Mr Skidmore. Divisional differences mark out her life, from Projects to Personnel and Presentation.

Her most terrible fear is that her precious routine will be disturbed, a fear which she can only voice in tones of mock-hilarity. 'I have to be on my toes because there's always some bright spark wanting to commandeer them and drag them off elsewhere,' she says. When Peggy learns from Mr Skidmore that the extra photocopying which she did was not for his benefit, she feels the carpet has been pulled from beneath her feet. To make things worse, she begins to feel sick after lunch and goes home. The next scene logs the beginnings of her physical decline, with her first visit to the doctor. The subsequent scenes now shift to a hospital bed. The diagnostic tests have obviously found something malignant.

Time is now running out for Peggy, whose appearance weakens with every blackout. When she says, 'Miss Brunskill says everybody is on their knees praying I come back soon,' we are left to infer that they may well be praying, but probably not for her swift return to work. Peggy becomes snobbishly fond of her specialist, Mr Penry-Jones, a 'very courtly oldish man, blue pin-striped shirt, spotted bow tie'. And amid the collapsing hierarchy of her old regime, which she tries desperately to reconstruct on the ward, her conversation continues to ricochet from one non sequitur to another. 'Nurse Trickett . . . She hasn't got a boyfriend. I've promised to teach her shorthand typing. Her mother has gallstones, apparently.' But Peggy has something worse.

Peggy's hold on life is getting looser and looser. She dozes off between sentences. And when she sees a fly, buzzing around her head, it is the clearest augury yet of her approaching death. *A Woman of No Importance* scored a huge hit when it was broadcast. The British TV-watching public seems to have an inexhaustible appetite for the failings of small-minded simpletons, busybodies and bores, and Peggy Schofield is all of those. They tend to be female, like the unspeakable Linda Snell in *The Archers*, or Ena Sharples in *Coronation Street*. Peggy is a scapegoat for our worst fears. A tiny minority of viewers, including this one, find the clues Peggy drops about herself oppressively heavy-handed, and done solely for our benefit, not hers, but her death throes held her TV audience spellbound. The final scene in *A Woman of No Importance* is of an empty bed, reassuring us that that was the end of Miss Schofield. But for Alan Bennett, it was just the beginning.

12

I want a future that lives up to my past

An Englishman Abroad, A Private Function, 1983–1985

On 11 January 1959 an article appeared in the *Observer*, written by the actor Michael Redgrave. It was a description of a visit to Russia which he, along with other members of the 'Stratford' company, now the Royal Shakespeare Company, had made the previous year, visiting Moscow and Leningrad. They performed *Hamlet* in Moscow, after which, writes Redgrave: 'I remember the face of Guy Burgess, his eyes red with tears and his voice only just in control . . . "I suppose it's partly because I haven't heard this glorious stuff in English for years, but, believe me, this is the most wonderful thing that could have happened." '

Guy Francis de Moncy Burgess went from Eton to Dartmouth College and then Trinity College, Cambridge. There he met Redgrave, who described him as 'one of the bright stars of the University scene'. A few years later he was one of the bright stars of the espionage scene by becoming one of the Soviet Union's most valuable double agents. His collaboration with the other members of the 'Ring of Five', to use the KGB's own term, sent relations between the UK and the USSR into a flat spin for the best part of two decades, and even affected Britain's relations with the United States.

The description of the encounter which Redgrave published in his 1983 autobiography, *In My Mind's Eye*, is more fulsome. 'On the first night of *Hamlet* in Moscow a rather noisy group of English newspapermen were gathered outside my dressing-room door. Out of their hubbub came one voice I thought I recognised. It could be Guy's – it was. He swept into my dressing-room, extending both arms to greet me. He had been crying. "Oh, Michael! Those words, those words! You can imagine how they carry me back. Magic!"

'His face underwent a sort of convulsion; he lurched past me and, with what looked like practised accuracy, was sick into the basin. An athletic-looking young man who had come in with Guy waved his hands in apology. "Oh Guy, you are a *peeg*," he said, with considerable force.' Redgrave describes how Burgess recovered instantly, and invited him for lunch the following day. Redgrave describes the flat as 'tidy and comfortable', with the current *New Statesman* on a coffee table, along with a pot of pâté de foie gras from France. Lunch was served, but 'Guy, who was already too drunk to eat, paced up and down the room, talking'. After lunch they went for a walk, which took in one of Burgess's favourite basilicas. Burgess came to see him several more times at the theatre. Redgrave writes that Burgess also made friends with Coral Browne, who played the Queen in *Hamlet*, and that 'She agreed to order him some clothes at Simpsons in Piccadilly when we got back. He said he still had some money in England.

'On the day we were leaving, he came to see us off at the hotel. As we drove away, he was near tears. "Write to me," he said; "it's bloody lonely here, you know." '

This atmospheric and strangely poignant encounter, in the depths of the Cold War, made a strong impression on the Australian-born Coral Browne too. In 1977 she came to see *The Old Country* and went backstage afterwards to see Guinness. From time to time, various people were provoked by seeing the play into retelling anecdotes about Kim Philby and his fellow spies, such as Burgess and Donald Maclean, and many of these were relayed to Bennett at second hand. But the story which struck him more than any other, told to him over dinner at the Mirabelle, was Coral Browne's version of her first meeting, was with Burgess.

The image of a once-sparkling undergraduate who had been put out to grass in Moscow by an ungrateful and unappreciative administration, his usefulness to the Party spent, made a big impact on Bennett, who perhaps thought back to the fallow days after *Beyond the*

Fringe and drew some comparisons. 'I find it hard to drum up any patriotic indignation about Burgess,' wrote Bennett in his introduction to the play. On Radio 3's *Third Ear*, talking to Paul Bailey, he said: 'I can't get worked up about Burgess, partly because he was a very funny man who caused gales of laughter. It shouldn't be an excuse, but it is.'

The themes of exile and disguise, of crime and punishment, fascinated him, and his attempt to dramatise that episode became Bennett's first historical drama, which, directed by John Schlesinger, was broadcast on BBC1 on 29 November 1983 under the title *An Englishman Abroad*.

Alan Bates was cast as Burgess, and Coral Browne played herself as she tried to find Burgess's apartment in some hideously bleak urban tower-block sprawl, shot in Dundee.

Bennett had decided that the flat needed a little roughing up. 'Hardly luxury's lap,' says Burgess. 'A pigsty, in fact. I used to live in Jermyn Street. Tragic, you might think, but not really: that was a pigsty too. By their standards it's quite palatial.'

Palatial is hardly the word we are meant to associate with Burgess's flat. Lunch, of two tomatoes, a grapefruit and several cloves of garlic, is burned and then served. He begins by saying that he has 'heaps of chums' up here, but a few moments later he admits, 'Actually, there's no one in Moscow at all. It's like staying up at Cambridge for the Long Vac. One makes do with whatever's around.' The ambiguity between 'guest' and 'captive' should already have sunk in.

Whatever's around is, for the most part, a good-looking accordion-playing young Russian called Tolya. 'At least you've found a friend,' says the sympathetic Browne. 'Tolya? I'm not sure whether I've found one or I've been allotted one,' says Burgess. (As he says at the end of the play, 'When I first came I used to be shadowed by rather grand policemen. That was when I was a celebrity. Nowadays they just send the trainees.') Burgess is bursting to chat, for which there is no penalty worse than not being able to. As he says, 'The comrades, though splendid in every other respect, don't gossip in quite the same way we do, or about quite the same subjects.' Spying is like a hasty marriage: one does it when quite young, thinking it beautiful and romantic, and then has to live with the consequences.

Hilary in *The Old Country* wanted to know if the institutions and places he remembered had changed. Burgess asks about people. Has

Browne seen Auden, or Connolly, or E.M. Forster? Also, Burgess arrived in Moscow without a partner, but with fellow spy Donald Maclean, whom he patently cannot stand. 'He's so unfunny, no jokes, no jokes at all . . . And here we are on this terrible tandem together . . . Debenham and Freebody, Crosse and Blackwell, Auden and Isherwood, Burgess and Maclean.' Ms Browne whips out her tape measure and starts taking measurements. 'Clothes have never been the comrades' strong point,' says Burgess, trying to be gracious.

Burgess utters the lament of every exile when he says: 'For charm one needs words. I have no words.' Not just for charm. He goes on: 'Sex needs language.' And besides: 'Boys are quite thin on the ground here.' Worse still, Browne has to tell Burgess that he is not even the subject of much gossip back home, a fate which might have appealed to the play's author, but not to its subject.

Eventually, Browne asks him why, if so many things displease him, he still likes it here. To which his quiet response is: 'The system. Only, being English, you wouldn't be interested in that.'

'I was a performer . . .' he says. 'But I never pretended. If I wore a mask, it was to be exactly what I seemed.' If Burgess and the Hilary of *The Old Country* differed in their attitudes to spying, Bennett doesn't make a distinction. As Hilary said: 'The best disguise of all is to be exactly what you say you are. Nobody ever believes that.' And so Burgess fooled his colleagues, whose attitude, as he says, is: 'How can he be a spy? He goes to my tailor.' In one of the most famous phrases in the play, Burgess continues: 'I can say I love London. I can say I love England. I can't say I love my country. I don't know what that means.' Browne says it's ridiculous 'pretending that spying, which was what you did, darling, was just a minor social misdemeanour, no worse'. So why did he do it? 'Solitude,' says Burgess. 'If you have a secret you're alone.' 'But you told people,' says Browne. 'No point in having a secret if you make a secret of it,' says Burgess, with Bennett obviously lurking behind. When Browne says she has to go, he pleads: 'Don't go yet. I don't want you to go yet.' She suggests that they go for a walk but, as with Hilary in *The Old Country*, he cannot go until he is given clearance, so to while away the time he plays her his record. Not *one* of his records, but the only one he has. And not even both sides: he plays one side only, which is – as Browne said to Bennett – Jack Buchanan singing 'Who Stole My Heart Away?' And so the old 78 is placed on the gramophone, and we hear the same crackly tune which provided the opening music, when it was cleverly illustrated with gigantic posters of Uncle Joe and other Communist heroes.

Back in London, an assistant in one of the shops on Browne's list tells her that Mr Burgess's account has been closed. 'Well,' he explains, 'we supply the Royal Family.' Browne does not understand. 'The gentleman is a traitor, madam.' 'Must traitors sleep in the buff?' objects Browne. 'Say someone commits adultery in your precious nightwear . . . What happens when he comes in to order his next pair of jimjams? Is it sorry, no can do?' She continues: 'You were quite happy to satisfy this client when he was one of the most notorious buggers in London . . . Only then he was in the Foreign Office.' The final scene in the film is of Burgess walking proudly down a Moscow street (in fact the Glasgow Suspension Bridge) dressed in his finery, as the sound of Burgess singing 'He is an Englishman' from Gilbert and Sullivan's *HMS Pinafore* swells into a full chorus.

Alan Bates's performance was simply magnificent. He perfectly embraced Burgess's mottled dandyism, a sentimentalist with a political stain, who worked hard to appear more interested in sexuality than politics, but of whom Bennett wrote that, even when pissed, 'there is a part of him that remains watchful and alert'. *An Englishman Abroad* was received rapturously in the press and won the Best Single Drama award at the 1984 British Academy of Film and Television Awards ceremony. Bennett also shared a Special Writers' award with John Tusa of the BBC's *Newsnight* programme. Alan Bates and Coral Browne won Best Actor and Best Actress. *An Englishman Abroad* also shared top honours with an adaptation of Paul Scott's sweeping Raj drama *The Jewel in the Crown* at the Royal Television Society Awards, reflecting glory both for the BBC and Granada TV. Bennett and *The Jewel in the Crown*'s screen-writer, Ken Taylor, shared the Best Writer award, and the Performance award went to Alan Bates. It was also named Best Single Drama of 1983 in the Broadcasting Press Guild TV and Radio Awards. *An Englishman Abroad* cost only £300,000 to make, but it brought Alan Bennett wider recognition, and more awards, than any other of his plays so far.

In August 1984 Bennett, now fifty, enjoyed his first West End rerun. It was a popular choice, being his first and best-loved play, *Forty Years On*, this time with Paul Eddington as the headmaster and Stephen Fry taking

Bennett's role of Tempest. Bennett didn't go to see the play on opening night, of course, but he did drop in towards the end of the party afterwards, and he even took the role of Tempest for five nights later in the year. The occasion was celebrated in the *Observer* with another penetrating profile, published on 12 August, though this time, unusually, several of his friends were canvassed for their views. All spoke behind a stiff screen of anonymity. The profile began by putting its finger on the nub of the whole matter. 'Bennett is a difficult man to fathom, and does not encourage an attempt to do so. He dislikes interviews, as he has made clear in the (quite numerous) interviews he has given over the years.'

The picture of Bennett was of a man able to cross continents as casually as counties. He still had his share in Keith McNally's Odeon restaurant in New York, though 'I don't get anything out of it except free meals'. He still rode a bike around London, and travelled up and down the M1 in a large Volkswagen. His mother, who had now lost most of her memory, lived in a home near his married brother in Bristol.

Much of the profile was an attempt to take Bennett's emotional temperament. It rephrased Wapshott's list of contradictions: 'reticent and forthright, gentle and sharp, generous and unforgiving'. One friend said: 'He does get angry and upset about things, and – though I haven't seen it myself – I gather his anger is awesome.' Another – or possibly the same – said: 'There is a weight of emotion, blackness, hurt that one senses and walks round.' Another, or the first, or a combination of the two, said: 'There is a demon that can get out of hand, and unless you're going to play the same game, you're sunk.' 'Alan's nuclear weapon', said another friend, 'is withdrawal of himself. He can simply disappear from people's lives.'

'Look,' said one friend, 'he's well off; he reads a lot, buys good pictures, eats good food, spends a lot of time in New York, and has complicated relationships with interesting people. I think he has a good time: though I think he'd be very cross to hear me say that.'

That same year, Bennett made his first proper foray into the world of movies, and he did so by signing a deal with a man who had come out of the same 1960s cultural revolution as he had. In 1963 the satirical Fab Four were joined by the popular singing Fab Four when the Beatles stormed Britain. Since then, Peter Cook and Dudley Moore had collaborated briefly with John Lennon in the first series of *Not Only . . .*

But Also. Now, albeit indirectly, it was Bennett's turn to pick a Beatle.

George Harrison was in many ways Bennett's temperamental equal. Harrison, a keen follower of Eastern spiritualism, recited the mantra of Hare Krishna every day and was visibly uncomfortable in the presence of journalists. Bennett had abandoned religion in his twenties, but the mantra of hating interviews was one that he recited on an almost daily basis.

George Harrison's company, Handmade Films, produced *Monty Python's Life of Brian* in 1979, *Time Bandits* in 1981 and *The Missionary* in 1982. (As well as *Privates on Parade* in 1984, over which a discreet veil will be drawn.) At the time, the British film industry was in dire need of such generous backing, since in 1983 the Thatcher government was four years into its task of dismantling the traditional British system of muddling through and trying to replace it with something more streamlined, profit-orientated and soulless. With the unions and the bosses at each other's necks, and seemingly set on choking the life out of each other, we seemed to be entering another dark age. Doubtless many people were feeling nostalgic at the time, and wondering where all this so-called progress – colour TV, supermarkets and traffic queues – was getting us.

There was good news too; at least we thought so. The marriage of Prince Charles and Lady Diana Spencer on 29 July 1981 was celebrated with street parties and cheering crowds. The British people, led by a media still sycophantically and uncritically fixated with royalty, thought it would usher in a new era for the royal family. Which in a way it did, though not as anticipated.

The film Bennett wrote became known as *A Private Function*, and it starred Michael Palin and Maggie Smith. It came, wrote Bennett, from an idea by Malcolm Mowbray, the director of *Our Winnie*, who wanted to make a film about the period after the war when life was, in a way, even tougher than the years they had just come through. *A Private Function* is set in Leeds in 1947, when Bennett would have been thirteen. Rationing was also still in place – bread until 1948, eggs until 1949 – so post-war austerity still bit deep. Some got round this by flouting the law. Bennett remembers his father over-conscientiously worrying that some customers would not get their fair share of pork, while knowing full well that a neighbouring butcher was getting in supplies from the flourishing black market. 'The butcher down the street from us was on the fiddle, and one of his customers was a stipendiary magistrate who was known to be hand in glove with him,' Bennett told the *Sunday Times* in November 1984. 'The people on the council did well out of the black market, and so did the police chief. My dad didn't. I wish he had in a way.' Bennett adds in his introduction to the film script that 'the weekly worry that his allotted supply would not be enough to cover the requirements of his registered customers eventually landed [my father] in hospital with a duodenal ulcer'.

The battlefield of *A Private Function*, as never before in a Bennett script, is between innocence and calculation, greed and need, the public face and the private sin, hunger for food and hunger for self-improvement. Gilbert Chilvers is a chiropodist, newly qualified and still full of ideals. 'Mrs Roach's in-growing toenail seems to have turned the corner,' he declares proudly. In the official, and thoroughly nice, biography of Michael Palin by Jonathan Margolis, Palin said of the part: 'Malcolm Mowbray [the director] kept on at me to be dull. Whenever I got out of line, he would say: "This man is not having a nice time – remember that." '

Part of the reason why he is not having a nice time is due to Dr Charles Swaby, the town GP and bully. He regards Gilbert as a quack and treats him like a threat. To compound Swaby's evil, he is also the driver of a car, whereas Chilvers proceeds everywhere by bicycle. In fact, Swaby's car seems always to make a beeline for the hapless Chilvers, who only just manages to pull his bicycle clear each time. Swaby, of course, bitterly resents Chilvers's ambitions to open a surgery on the high street. 'You can't call a fly-blown room where you cut toenails a surgery,' he sneers.

Gilbert has his own combustion engine in the form of his socially aspiring wife Joyce, played with brilliant small-town hauteur by Maggie Smith. Whereas the retired couple in *Sunset Across the Bay* were in retreat from city life, this younger couple are trying hard to embrace it. The excuse for the private function of the film's title is the forthcoming royal wedding between Princess Elizabeth and Prince Philip Mountbatten of Greece. Swaby, of course, holds the royal couple up as the ultimate ideal of purity. 'In Westminster Abbey tomorrow morning a young couple are getting married, of a purity and nobility scum like you just can't comprehend,' he says tauntingly to Gilbert. He and his accomplices, Mr Allardyce the accountant and Mr Lockwood the solicitor, plan to celebrate the royal wedding by slaughtering a pig and serving it up to their guests, but in these days of rationing the pig has to be reared secretly. Gilbert and Joyce are, of course, not on the guest list, the main characters marginal, as so often in Bennett's writing, to the main thrust of the story.

The other overzealous authority figure is the Ministry of Food inspector Mr Wormold, played, as austerity personified, by Bill Paterson. Though he maintains the appearance of monastic probity, he necessarily operates through a system of nods and winks. Most of these come from his landlady Mrs Forbes, a woman in her sexual prime whose conscript husband is missing in Malaya. In a world where everyone is living with a compromise of some sort, and food is not the only thing in short supply, Gilbert is a beacon of innocent goodness, trying only to advance his business opportunities.

In *One Fine Day*, Dave Allen fell for a building. In *A Private Function*, the tenderest emotions to be stirred are those between the pig (Betty) and Mr Allardyce, beautifully played, just prior to his *Withnail and I* apotheosis, by the suitably porky Richard Griffiths.

When Betty falls ill, and Gilbert is called in for medical assistance, Swaby (Denholm Elliott at his sneering best) is furious. 'Jaunty toenail-clipping little sod,' he fumes. 'Festering, bunion-scraping little pillock.' Just as Gilbert is beginning to think that they are 'in', Swaby makes his influence felt and Gilbert's shop is closed down. Joyce is, of course, furious. 'They're going to have to be made to realise who we are. My father had a chain of dry-cleaners.' And she utters that unmistakable cry from the heart of so many of Bennett's characters: 'I want a future that will live up to my past. Only when's it going to start?' Tremulously determined, Gilbert and Joyce snatch the pig at night and secret it in their house, which gives rise to some of the richest, and lowest, comedy of Bennett's career.

The single elderly parent was already one of Bennett's leitmotifs, but this was deployed to devastating effect when the pig comes up against Joyce's mother, played with sublime decrepitude by Liz Smith. After one particularly fetid bout of diarrhoea from Betty, it is Mother, of course, who suspects herself of having farted. Later, her flailing attempts to convince Dr Swaby – who, she is convinced, has come to certify her as suitable for transportation to an old folks' home – that she hasn't seen the pig ('No pig, no pig!') are hilarious. Luckily for Gilbert and Joyce,

Mr Wormold is unable to sniff anything untoward owing to infantile German measles, but their problems are far from over. The pig is now Gilbert's friend; it has migrated from 'it' to 'her'. To kill Betty now would not be butchery; it would be murder. Bennett said later that after writing *A Private Function* he had no longer been able to eat pork, a view that George Harrison – the author of the socially barbed song 'Piggies' – and his former colleague Paul McCartney, and certainly Paul's wife Linda, would no doubt have endorsed.

The penultimate scene finds Gilbert and Joyce, and Mother, happily established at the wedding banquet, albeit near the lavatories. Joyce even gets to dance with Swaby, and does not object to having her bottom squeezed by the lecherous doctor. In the final scene, Bennett tries to repair the damage inflicted on the porcine community by having Allardyce and the childless Gilbert cuddle a little piglet.

It is a shame that the film does not figure prominently in the many biographies of George Harrison, because *A Private Function* was one of the best British films of the 1980s. What was so impressive about Bennett's writing was the depth of characterisation. No character was blemish-free, but they all had redeeming qualities. It was a personal triumph for Bennett, together with his director Malcolm Mowbray. Bennett had shown that the spirit of Ealing comedy, in which David tended to beat Goliath, was still vibrant. Maybe that was why it received a royal premiere on 21 November, with Bennett photographed by Snowdon. It was notable that a man who had written about spies and closet homosexuals could be considered suitable viewing by the Windsors. The man who still cringed at using a rude word in the presence of royalty had written a film about adultery, contraband and farting pigs, and the royals were queuing up to see it. Even references to incontinent grannies were considered fair game. (The Queen Mother was eighty-four: rumours about her colostomy bag were widespread.) Perhaps what it proved was that you could say almost anything these days, provided you did so with wit.

Unfortunately, although he and fellow Leeds man Michael Palin remained good friends, Bennett's relations with Handmade Films were less happy. He wrote dismissively of the press release for the film in which, always with a keenly critical eye for the humbug of cod writers, he saw himself described as 'This flaxen-haired Northern lad'. It was a description he had tolerated when it was scribbled in the Exeter College

JCR Suggestions Book, but he clearly felt it ought to have been buried in the Fellows' Garden. Some time later, when he received a royalty statement from Handmade stating that the film had lost £2 million, he wrote back to them suggesting they submit it for that year's Booker Prize for Fiction.

To crown the success of *A Private Function*, the film was chosen to open the British Film Week at the Los Angeles Film Festival. In his diary on 13 March 1985 Bennett recorded a chaotic sequence of disasters, from missed limousines to faulty microphones at the ceremony, culminating in his rising to his feet in the near darkness, somehow missed out by the spotlight, when his name was called. 'Sit down, you jerk,' shouted someone behind him. Bennett obeyed, but he wasn't to be out of the spotlight for long.

13

Dyeing won't do you any harm

The Insurance Man, Kafka's Dick, 1986

Throughout the 1970s, Alan Bennett wrote intimate histories of northern life. With *An Englishman Abroad* and *A Private Function*, he had begun to move closer towards interweaving fictional and historical events. The next period of his development was perhaps his most ambitious yet, as Bennett explored various literary or historical puzzles. Jonathan Miller used to say that *Beyond the Fringe* was the show which rejected 'Wouldn't it be funny if . . .?' in favour of 'Isn't it funny that . . .?' Bennett and Peter Cook often said how much they missed the old-style comedy that *Beyond the Fringe* had killed off. Bennett was about to attempt an updated version of that formula.

Despite the references to Kafka's underpants in *On the Margin,* the leap from the Anglican Leeds-born owl to the Jewish Prague-born jackdaw ('Kavka', in Czech) is not an obvious one. And yet there are some parallels. The statement of Franz Kafka that 'everybody made me feel afraid' has a familiar ring, as does his complex relationship with his father. Kafka, in his most famous novel *The Trial*, tries to reduce his own presence down to the single letter K; Bennett adopts a similar device towards his friends in his own diaries. Kafka, like Bennett, was a hypochondriac, and religion features prominently in the writing of both. Their families share certain features too. While most of the 70,000 Jews in what was then known as Bohemia were pedlars, Kafka's father

Hermann had hauled himself up from dealing in buttons, threads and shoelaces to owning a fancy goods shop in Zeltnergasse, so he and Walter Bennett were of an equivalent social class. Kafka's paternal grandfather was a kosher butcher, and Kafka records many times in his diaries the image of a butcher's knife cutting into his flesh. Bennett was clearly intrigued by the world of Kafka, and he worked hard on a project to adapt Kafka's *The Trial* for TV. That was stillborn, but while he was reading around the subject Bennett made the sort of discovery which can only be described as a gift horse.

In October 1907, aged twenty-four, Kafka went to work for the insurance company Assicurazion Generali. Supplicants or claimants would bring their grievances to him, and he would judge whether or not they had a case. Many of these cases involved suspected tuberculosis, which was widespread at the time, as well as other symptoms which fed his well-established feelings of physical repulsion. In 1911 his brother-in-law Karl Hermann, who had been trading in asbestos, opened Prague's first asbestos factory. The first studies of the effects of asbestos on occupational health were not publicly available before the 1930s. Until then, the benefits of the magical mineral were too great to let vague and unproven grievances from breathless workers get in the way of profits.

The idea that Kafka, a man obsessed with dying, could have been connected with a factory which unwittingly condemned many of its workers to a slow death was too tempting a subject to go unexplored, and it was this which provided the basis for Alan Bennett's next TV play, *The Insurance Man*. Directed by Richard Eyre, with whom Bennett was to establish one of his most fruitful working relationships, it was first broadcast on BBC2 on 23 February 1986. Bennett postulated the existence of a factory worker – confusingly called Franz – who flings himself on Kafka's mercies at the insurance institute, and whom Kafka thinks he is saving by redirecting him to the newly opened asbestos factory. Franz doesn't die, but years later he has breathing problems and goes to see his doctor. The doctor looks at the X-rays of Franz's damaged lungs. 'You weren't to know,' he says. 'You breathed, that's all you did wrong.'

Just as with *An Englishman Abroad*, much of the shooting took place in stand-in locations, so that Prague was represented by Bradford – 'where every other script I've written seems to have been shot,' wrote

Bennett – and Liverpool, a city he did not know and came to like less, bored by the locals' cocky perkiness.

Whereas in *The Trial* Joseph K is obsessed with the answer to the question 'What have I done wrong?', in *The Insurance Man*, the question is 'What is wrong with me?' Franz, played with a commendably anguished expression by Robert Hines, works at a dye-works, and wakes up one morning to find a rash on his chest. When he goes to the factory doctor, the doctor says it is nothing to worry about. 'Dyeing won't do you any harm,' says the doctor in a typically Bennettian play on words. But the rash begins to spread all over his body. How can he make people take his complaints seriously?

Franz gets the sack (for being sick) but doesn't want anyone to find out – least of all his fiancée, Christian. In an impressive five-minute tracking shot, we see him entering the Workers' Accident Insurance Institute on Poric Street, an imposing building – actually St George's Hall, Liverpool – into which every invalid in Prague seems to be hobbling. Bennett felt that he was returning Kafka's world to its original dimensions by cutting out the vast spaces and echoing chambers which film-makers like Orson Welles had grafted on to it. 'Kafka's fearful universe is constructed out of burrows and garrets and cubbyholes on back staircases,' wrote Bennett in his introduction to the film. Watching Welles's Kafka made one feel agoraphobic. Here, the claustrophobia is restored. Once inside, his problems have only just begun, though, as insurance clerks lazily fall over each other to assert that they cannot possibly do anything about his problem, and so try to shift it to another department on another floor.

The three main clerks are Gutling, Pohlmann and Culick – Kullick was the name of one of the three examining clerks in *The Trial*. 'Now, it's possible that your firm will try to put the blame on you,' says Pohlmann to a stunned worker. He continues: 'Just because you're the injured party doesn't mean you are not the guilty party.' Bennett has got to the watering hole early again, and by finding the comedy in Kafka has the whole field of Kafka studies in which to play. This study of the little man fighting against the giant of bureaucracy shows the acute reversal of the breezy Ealing comedy victory of *A Private Function*. We know that David can only be crushed by Goliath this time.

Dr Kafka himself, a German among Czechs played by Daniel Day-Lewis with a tinge of an accent to emphasise his foreignness, gets to muse over many Kafkaesque epigrams. 'Have you noticed,' he says to Gutling, 'how often when claimants are telling you about their accidents, they smile? Why do they smile? They're apologising. They feel foolish. Utterly blameless, yet they feel guilty.' With Franz increasingly distracted by the creeping metamorphosis that is turning him, if not into a beetle overnight, at least into some kind of insect, he so shocks Christian by stripping naked in front of her family that she abandons him.

Making cameo appearances are characters from Bennett's own life, such as Lily, a sort of prototype Miss Shepherd, played by Vivian Pickles, who is convinced her case will be heard, but who is waiting outside the door of what turns out to be an empty room. 'My documents have just gone in. They're studying them now, possibly,' she says. But the best, most passionate speech is spoken by an angry doctor, played by Geoffrey Palmer, which captures the essence of the play:

> Has it ever occurred to you that everyone who comes before this panel has, prior to their accident, been of a sunny and equable disposition, capable of long periods of sustained attention, unvisited by headaches or indeed any infirmity at all, the mind alert, the body in perfect order, a paragon of health? Take this young woman. Previously a cheerful soul, she is now said to be anxious and depressed. So? Previously an optimist, she is now a pessimist: is that such a bad thing? One could say that this accident has brought her to her senses rather than deprived her of them. She now takes a dim view of the world. So do I. She can't keep her mind on the matter in hand. Nor can I. She winces when she looks in the mirror. So do I.

(So did Kafka. And Bennett.) ' "But I was not like this before my accident. I had no quest," ' he says, in Lily's voice. ' "Looking for what is wrong with me is what is wrong with me!" ' 'People will be wanting compensation for being alive next,' says one of the secretaries.

At long last, Franz finds Dr Kafka, who thinks he has the perfect short-term solution: a job in his brother-in-law's new factory. Franz asks what the factory produces. 'Asbestos,' replies Kafka. 'Thank you,' says Franz. 'You saved my life.'

Hugh Hebert in the *Guardian* described it as 'one of the most remarkable pieces of television drama of this, or last, or – for my money – any other year'. *The Insurance Man* was a monumentally impressive work, simultaneously quirky and crushingly sombre, grasping the immensity and the littleness of private tragedy with great subtlety and stealth, and it won a second Royal Television Society award for Bennett.

Bennett's diaries from 1985 and 1986 record the small comedies and tragedies of life around him in Camden Town, Yorkshire and New York. He fills time during the filming of *A Private Function* entertaining the cast or being entertained by those more given to free-range anecdotage. One actor describes him as 'continuity giggles', which delights him. Miss Shepherd continues to leave her dotty notes expressing her ambition to stand as a Member of Parliament, or at least vote for the still fresh-faced Alliance Party. As ever, his ear is trained for on-air cant, such as the radio treatment of a helicopter crash on 8 April 1986. ' "But what did it look like?" persists the reporter [to an eye-witness]. What he means is, "What did it look like seeing six people burn to death?" ' In June he gruffly writes that the Guards beat the retreat to the signature tune from *EastEnders*. In July he complains that Marks & Spencer now sell 'ruby-red orange juice, shoppers presumably being considered too squeamish for blood orange juice'.

In April 1986 Bennett went to Ypres to try to find the last resting place of his uncle Clarence, a moving account of which later appeared in the *London Review of Books* under the title 'Uncle Clarence'. He also read it on radio. With ambitions for adapting *The Trial* now firmly on the back burner, and after their success with *The Insurance Man*, Alan Bennett and Richard Eyre collaborated on a second sidelong look at the myth of Franz Kafka, this time for the theatre. The stage play was first performed exactly seven months after the TV play was seen. And for Bennett it was out of the dark and into the light.

In recent years Bennett had shown an increasing desire to get away from the young man whom Peter Cook remembered stuffing a handkerchief into his mouth. Cook must have been trying harder than ever to make Bennett reinsert that handkerchief in the recordings he released during the 1970s of Derek and Clive, Pete and Dud's foul-mouthed alter egos. Now, though, it was the turn of Alan Bennett's public to reach for their handkerchiefs. The new play, which opened at the Royal Court on 23 September 1986, was called *Kafka's Dick*.

It is a play about posterity. It includes a posthumous trial scene, just as in *Forty Years On*, and it also deals with literary reputations, as would *Prick Up Your Ears* in 1987. But where *Prick Up Your Ears* was concerned to paint a portrait of a swinging London scene – the sort of scene which almost entirely passed Bennett by – *Kafka's Dick* is mostly set in suburbia, and in the minds of its protagonists. There are two couples in the play. One pair is Franz Kafka and his friend Max Brod, who was a more successful writer than Kafka during the latter's life, but after Kafka's death became such an effective executor that he all but obliterated traces of his own literary heritage. The other pair is a modern suburban couple, Sydney and Linda. Sydney is a Kafka maniac, ready to pounce on any lurking biographical crumb. Kafka himself is also concerned, obsessed you could say, with what he thought was his unfeasibly small penis. So Kafka's dick has two immediate applications.

Bennett's play begins with a challenge from Kafka to his friend. 'I want you to promise me something,' says Kafka. 'You must burn everything I've ever written.' Brod challenges this by saying that he doesn't need to worry about burning the books, as the Nazis will take care of that. 'Burn books?' exclaims Kafka. 'Who in his right mind would want to burn books? They must be sick.' Never mind, says Brod the fixer. He can help. He will ensure that the Nazis burn Kafka's books, with his name prominently displayed. As he says: 'Burn one and you sell ten thousand. Believe me, if the Nazis hadn't thought of it the publishers would.'

Of course, Brod doesn't burn all the books, and when Kafka discovers this he is apoplectic. 'I say burn them; what do you think I mean, *warm* them?' At last Linda gives Kafka something to be happy about. 'I have to confess, I've never read a word you've written,' she says. When Bennett finally opened the door on his relationship with Anne Davies he admitted that one of the reasons he liked her was because she didn't want to be a literary wife.

In the play's final twist, Sydney's father persuades Hermann that no one got anywhere by having an 'average' father. He decides he wants to stay on as the villain, the bad father, because, 'So long as my son's famous, I'm famous. I figure in all the biographies, I get invited to all the parties.' The play ends with the much-criticised celestial party, in which his father is of course God. 'I'll tell you something,' says Kafka. 'Heaven is going to be hell.' *Curtain*.

The critics loved it, give or take the final scene. 'It is a bold and original conceit even if there are times when the spray of verbal jokes is not sustained by the necessary internal dynamic,' wrote Michael Billington in the *Guardian*. Michael Ratcliffe in the *Observer* described it as 'a paradox: a mordant attack on twentieth-century trivialisation and barbarity by a playwright who cannot resist blunting the force and intensity of his attack by a constant stream of gags, some of which are very good, but many of which are surprisingly cheap and feeble from one of the funniest and most fastidious writers working in England today'. John Peter in the *Sunday Times*, who described the play as being about 'literary criticism as a form of piracy', added that 'My feeling is that Bennett has taken more on board than he can deal with.' His objection was that 'When it is a question of looking forward, the anachronistic comedy works beautifully. But not when it comes to looking back.' For Jack Tinker in the *Daily Mail*, it was 'all good, if never quite clean, fun'.

The play's success was helped by an inspired cast. Roger Lloyd Pack as Kafka was a revelation, his eyes appearing to try to tear themselves away from his body. Andrew Sachs played Brod, Jim Broadbent was Hermann Kafka, Alison Steadman was Linda and Geoffrey Palmer was Sydney – some of the best actors of their generation. *Kafka's Dick* contains some of the funniest writing Alan Bennett ever composed, while also continuing to pick away at issues of generational rivalry, literary immortality and a barely concealed hostility to attempts to 'understand' writers (such as this book is attempting to do). It also drew the most sustained criticism so far from the press that Bennett was far too preoccupied with jokes at the expense of character and plot. The title of *Kafka's Dick* had caused offence to many, including Steven Berkoff who wrote an angry letter to Bennett before the opening night, castigating him for being a 'hack' and for misrepresenting Kafka's life and trial to comic effect. Bennett cheerfully wrote back to him pointing out that he should reserve judgement until he had seen the play. Bennett also chatted about the play to his good friend Russell Harty for an article in the *Sunday Times*. 'If it has a theme, it's biography,' he said. 'It's to do with the way that, these days, biography is all about cutting people down to size.' He also said he liked Kafka because: 'When he got up in the morning and looked at himself in the mirror, he winced. And even in the worst moments of his life, he couldn't help making jokes.'

Bennett confessed to feeling sympathy for Hermann Kafka. 'There came a time, reading about Kafka's dad, when I just began to get warm towards him,' he said. 'He's so maligned, such an ogre, that I thought I'd tip the balance a bit in his favour.' If *The Insurance Man* is Bennett at his darkest – Woody Allen's *Shadows and Fog* came somewhere close to creating the same atmosphere in 1992 – *Kafka's Dick* is Bennett at his most cheeky. As saucy as a seaside postcard, it may have shocked some people, but he was within a year of unleashing something far racier. The headmaster in *Forty Years On* had warned: 'Mark my words, when a society has to resort to the lavatory for its humour, the writing is on the wall.' Bennett was heading in just that direction.

14

The thinking man's *Sid and Nancy*

Prick Up Your Ears, Talking Heads, 1987

'Went up to see Joe Orton & Kenneth [Halliwell],' Kenneth Williams confided to his diary on 23 July 1967. 'They were v. kind. We chatted about homosexuality and the effect the new clause would have. We agreed it would accomplish little. Joe walked with me to King's X. We also talked about his inability to love, his horror of involvement, & his need to be utterly free, and Ken H. disagreed with this, saying that love is involvement, and you can't live without love.'

Williams, who had known Orton and Halliwell since playing the part of Truscott in the (disastrous) first staging of Orton's play *Loot* in 1965, sent them a nice letter the next day thanking them for listening. Two weeks later, on 9 August, Orton and Halliwell were dead and Williams was in shock. 'There is something so dark and horrible about the circumstances,' wrote Williams. 'Joe Orton – in pyjamas with head injuries, a hammer nearby – and on the floor the body of Ken Halliwell, dead from suicide. Did he have a hallucination or something? Did he fear J. might drop him? It's all so odd. When I think of the generosity of Joe – his warmth and affection – his kindness to me when I was so depressed – I just want to cry.'

The *Evening Standard*'s account of the case read as follows: 'Joe Orton, the 34-year-old award-winning playwright, was battered to death with a hammer in "a deliberate form of frenzy". The murderer: his 41-year-old flat-mate, Kenneth Halliwell, who committed suicide with "an enormous overdose of drugs". The St Pancras deputy coroner, Dr John Burton, recording the verdict at the inquest today, said: "It is quite clear Mr Halliwell struck Mr Orton while he was asleep. There is no question of a suicide pact – nothing to suggest that Orton was a party to this. The evidence is overwhelming that Orton was killed by Halliwell. In a note he said he had done it intentionally. By inference there was trouble between them for some time. It appears it came to a head." '

Unless Dr Burton was making a very dark joke indeed, he should perhaps have reworded his final sentence. The police pathologist established that there had been nine blows to Orton's skull. After he had done it, Halliwell made good the threat which he had been making on and off for years and took his own life, the twenty-two Nembutals washed down with grapefruit juice having done the trick within thirty seconds.

'Curiously I have no anger for Halliwell,' wrote Williams on 4 September, 'only sorrow – though the more one considers it, the more horrible it all seems. Now, that is the end. No doubt someone will write a book about it all – and time will eventually heal the terrible pain of those who cared for them.'

Williams was right about the book. On 26 August 1971 Williams had his first meeting with the man who would become Joe Orton's biographer, John Lahr. 'All this raking over the old ground,' he moaned in his diary. It took Lahr about seven years to finish the book, but it was published to tremendous acclaim and considerable controversy, not least because of its title, *Prick Up Your Ears* (drawn from a phrase jotted down in one of Orton's exercise books for possible later development). The screenplay option eventually ended up on the desk of two men with a far less fraught working partnership than Orton and Halliwell: Stephen Frears and Alan Bennett.

Orton's contribution to the theatre rests largely on three plays, *Entertaining Mr Sloane* (1964), *Loot* (1965) and *What the Butler Saw* (1969), the last produced posthumously. His plays shocked and teased audiences with what the *Oxford Companion to the Theatre* describes as 'the contrast between [their] prim-and-proper dialogue and the violence and outrageousness of [the] action'. Orton's contribution to theatrical legend was in the shocking manner of his death, the seeds of which lay in his relationship with his boyfriend, the temperamental, depressive Kenneth Halliwell. Writing the screenplay meant that Bennett was obliged to look hard at Halliwell, an older man who could not bear the thought that his own artistic efforts were irredeemably mediocre compared with his lover's. In the introduction to the screenplay Bennett writes: 'I admired [Orton's] plays . . . but from what I read in Lahr's biography I had mixed feelings about the man. I felt I didn't like him, or (it amounts to the same thing) I felt he wouldn't have liked me. I didn't object to the promiscuity and the cottaging; what I found hard to take was his self-assurance and the conviction (however painfully and necessarily acquired) of the superiority of his talent.' In his postscript to the collected *Beyond the Fringe* scripts (first published in 1986), Bennett wrote: 'I have just finished a script about the life of Joe Orton, murdered by his lover and teacher Kenneth Halliwell. Whereas in private Orton readily acknowledged his debt to his friend he never did so in public. No wonder Halliwell battered his brains out; there were times in those years 1961–64 when I felt like that myself.'

It was with much relief that Bennett finally handed the screenplay over to Frears, since he had been struggling with it, on and off, since 1980, unable to decide to whose story to give the greater emphasis. In one early draft, the character of Halliwell became the hero and Orton the villain. But this, Bennett later decided, 'was not true to the facts', so, at John Lahr's suggestion, Lahr entered the story as a character writing the biography. This made it more of a detective story, *Orton's Dick* perhaps, and the film is paced like a search movie, in which we discover more through our questing narrator. The final trick was to keep Lahr but to introduce the awesome Peggy Ramsay, Orton's agent (played by Vanessa Redgrave in the film). A good agent can often help an embattled writer, and Ramsay was one of the great agents of her day. Even at that distance, the Ramsay effect worked on Bennett, and the block lifted.

Eventually, filming went ahead in July 1986, starring Gary Oldman and Alfred Molina as Orton and Halliwell, and Bennett's old collaborator Stephen Frears – who happened to come from Orton's home town of Leicester – directing. Having defended the title of his play *Kafka's Dick*, Bennett and Frears decided to take John Lahr at his word, and the film was called *Prick Up Your Ears*.

The film starts, as the book does, with the last scene. Halliwell's face, in spectral half-light, calls out Joe's name in the darkness, and then, more hesitantly, refers to him by his original name: 'John?' It is as if, having killed Joe, he is hoping that he might have resurrected John. But he hasn't, of course. Halliwell's suicide note was also a confession of murder. He said as much in the note that was found on top of Orton's diaries:

> If you read his diary all will be explained. KH.
> PS. Especially the latter part.

The trouble was, not everything was *in* those diaries. We know from reading them that Orton was discovered by Halliwell when they were both at RADA, the Royal Academy of Dramatic Arts. The entry for 16 June 1951 reads 'Move into Ken's flat', and the following three days' activities are summarised by the curt but euphoric 'WELL!' For the next ten years, though, the pair lapsed into silence as they worked on their craft, and each other. They only surfaced in 1962, when they were found guilty of defacing Islington Council library books and sentenced to six months each in jail. At least Bennett had a beginning and an end, though. Between these, he constructed a rope bridge of intelligent speculation concerning Orton's ascendancy as a writer and Halliwell's slow disintegration. Bennett portrayed Orton's arrival in London, at RADA, as a gauche Midlands lad who nevertheless possessed a spark of something vibrant. Halliwell, seen in his audition doing Hamlet in an ornately purple voice, produces yawns within seconds – too quickly, in fact. But in the strange confinement of a gents' lavatory, Orton – described by Lahr as 'a voluptuary of fiasco' – found the casual intensity of desire that he sought. Bennett suggests that in their different approaches to sex lay the seeds of their destruction. Orton excitedly advances on any feasible sexual prospect, whether on the Holloway Road or on the beach at Tangier. He encourages Halliwell to take his chances too, and even treats a police raid as a bit of a joke. Halliwell is forever, maddeningly, holding back, trying to engage potential pick-ups in humdrum conversation when it's clear, even in Morocco, that they are interested in only one thing.

Orton and Halliwell were pioneers of the type of travel known nowadays as 'sex tourism' and practised by all sorts of English travellers, from the high to the low, writers, actors, even critics, on beaches from Morocco to Thailand. Abroad, a level of freedom existed which was not to be found at home. In England, where the age of consent for gay sex was fixed at twenty-one in 1967, men could have been arrested for having sex with each other, and frequently were.

Claustrophobia is a word often used in discussions of Bennett's works, whether of couples pining to escape from Leeds, or of the world of Franz Kafka. In *Prick Up Your Ears*, the stifling atmosphere of the poky little flat they shared in Noel Road, Islington, is perfectly evoked. In one of the film's earliest scenes, though only weeks before their catastrophic final hours, Orton arrives home late to find Halliwell waiting impatiently for him. 'What sort of a day have you had, Kenneth?' Halliwell asks rhetorically. He can then go into his carefully rehearsed accusatory rant: 'Well, not unproductive, Joe, actually. I caught up on a big backlog of dusting. Then I slipped out to the end of the road to replenish our stock of corn flakes. When I got back I rinsed a selection of your soiled underclothes, by which time it was four o'clock, the hour of your scheduled return. When you failed to appear I redeemed the shining hour by cutting my toenails.' If Bennett's sympathies were with Halliwell, they enabled him to produce a more life-sized study of Halliwell's neurotic mediocrity than of Orton's live-for-the-moment priapism.

Alan Bennett was in the fortunate position of being able to write his own publicity in an article for the *Sunday Telegraph* magazine. Not only was this more of a scoop than an interview with the film's writer, but it also allowed him to duck out of answering any questions he didn't want to answer. Bennett saw the film as 'not a commercial for the homosexual life so much as the story of a marriage'. He speculated on what drew Orton to the seedy, and came to the conclusion that the one thing Orton was in search of was risk. 'There are precious few places in society when one can find risk,' he wrote. 'A casino is one, I suppose, and a public lavatory is another.'

Not surprisingly, Bennett did not speculate on what people who had enjoyed the comparatively mild atmosphere of his earlier films might have made of this one. 'The question people ask now is what the film is going to seem like in the age of AIDS,' he wrote, though that might not have been the first question in an interviewer's mind. This was Alan Bennett, for goodness' sake. Until now, the nearest he had come to on-screen sex was Maggie Smith, towards the end of *A Private Function*, announcing to Michael Palin: 'Gilbert, I think sexual intercourse is called for.' The rest of the time, sex, especially gay sex, was something that took place off camera, or offstage. In the past, the lavatory was the scene for some gentle domestic baiting. But *Prick Up Your Ears* celebrated extra-domestic masturbation, and much more. What were the members of the Settle Civic Society – still in shock from seeing the word 'dick' in the title of a Bennett play – meant to make of cottaging scenes such as the one that took place in half-light in a public lavatory just after Orton stole away from an *Evening Standard* awards ceremony. In the words of the script: 'Orton goes up to the man and puts his hand down to his cock . . . Someone is sucking Orton's cock. He comes. Zips up his fly.' It was like an Ealing comedy directed by Rainer Werner Fassbinder.

By contrasting Orton's libertine sexuality with Halliwell's guardedness, Bennett found a new freedom. When Peggy Ramsay tells John Lahr that the Festival of Britain marked the time when 'it all came off the ration', from food to sex, it was also Bennett marking a change of direction from *A Private Function*, when food and sex were most definitely *on* the ration. When Dr Wicksteed in *Habeas Corpus* declared 'King Sex is a wayward monarch', the randiness was purely farcical. No eroticism was intended. In *Prick Up Your Ears*, Bennett was not commenting on his sexuality, any more than Stephen Frears or John Lahr were. But it showed that he could embrace sex as eagerly as could any of his contemporaries. It was a genuine and daring break for Bennett. In particular, it made a nonsense of any future attempts to diminish Bennett's 'cosy little world' of tea cosies and cupcakes. There was a place for all that, but the reality was more complex. It was a reality that the media were determined not to embrace, of course.

Bennett has not yet written – or seen published – a conventional love story. This, or *Me, I'm Afraid of Virginia Woolf*, is the nearest he has come to it. As a story of obsessive love, this is very direct indeed. And yet it is hard to disagree with the verdict of David Thomson, in his magisterial *Biographical Dictionary of Film*, that *Prick Up Your Ears* 'chose to dramatize writer John Lahr's inquiry into the life [of Joe Orton] and thus missed too much of the life'.

After he has smashed Orton's head in, Halliwell sees the *Evening Standard* award for Best Play of 1966, which Orton had won for *Loot*. 'I should have used that. More theatrical. You'd have spotted that straight away,' he says to the now-dead Orton. There is perhaps more of Bennett than Halliwell in there, but it makes the point none the less. *Kafka's Dick* and *Prick Up Your Ears* briefly meet towards the end of the film, when John Lahr asks Peggy Ramsay if she feels like the second wife. 'Better than that, dear,' she says. 'The widow.'

The British critic Adam Mars-Jones, one of the few openly gay film critics writing for a national paper, had reservations about the prospect of Bennett writing a screenplay about Joe Orton's life and death, since, as he said, 'Bennett . . . sometimes seems to think that there is nothing to sex except embarrassment.' However, he soon admitted that 'Bennett has done Orton proud'. Giving praise to Frears for avoiding 'the false nearness of nostalgia', Mars-Jones hailed 'a remarkable double act'.

Others felt differently. If the aim of *Prick Up Your Ears* had been to *épater les bourgeois*, Godfrey Barker, writing in the *Daily Telegraph*, came close to giving himself a hernia in print, describing the film as 'smug, sordid, obscene and self-admiring. The unhappy reality is that *Prick Up Your Ears* is a masterpiece of nullity, a triumph of interminable and most intense triviality. It is an act of embarrassment, a shame to the British film industry and to Mr Alan Bennett and Mr Stephen Frears.' This tirade against a film which he describes as 'superficial as the smears on a lavatory wall' is overheated but no doubt deeply felt:

> Retracing the sod's diary that Orton so coyly wrote in Pitman shorthand, the camera wanders lovingly in his shirtlifting wake as he drops his trousers in Leicester, strokes his literary darling in Islington, grins, sniggers, sucks and kisses until his boyfriend batters him to merciful death in 1967.

Barker resented the fact that it was 'implicit, of course, that all truly liberated souls will regard open homosexual masturbation on screen as, heavens, rather amusing, suave and soigné'. Building to a climax, he continued: 'I loathed the writhings of these cocksure rentboys, am unashamed about my loathing, and was lifted into the stellar regions of boredom rather than shock by their unnatural practices.'

Not since *On the Margin* had Alan Bennett incurred the rage of the Home Counties apoplectics so violently. And yet the film didn't meet universal delight in gay circles either. Simon Shepherd's book *Because We're Queers,* which appeared in 1989, accused 'the Orton industry' – by which he meant Lahr and Bennett – of demonising Halliwell by conducting interviews which 'were already prejudiced against Halliwell' and of taking statements 'without it being explicitly asked how much of that evidence came from a sexist or homophobic bias'. Bennett, said Shepherd, had simply swallowed Lahr's version of events without asking any questions.

Of course, portrayals of Halliwell that emphasise him as a screaming, hysterical queen *are* hackneyed, as is the idea that, in Shepherd's words, 'queer love is doomed to destruction'. But the portrait of Halliwell is far from being unsympathetic, and he *did* bash Orton's brains out in a jealous rage. For another thing, many of the witnesses that Lahr spoke to were gay themselves, and perfectly happy to be so, so Lahr and Bennett could hardly be accused of homophobia. And despite all of Shepherd's reservations, it is hard to disagree with Alan Bennett's verdict that Kenneth Halliwell could be an extremely irritating man.

Prick Up Your Ears, which Barker described as 'the thinking man's *Sid and Nancy*', was selected as the British entry for the Palme d'Or at the 1987 Cannes Film Festival.

In the same year, Bennett slipped comfortably back into his old clerical garb when he played the Bishop in Christine Edzard's sprawling two-part film of *Little Dorrit*. He also played Lord Pinkrose in a version for television of Olivia Manning's *The Fortunes of War*. Bennett was still available for acting roles, whether high profile or – as when he played the part of Posner in Nigel Williams's play *Breaking Up* – just interesting.

It was at about this time that the press began to write about a disease which was cutting swaths through the ranks of his fellow performers. In Kafka's time they had tuberculosis and syphilis; the health scare of the 1980s was AIDS. From being unknown at the start of the decade, by 1987 the disease seemed to be developing into a pandemic. The theatre community was hit hard, and soon the red ribbon was an essential lapel accessory worn by people to express their concern and their desire to help. In the circumstances, the gay community felt that silence implied indifference, and the tactic of 'outing' people who were suspected of being gay but hadn't yet admitted it was widely employed, especially in the United States. Alan Bennett was hardly the sort of man given to shouting his sexual preferences out loud. Back in Britain, one of the gay community's most dynamic figureheads was the actor Ian McKellen. At an AIDS benefit, McKellen publicly challenged Bennett to state whether he was heterosexual or homosexual. Bennett responded by saying it was a bit like asking a man crawling across the Sahara whether he would prefer Perrier or Malvern water. 'I was rather pleased with that,' Bennett later told Charles Nevin of the *Independent on Sunday*. 'It put him in his place as well. I don't think people should make these great revelations about their private lives.'

In June 1987 Bennett was to be found at the kettle again, this time preparing tea for Jill Parkin of the *Yorkshire Post*, who had travelled down to London to see how Bennett was coping with the news that *Getting On* was to be performed at the Stephen Joseph Theatre in Scarborough, and that *Enjoy* was being revived – 'resuscitation' might be a better word, they agreed – at the Library Theatre in Manchester. Bennett said that there were only three of his plays which he could look back on without wanting to change them: *Habeas Corpus*, *An Englishman Abroad* and *A Woman of No Importance*. He was puzzled, bemused perhaps, that none of his plays had yet been performed in Leeds. Parkin spotted the obligatory donnish clothing gaff, a huge double ink blot on the right elbow of his shirt. 'Yes, I'm drowning in paper,' he said. 'My work is rather like the trenches. I have this enormously long front of started plays and I move along horizontally, occasionally . . . making progress but never actually reaching Berlin.'

On 2 September 1987 the *Daily Star* made a more interesting discovery. 'We learn of the kindness of the dramatist Alan Bennett, who has a permanent visitor in the driveway of his comfortable period home in London,' wrote its diarist. Adopting a more arch style than the paper has affected in subsequent years, he 'found a crumbling caravanette, inside of which was residing a Miss Shepherd'. Having noted that she was even sharing Bennett's electricity supply, the diarist concluded that 'should Mr Bennett ever run dry of ideas for his next play he might find fertile inspiration in the circumstances of his very own driveway'. This is possibly the first and only case of accurate literary prediction in the entire history of the *Daily Star*.

If the raucousness and squalor of *Prick Up Your Ears* appeared to represent a reaction against Bennett's apparent reputation as being the voice of Middle England, his followers did not have to wait long for him to give them more of what they wanted. *Talking Heads* was broadcast on BBC1 between 19 April and 24 May 1988, and the programmes bounced Bennett on to a previously unthinkable level of public and critical acclaim, a level he has been on ever since. In structure, they were a straightforward development from the success of *A Woman of No Importance*. In that play, Patricia Routledge talked straight to the camera, from a limited range of scenes, and from an even more limited point of view. The confessions and failures of a cast of low achievers were a raging success, perhaps because so many people sit watching the telly and wondering why their lives are so awful. Here was someone they could point to and say: 'There's always someone worse off than yourself.'

The first monologue in *Talking Heads* was called 'A Chip in the Sugar', and starred Alan Bennett himself as Graham Whitaker, a middle-aged bachelor who lives with his seventy-two-year-old mother, Vera. Vera is getting a little forgetful but is still lively enough to enjoy outings and occasional visits to small restaurants or cafés. Graham's mental health has been unstable over the years, and when he and Mam bump into an old flame of hers, a rather sharp semi-retired gent's outfitter called Frank Turnbull, the prospect of her leaving him is something he cannot face. Graham further suspects the house is being watched, a suspicion which his mother greets with the suggestion that he should 'take another pill', but his suspicions are vindicated when the prowler turns out to be Mr Turnbull's daughter, who has come to warn Mam that Frank Turnbull is a philanderer and a cheat. In *Intensive Care*, the knowledge that Midgley's father had had an affair briefly liberated him. It works in a similar way for Graham, too, though here it means that life can go back to normal: he has his mam back. Bennett's Graham was all raised eyebrows and suppressed shudders, and it was widely praised in the press. Nancy Banks-Smith in the *Guardian* called it 'a little miracle. You would not have thought that desolation and laughter could coexist so cosily.' Comparing it with a portrait of another writer that same week, Christopher Tookey, a long-term fan of Bennett's, wrote in the *Daily Telegraph* that 'Bennett's skill with words . . . could not have been further removed from Barbara Taylor Bradford's conveyor belt prose'. Which might have given the two writers something to chat about while they were both waiting to collect their literature doctorates from Leeds University ten years later.

In 'A Lady of Letters', Patricia Routledge finally gets her hands on the half-hour monologue which she and Bennett had been circling like hawks in *Doris and Doreen*, *A Visit from Miss Prothero* and *A Woman of No Importance*. Routledge plays Irene Ruddock, who starts out as a nosy neighbour and winds up receiving a custodial sentence and then sharing a prison cell with a prostitute who has killed her own child while under the influence of alcohol. So many of Bennett's characters dream of escape. For Miss Ruddock, the prison sentence is the best possible outcome for her. She is liberated, and enjoys learning jailbird skills like smoking and swearing, even though she, somewhat unconvincingly, gets it wrong, telling her friend to 'fuck up'. Her last speech is a bucolic fantasy from the depths of her prison cell that has an echo of Ms Craig's final speech from *Enjoy*: 'I can hear the wind in the poplar trees by the playing field and maybe it's raining and I'm sitting there. And I'm so . . . happy.'

In 'Bed Among the Lentils', Maggie Smith plays a vicar's wife – and nothing to do with the abortive Cary Grant project from 1967 – called Susan. Partly out of frustration at the inertia of her own life – not having turned into 'a wonderful woman at the stroke of fifty' – Susan has become an alcoholic. Susan, to put it lightly, finds being a vicar's wife a bore. She no longer has sex with her husband Geoffrey, who seems more interested in ingratiating himself with the local diocesan bishop than with tending to her physical wellbeing. Her descriptions of Geoffrey's godliness, and his popularity with the faithful, are hilarious, and very bitchy. Susan tries to pick fights with some of the ladies on the vestry duty rota, but frequently she is too drunk to operate effectively. She knows, more than most of the other characters in the series, what is really happening to her. Liberation, of a sort, comes when she has a brief affair with the Pakistani owner of a corner shop in a different part of town. Like Trevor in *Me, I'm Afraid of Virginia Woolf*, a corner has been turned. Unlike Trevor, we cannot be sure that she won't find herself back in the same place where she was before.

In 'Her Big Chance', Julie Walters plays a small-time actress called Lesley, who doesn't realise that she has been cast to play the lead in a pornographic movie. Lesley is a confusing cross between wide eyed and wide open. 'The parts I get offered tend to be fun-loving girls who take life as it comes,' she says, like the description of life in Sweden which Dad read out in *Enjoy*. Lesley is, of course, inanity incarnate, but she has a thirty-eight-inch bust, and so is invited to audition for a movie, a role which she is thrilled to be offered. When she finally agrees to take her bra and panties off in front of her on-screen boyfriend Alfredo she is told that by doing so 'she is showing her contempt for his whole way of life'. Bennett doesn't credit her with the self-defensive instincts which most women, let alone large-breasted women, have. She ends up in bed with the director, whose name is Gunther, and her parting gift is to leave a postcard for the cast that says, 'Goodbye gang! See you at the premiere.' Sadly, we are forced to conclude that Alan Bennett has never met an aspiring but unsuccessful actress who has been tricked into playing a very small part in a soft-porn movie. 'Her Big Chance', for all that it is funny in places, rings the least true.

In the other monologues, Thora Hird in 'A Cream Cracker under the Settee' gave one of the best Senior Citizen in Crisis performances of her life, as a proud but elderly lady whose excessive tidying has led to her suffering a fall. And in 'Soldiering On', Stephanie Cole does just that after the death of her husband, while trying to shield from herself the unpalatable thought that her son is making improper use of her late husband's financial remains.

Talking Heads was such an overwhelming success that it has become sacrosanct, beyond criticism. David Thomson (again) describes the six dramatic monologues ('no, adramatic') as 'shattered lives, no matter that the broken pieces are held politely together in the way a humble soldier on the Somme might have held his privates in place waiting for his turn with the surgeon'. There was a barrage of praise in the press: normal critical judgements seemed to have been put on hold. 'The form is as poignant as the words or the performances,' wrote Thomson. 'There is a passivity here that must count as Bennett's most profound limitation.' No one criticised Bennett's subjects for being able to adduce all the right evidence about their dismal lives but, absurdly, none of the conclusions. 'Bed among the Lentils' aside, this writer has always felt strangely unmoved by *Talking Heads*. But he is in the minority.

In Bennett's introduction to the collected edition of *Talking Heads*, the president of the Settle Civic Society rails against 'The mock Georgian doorways that disfigure otherwise decent houses, the so-called Kentucky fried Georgian' and lace ('or more likely nylon') curtains which, gathered in the middle, 'look to me like a woman who's been to the lav and got her underskirt caught up behind her'. And, of course, trendy clergymen get a ticking off. 'Along with postmen and porters I wish they had not abandoned black,' he says. 'If a parson submits to the indignity of a dog collar the chances are it has gone slimline, peeping coyly above a modish number in some fetching pastel shade.' Were all Bennett's fans safe from such décor gaffes? One is forced to the conclusion that for many readers, one of the pleasures of reading Bennett is a sort of masochism.

Such was the success of *Talking Heads* that by 1995 they had found their way on to the schools' A-level syllabus, where they have been ever since. In 1999 an edition of *York Notes* was published to steer students through the text. The author, Delia Dick, is a clear and patient teacher. 'Make careful notes on themes, character, plot and any sub-plots of the play,' she advises. 'Why do you like or dislike the characters in the play? How do your feelings towards them develop and change?'

Ms Dick also glosses some of the more remote elements of Bennett-ese, from explanations of defunct political states like West Germany to dialect phrases such as 'side the pots' ('to clear the table'). The character with the longest glossary is Muriel in 'Soldiering On', and one of Bennett's most indubitably southern characters. His Home Counties character's speech needs translating more than the Yorkshire-born ones.

Talking Heads fans ranged from distinguished film critics to Bob, or Sir Bob, Geldof, who tapped Bennett on the shoulder in a bookshop to say how much he'd enjoyed the series. 'Someone as famous as that coming up to me,' Bennett told Michael Hickling. 'I went bright red.'

15

A Wapping scrap

Dinner at Noon, 1988

'Alan Bennett pays respect . . . to the right to attention of the "little" person in society,' writes Delia Dick in her *York Notes*. *Talking Heads* was certainly that. If *Talking Heads* were a chat show, it would have been Russell Harty rather than Michael Parkinson. Whereas Parkie only ever went for the big names, Harty was more than happy to drop in for a cup of tea with an old lady in a Leeds back-to-back who would probably have produced more funny stories than most of the celebrities with whom he was paid to converse.

Russell Harty and Alan Bennett had shared good moments, such as their exuberant mini-Grand Tour of Italy undertaken after Oxford, as well as sad moments such as when Harty accompanied Bennett to Walter Bennett's funeral. Harty's public skill was asking people questions, which, to Bennett, was increasingly an anathema, and yet the two were the best of friends, the external trappings of their professional lives kept in separate compartments. Harty's broadcast triumphs included interviews with J.B. Priestley, Jonathan Miller, Gloria Swanson, Charles Aznavour and Franco Zeffirelli, and he even got to present *Songs of Praise* for the BBC. But in 1987, a personal disaster befell him which left him feeling convinced that his career was beyond the reach of prayer.

On 1 March of that year, the *News of the World* ran a story based on a statement by 'handsome six-footer' Dean Craddock, a twenty-year-old rentboy working for the Ecstasy escort agency, which, according to Peter Chippindale and Chris Horrie, authors of *Stick It Up Your Punter: The Rise and Fall of the Sun*, 'ran magazine ads offering "especially selected stunners" for "home/hotel visits" '.

Under the headline 'Smack Happy Harty, My £60-A-Night Lover' and the strap 'Exposed: the secret sordid life of chat-show king who mixes with the mightiest in the land,' a painfully thin 'Exclusive' followed, alleging that Harty had met the boy at a party in Earls Court, and that Harty 'asked me to massage him, and smacked me'. All that for £60.

Harty, not unreasonably, panicked. Thinking that rumours of homosexuality would shatter his TV image, he assumed that it was all up, and so he took on more and more work to protect himself against a time when offers would slow to a trickle. But they didn't. Commissioning editors took an unhysterical view of the unremarkable scoop, the newspaper-reading public seemed to treat the whole thing as a bit of a joke, and Harty found that he was working, if anything, harder than ever.

Reporters from the *News of the World* converged on the little town of Giggleswick, anxious to dig up any dirt, or background information. 'Reporters sat on his doorstep, searched through his dustbins, harassed neighbours, chased his car and forced their way into the public school in the village, where he had once been a master,' wrote Chippindale and Horrie. 'The attempted bribe to the vicar was in the devious form of the offer of a large "anonymous" contribution to the restoration fund for the church roof. But the reporters were disappointed. The villagers closed ranks and displayed a fierce loyalty to his privacy, appalled by what was happening.'

Over a year later, in the early hours of 4 May 1988, the exhausted Harty fell ill and was admitted to the St James's Infirmary, Leeds, suffering from an undisclosed condition, eventually confirmed as Hepatitis B. On the same day, the *Sun* ran a feature headlined 'The life and times of Russell Harty'. It alleged: 'Over the past eighteen months Russell has been linked with teenage rentboys and was reported to have been sharing his home with a teenage boy.' Strange, the combination of the deviousness of the allegations and the familiar, almost affectionate use of the first name.

The media feeding frenzy continued. If anything, it increased.

St James's, or 'Jimmy's', to give it its nickname, had been the subject of a fly-on-the-wall treatment by Yorkshire TV. Now, it was about to be visited by yet more cameras, though this time most were at the gates or peering through the windows.

Various tricks were played. Harty's Yorkshire neighbours soon tumbled to the low cunning of the breed when they realised that various overweight men, supposedly playing football in a field overlooking Harty's garden in Giggleswick, kept kicking the ball over the wall and then taking rather a long time to get it back. This was meant to provide 'colour' for the exposé that ran the following Sunday. 'Another time,' wrote Chippindale and Horrie, 'a large bouquet of Get Well Soon flowers was sent to another patient in the intensive care unit, within which was concealed the number of a Manchester paper's newsdesk and some money.' Not only was the patient too sick to read the note, but the hospital, 'gallantly struggling to maintain good relations with the press, refused to reveal the identity of the paper responsible'.

Harty's health deteriorated rapidly, and Bennett's notes about him in his diary became more and more concerned. By May, Bennett was writing: 'Some signs yesterday that Russell was coming out of his coma, and today he is sitting up and taking notice, even trying to write notes.' Visitors were told that they could wave at him through the glass, but no one was allowed in. On 7 May, a day after a consultant told Bennett that Harty was 'not yet out of the wood', the hospital over-optimistically held a press conference to announce that Harty had 'turned the corner'. This particular corner, it turned out, would be of the wrong kind, but the precipitate decision had been taken, it was widely felt, principally to deter the press. In particular, it was hoped to forestall the efforts of the long-lens photographers, who had gone to the effort of hiring a flat opposite from which they could pry through the window of Harty's ward. Bennett's concern for his dying friend is one of the most touching aspects of the extracts published in *Writing Home*. And Harty's faltering efforts to reassure those around him were typical of the man: 'Russell . . . keeps scribbling indecipherable notes on the lines of "Tell the world I am grateful to the doctors of St James's Hospital and all staff and cleaners on Ward 17".'

In May 1988 Bennett spent ten days visiting the Soviet Union on a visit organised by the Great Britain–USSR Society, a post-Cold War version of the trip that Michael Redgrave and Coral Browne had gone on in 1958. It was his first visit to the country whose language he had studied before Oxford. With him were literary luminaries such as Craig Raine, Paul Bailey and Timothy Mo. They were also joined by Sue Townsend. They saw the Bolshoi, and Turgenev's birthplace, but they didn't – so far as we know – meet any former spies. They returned to England on 20 May. Harty must have been on Bennett's mind, but he had other matters to think about that month, too, such as a visit to Leeds to open the new theatre of Leeds Grammar, the school which had rejected him for confusing Job and job. He was also pleased to be informed that an Alan Bennett play would finally be performed at the Leeds Playhouse: it was *Kafka's Dick*, in a short run lasting until 4 July.

Time was running out for Russell Harty, though, and he died from liver failure on 8 June. The funeral was held in Giggleswick on 11 June. By Alan Bennett's side was an attractive dark-haired woman. Her clothes were probably a shade unusual, with more than a touch of the Gypsy in them. She was not named in any of the press reports, but it was Anne Davies. Harty was buried in Giggleswick churchyard, a beautiful spot, in a small plot almost equidistant from St Alkelda Church and the sports field of the school where he taught, and where he had been so happy before he found fame, and eventually torment, through TV. Harty's obituary notices celebrated him for mastering a new style of interviewing: less formal, less stuffy.

Harty's last outing on TV had been *Mr Harty's Grand Tour*, broadcast in 1988. It was an attempt to celebrate the simple joys of life like walking through villages, unaccompanied except for a large camera crew. In the same year, Bennett tried something similar. Until now, he had been first and foremost a dramatist. And yet so many of his plays revolved around phrases borrowed from other people – the famous 'black book' figuring strongly in colleagues' reminiscences of him – that it seemed almost a logical next step to make a fly-on-the-wall documentary. It was his most sustained attempt to do a TV documentary since the marvellous spoof documentary 'The Lonely Pursuit' for *On the Margin* in 1966. This time, he remained in the north, but relocated himself and Jonathan Stedall's film crew to the plush surroundings of the Crown Hotel, Harrogate. The title of the programme was *Dinner at Noon*.

Bennett saw *Dinner at Noon* as his chance to capture on camera some of the theories recorded by Erving Goffman, Sociology Professor at the University of California in the fifties and then at Philadelphia. Goffman had carried out important field studies while based on the Shetland Isles between 1949 and 1951. His books included *The Presentation of Self in Everyday Life* (1959), *Encounters* (1961) and *Behavior in Public Places* (1963).

Bennett wanted the cameras to capture snapshots of the lives of staff and guests. The idea was that the guests should speak for themselves, though as the filming continued it became apparent that much of what was being recorded was too stilted or banal to be used. The problem is that hotels are difficult enough places in which to behave 'naturally', and the presence of TV cameras would have made it even more problematic. Besides, even when they do not intend to, camera crews have a tendency to take up more than their allotted space, blocking the lifts with their equipment, shushing people when their voices are not those wanted, or beckoning onlookers away from the sacred frame of filming.

No doubt Stedall's crew behaved with more than usual tact, but the footage still looked ponderous and 'composed', and they didn't have that much time, only ten days. It was at this point that Stedall or Bennett realised that there was a solution near at hand: if Bennett could write his own commentary, they might be able to dovetail that with the pictures and somewhat strangled snatches of dialogue. Bennett rose magnificently to the challenge, and *Dinner at Noon* is still one of his quirkiest TV triumphs.

The first line – 'I was conceived in a strange bedroom' – is spoken as the camera pans round a very fancy hotel bedroom, as if Bennett were hiding in the cupboard, hoping not to be found. It was, he goes on, 'in a boarding-house bedroom in Morecambe, or Flamborough, or Filey – oilcloth on the floor, jug and basin on the wash-hand stand, the bathroom on the next landing. Nowhere like this, anyway, a bedroom in the Crown Hotel, Harrogate.'

It was broadcast on BBC1 on 9 August 1988. For the TV reviewers, hot on the heels of his success with *Talking Heads*, it was another triumph. Andrew Hislop in *The Times* commented approvingly that, having set himself up to record snatches of speech, 'the brave new hotel world . . . in homage comically sent up itself as though scripted by the bespectacled, limpid but yet so precise manipulator of its manners'. The *Telegraph* called it 'a memorable experience'. Peter Paterson in the *Daily Mail* welcomed the programme as a change from the conventional series 'which normally allows a well-known journalist to bang on about a particular subject which his, or her, own paper shows not much interest in. Last night, however, was gloriously, wondrously different.' Paterson described Bennett as 'a seer, a prophet, and a very great artist'. His favourite moment – and it is certainly one of the highlights of the film – came during a presentation made by a visiting French dignitary. The Yorkshire lady who was compelled to listen to it spoke no French, and her Gallic counterpart spoke no English. The English lady, having endured the speech, drew herself up, pursed her lips, did all those other things that Goffman had noted earlier, and said, 'Well, I'm very glad you came.' As Paterson said: 'It was a scene worthy of Chaplin, Keaton, Laurel and Hardy, and Monsieur Hulot. Or Alan Bennett.' Alan Bennett was now a reference point in his own right.

The *Yorkshire Post*, lucky enough to view the programme from within the Crown Hotel itself, reported that it drew a 'mixed' reception. 'Some viewers suggested that the people portrayed in the film had been sent up to a certain degree, and the former Mayor of Harrogate, Councillor Douglas Muscroft, who made a fleeting appearance, thought the writer had been "a bit cruel at times" with his insights.' Others thought such claims were 'a load of tripe'. The fact is that the camera is a dangerous interloper, which makes fools of us all. The best solution is to stay well out of the limelight. Bennett himself was just about to do the complete opposite.

Russell Harty's memorial service was held on 11 October 1988 at St James's, Piccadilly. The audience included Sir Ian Threthowan, the former director-general of the BBC, together with Melvyn Bragg, the Earl of Snowdon, Frank Muir, David Frost, Penelope Keith, Esther Rantzen and Stephen Fry. Ned Sherrin, Sue Lawley and the deputy director-general of the BBC, John Birt, gave readings. The protocol with memorial services is normally pretty clear. They should present a collage of different impressions to remind us of the person we have lost. They should be occasions for laughter, and for sadness. And, like maiden speeches in the House of Commons, they should not be political, or controversial.

Bennett had never had a reputation for being a flag-waver. He had refused to take Ian McKellen's bait and so would not be enticed into marching with one camp or the other. If he got angry, it was usually a sort of dry anger, scornful in print rather than anywhere else. But the passion that had been simmering since Harty's confinement and death could not be suppressed. In front of the assembled great and good, and several extremely interested newspaper reporters (and Andreas Whittam Smith, editor of the then new and radical *Independent* newspaper), he broke ranks. He praised Harty's ordinariness, and he lauded him as a man who could trust his instincts. '[Russell] understood that most people are prisoners in their lives and want releasing,' he said. He admired the fact that Harty 'never kept people in compartments'. He went on: 'Russell never made any secret of his homosexuality . . . He didn't look on it as an affliction, but he was never one for a crusade either . . . He had never read Proust, but he had somehow taken a short cut across the allotments and arrived at the same conclusions.'

Some newspapers, particularly the *Daily Telegraph*, seemed to have stopped their ears to any further comment at that stage, merely filing a report that relayed lots of Bennett's affectionate stories about his old friend. It would have been as much use to describe the Nuremberg Rallies as a lively assortment of flags and synchronised marching. The paper had simply re-emphasised Alan Bennett's public image at the expense of anything new he might want to say. What it left out, though, was an impassioned denunciation of the 'gutter press systematically trawling public life for sexual indiscretion'. He went on:

> Reporters intermittently infested his home village for more than a year, bribing local children for information about his life, even (there is a terrible comedy in it) trying to bribe the local vicar. Now as he fought for his life in St James's Hospital one newspaper took a flat opposite and had a camera with a long lens trained on the window of his ward. A reporter posing as a junior doctor smuggled himself into the ward and demanded to see his notes, and every lunchtime journalists took the hospital porters over the road to the pub to try to bribe them into taking a photo of him.

To describe reporters as 'infesting', which is the sort of language normally associated with head-lice or rats, is shockingly emotive. His most ringing phrase, and his most stinging accusation, was that 'One saw at that time in the tireless and unremitting efforts of the team at St James's the best of which we are capable, and in the equally tireless, though rather better rewarded, efforts of the journalists, the worst.' Bennett mockingly sympathised with their fury. 'Russell, with his usual lack of consideration, was dying of the wrong disease.'

Bennett acknowledged that some people might think that such comments were out of place at a memorial service. Others were intrigued. The speech was reprinted in *The Listener* in full. A digest also appeared in the *Guardian*, written by Peter Fiddick, the very man under whose leadership *The Listener*, already failing, would finally, in 1991, collapse and die.

The Murdoch papers seemed reluctant at first to react to this slur on their reporters. The *News of the World*'s sister paper, the *Sun*, used the occasion simply to repeat Bennett's statement about Harty's sexuality, as if it had secured a coup in being there while Bennett 'outed' his old friend. 'Gay Harty – by Bennett' ran the headline on 12 October. The *Sun*, referring to Bennett as 'The bachelor playwright', either chose to ignore the accusation, or dim-wittedly failed to spot the charge. But the *News of the World* came out again the following Sunday, and by then it was in no mood to apologise.

'Lessons to Learn' ran the lead editorial in the *News of the World* on Sunday, 16 October 1988. 'At a star-studded memorial service this week, bachelor playwright Alan Bennett blamed the *News of the World* for the death of chat-show host Russell Harty,' it began.

'Today we'd like to teach Mr Bennett a lesson in medicine: nobody ever caught Hepatitis B from a newspaper.' The next paragraph was equally short.

'Harty caught his killer virus because he was gay.' Time for another paragraph.

'And more importantly he was a gay who broke the law by having sex with an underage rentboy.' Finally:

'It was for breaking that law that this newspaper exposed him and we make no apologies for that.'

The following Monday, the *Sun* rode to the rescue of its sister paper, and this time there was no question over the tone of the article. 'Russell Harty paid a high price for his homosexuality,' it said in a leader. 'His death from Hepatitis B was a long and lingering one. But . . . the truth is that he died from a sexually related disease. The press didn't give it to him. He caught it through his own choice. By paying young rentboys to satisfy him, he broke the law.'

The *Sun* concluded: 'Some, like ageing bachelor Mr Bennett, can see no harm in that. He has no family. But what if it had been YOUR son whom Harty bedded?' The terrifying thing about the *Sun*'s editorial line was its clear thinking. In the *Sun*'s eyes, either you were a proud upstanding family man or you were an uncontrollably volatile queer, lunging at small boys in doorways or back alleys.

Few public figures have dared to take on the tabloids. When they are under attack, the tabloids form a powerful, aggressive, sanctimonious and brutally efficient fighting team. They have long memories and short tempers, and they will go to any lengths to feed a vendetta. Speaking out about the media's treatment of his late friend was a more courageous gesture than any response Alan Bennett could have offered to Ian McKellen. The consequences could have been horrific. Bennett could have been pursued, telephoned, spied on, found himself the object of long-distance lenses, hounded twenty-four hours a day. And yet he wasn't. Bennett had declared war, and yet the fight never came to anything. It was perhaps fortunate that Bennett's outburst came so soon after the success of *Talking Heads*, when Bennett's popularity was at an all-time high. For another thing, Harty was dead, and the *News of the Screws* had its story. Perhaps there was nothing more to be said. Leaving aside the unlikely possibility that Bennett's volley may have struck a chord with the fiercely self-righteous souls at Wapping, one looks in vain for explanations for the paper's failure to go for him. First, they may have done some preliminary snooping and concluded that Alan Bennett had no sexual peccadillos beyond looking out through the venetian blinds of his Camden Town window. No rentboy honey traps for him, then. A second possible reason is that, with skewed tabloid logic, the *News of the World* still had a remnant of respect for the taboo-shattering Bennett of *Beyond the Fringe*, and so held off for that reason.

In those days, *Private Eye* was still laying waste to dozens of British rogues. And *Spitting Image* was four years into its thirteen-year assault on all those deemed publicly venal. Yet Bennett had escaped any such put-downs. Could it be that, by 1988, just as *Talking Heads* was deemed above criticism, so Alan Bennett himself had reached the stage in public life where his personal foibles were simply considered beyond reproach? Could such a lofty position really be said to exist in Margaret Thatcher's Britain?

16

One is, to some extent, kicking one's heels

Single Spies, 1988–1989

As the shadows lengthened on the 1980s, Alan Bennett deserves praise for his creative attempts to reduce the telephone bills of some of our national newspapers. In the absence of an answerphone, foreshortening journalists' enquiries was to become one of his most widely deployed weapons, and the *Daily Mail*'s jovial gossip columnist Baz Bamigboye was one of the first victims. Just a week after Russell Harty's memorial service, and having heard an early rumour about his next play, Bamigboye tried to persuade Bennett to embroider his speculation. 'It's too early to talk. I'm going to put the phone down – nicely,' said the playwright. But Bamigboye had enough in his notebook, and the story was filed. 'Alan Bennett is the surprise performer picked to play one of the National Theatre's most coveted parts of the year – that of Anthony Blunt,' Bamigboye declared. His information would turn out to be pretty accurate. Bennett was indeed writing a play about the former keeper of the Queen's pictures who spied for Russia and was stripped of his knighthood by Margaret Thatcher. One of the stars would, he correctly predicted, be Simon Callow.

The double bill was one of the first commissions by the National's new chief, and one of Bennett's chief doubles partners, Richard Eyre. Bamigboye's story was overtaken by events in only one respect. The provisional title that the columnist quoted – 'Spy Stories' – was superseded when Callow suggested a better one: *Single Spies*. And so *Single Spies* it was.

Two plays were presented. The first was a newly staged version of *An Englishman Abroad*, directed by Bennett, with Prunella Scales taking the place of the ailing Coral Browne, and Simon Callow as Guy Burgess. Bennett described the birth pangs of the second play, *A Question of Attribution*, in an article which, strange as it may appear, he wrote for the *Evening Standard* in February 1989. It all began in the Rameses Hilton Hotel in Cairo, in January 1987, where he had gone to film an instalment of *The Fortunes of War*. Between shots, says Bennett, he made notes on the back of the hotel's laundry cards about an imaginary dialogue between the Queen and Blunt. But it wasn't until a few months later, in one of the curious cage-like upper recesses of the London Library, that he came across a copy of the *Burlington Magazine* which contained a discussion concerning Titian's *Triple Portrait*, and how, when the painting was taken away to be cleaned, and then X-rayed, three extra figures were revealed in the background.

The amateur art lover in Bennett must have been intrigued by the aspects of the painting behind the painting, of the scraping away of later secretions in search of the unlacquered truth. But the dramatist Bennett suddenly made the connection between the painting, which was in the possession of the Crown, and Sir Anthony Blunt, who was the Surveyor of the Queen's Pictures from 1952 to 1972 (having been Surveyor of the Pictures of King George VI from 1945) and Adviser for the Queen's Pictures and Drawings until 1978. Blunt was stripped of his KCVO in 1979 when it became known that he had been a spy during the Second World War, years after he had confessed in 1964 and was granted immunity in return for weekly interrogations. 'As I read the article it seemed such a perfect metaphor for Burgess and Maclean and Philby, and the fourth man and the fifth, that I could hardly believe someone had not come across it before,' he wrote, as he researched the idea at the London Library. 'I half expected other playwrights to come clattering up the iron steps in pursuit of the same idea. Even now the existence of the painting seems to me such a curious coincidence that I think the audience may assume it's all been made up.'

The double bill opened at the National Theatre on 1 December 1988. Callow's performance as Burgess was lighter than Bates's, and most of the theatre reviewers missed the outside shots from the TV original – except for *The Times Literary Supplement*, which preferred it – but it was a witty and penetrating play none the less.

On its own it would have been an enjoyable evening in the theatre. Bennett, though, was about to enjoy one of the most spectacular theatrical triumphs of his career, while also performing in a new stage play of his own for the first time in twenty years. *A Question of Attribution* is set in the late 1960s and starts with Blunt being quizzed, in somewhat lacklustre fashion, by a government official called Chubb (played by Callow, who also directed). As they look through Chubb's collection of slides – Bennett's first dramatic use of slides was in *The Old Crowd* – Chubb pursues Blunt with the vigour of someone chasing peas round his plate. 'Why did you do it?' he asks, to which Blunt, in his patrician tones, loftily replies: 'It seemed the right thing to do at the time.' Chubb, who lives in the drab suburb of Purley, is clearly rather in awe of Blunt, and asks if he has ever met the Queen. Blunt replies that it is 'like asking a shopgirl if she sees Swan or Edgar'. 'I wonder what she's really like,' says Chubb.

In the next scene, a newly cleansed Titian has revealed the presence of a third head. Blunt decides to send it for an X-ray, as he is still not happy with the composition. The scene then moves to Buckingham Palace, where Blunt and one of his students, Phillips, are studying some more pictures. Blunt mounts a ladder to scrutinise one of the paintings. It is only from there, with his vision partly obstructed, that he cannot see that a corgi, a comic shorthand for royalty, has trotted onstage. While everyone else runs for cover, Blunt carries on talking, airily asserting that 'there is no such thing as a royal collection. It is rather a royal accumulation.' Upon which statement, and provoking a gasp of shock from the audience, the figure described as 'HMQ' walked slowly on to the stage. Handbag, coat, very much a queen. It is, to be sure, one of the most dramatic entrances in modern British theatre, and one which no serious British mainstream playwright had successfully attempted until now.

Blunt, still up the ladder, demands his glasses: 'Come along – we haven't got all day.' HMQ, uncertainly at first, eventually hands the glasses up, to barely suppressed hysteria from the audience. Descending, still unsighted, he complains: 'You're supposed to be holding the steps. I could have fallen flat on my face.' To which HMQ replies: 'I think you already have.'

Bennett's reaction as Blunt was perfect. He stepped back elegantly and bowed. Her Majesty explained her presence, or rather the cancellation of her absence. The swimming pool which she was due to open had sprung a leak. 'So this afternoon one is, to some extent, kicking one's heels.' Bennett later said in an interview with Terry Coleman of the *Guardian*: 'Somebody told me about the Royal Family, that they are very much at a loss unless they have a programme, even if they're staying with people. They do actually want it laid out.' This is where Bennett got his chance to lay it out. His latest interrogator is the monarch herself.

HMQ: And how did we 'accumulate' this particular picture?
Blunt: It was thought to be by Titian.
HMQ: And now it isn't?
Blunt: Not altogether, Ma'am.
HMQ: I suppose that is part of your function, Sir Anthony, to prove that my pictures are fakes?

Scales's ability to look stiff but comfortable in her stiffness was remarkable enough. But what made the performance so maddeningly funny was that HMQ seemed not to have, or need, a sense of 'humour'. It was like a version of Miss Prothero: HMQ 'is one of those people who only see jokes by appointment'; by royal appointment, of course. Her mask, as Guy Burgess in *An Englishman Abroad* and Hilary in *The Old Country* say, was to be herself.

Blunt's response sets the dynamic for the rest of their exchange. 'Because something is not what it is said to be, Ma'am, does not mean it is a fake.' HMQ vaguely wonders, now that it is a fake, 'what are you planning to do with it? Put it out for the binmen?' Blunt tries to change the conversation, to ask her what she would have been doing this afternoon. HMQ begins a short guided tour of the royal collection. She stops at one exhibit. 'This ostrich egg was given us by the people of Samoa. It hasn't quite found its place yet.' It was the Queen as a Talking Head. The impersonation of the Queen used to be a treasonable offence, and no wonder. It was fantastically, liberatingly, radically funny.

'The trouble is,' says HMQ, with a line borrowed from *Dinner at Noon*, 'whenever I meet anybody they're always on their best behaviour. And when one is on one's best behaviour one isn't always at one's best.'

HMQ doesn't, it turns out, have any paintings by Poussin. Whereas Sir Anthony does. 'You mean you have one and we don't? Something wrong there.' Sir Anthony saying he has two Poussins is not funny at all. The Queen saying that she hasn't is.

Throughout their dialogue an unspoken question hovers. Did she know that the keeper of her collection had been conspiring, in effect, against her? Bennett is making a royalist assumption that the work of a spy inflicts more damage on the Head of State than on his or her subjects, but the assumption is worth going along with to see what dramatic possibilities it throws up. Suddenly we have a game of poker, with both players holding their cards close to their chests. 'Portraits are supposed to be frightfully self-revealing, aren't they?' she says.

HMQ: Have you had your portrait painted?
Blunt: No, Ma'am.
HMQ: So we don't know whether you have a secret self.

Blunt, whose only concession to nervousness is to pat his forehead occasionally with a silk handkerchief, replies that 'the only person who doesn't have a secret self must be God'. HMQ's response is: 'I suppose for me heaven is likely to be a bit of a comedown.' (The joke is 'borrowed' from Cook and Moore's 1967 film *Bedazzled*, though we can hardly begrudge Bennett that.) Then HMQ says: 'What about you?' He responds: 'I'm not sure I'll get in, Ma'am.' They discuss another painting. 'Where's it been? In the cellar?' 'Hampton Court,' says Blunt. 'Same thing,' says HMQ.

'You see, what I don't like is the assumption that one doesn't notice, one doesn't care,' she says. 'Still, we're off to Zambia next week, so that will cushion the blow.' Eventually, she lets him take the Titian down. 'One never stops, you know,' she adds. 'Governments come and go. Or don't go.' The Thatcher government had by then been in power for eight years. The line was greeted with a huge laugh, and even, on some nights, a blood-curdlingly sincere cheer. It had been suspected for some time that the Queen was not an ardent fan of the Iron Lady. Bennett had formed a satirical double act with the monarch! How much more anti-Establishment could one get? It was some return, at any rate, for the damage done to his stomach by Mrs Thatcher, whose period in power Bennett blamed for the worsening of his duodenal ulcer.

'Strange about the royal family,' says Blunt, after she slips regally away. 'They ask you a great deal but tell you very little.' A footman called Colin enters. 'What were you talking about?' he asks. 'I was talking about art,' says Blunt. 'I'm not sure that she was.'

The encounter quickly became referred to among the critics as 'that scene', a sure sign that it had created a sizeable blip on the public radar. The play even came to the attention of Frank Rich of the *New York Times*, who wrote that the scene with Blunt and HMQ had become 'the talk of the town' and correctly noted that the audience 'all but gasps' when HMQ walks onstage. Michael Ratcliffe in the *Observer* called it 'brilliantly sharp and funny'. Nicholas de Jongh in the *Guardian* called *A Question of Attribution* 'a true work of art in its own right, a theatrical metaphor turned into a play, a disruptive meditation upon our quest for certainty and identification'. Michael Billington, moonlighting for *Country Life*, felt that the second play was 'So full of ideas that one feels the need to read the text or to see the play twice'. On Radio 3's *Critics' Forum* (unforgettably parodied in *On the Margin* thirty-two years earlier) all agreed that Prunella Scales was brilliant in both roles. Bennett's role as Blunt was highly praised too, but William Feaver, art critic of the *Observer*, found *A Question of Attribution* 'a rather childish view of art history, a send-up of the sort of elevated people with snooty accents'. Margaret Walters said, 'Bennett can never resist a one-liner. He writes the best jokes . . . in the business. They're hilariously funny and in a funny sort of way that does slightly detract from anything more serious.'

Baz Bamigboye had another bite at *Single Spies* on Christmas Eve 1988. 'Director of National Theatre Threatened to Quit' ran the headline. It turned out that some of the National's governors were so concerned about the content of the play that they were considering either banning it or cutting the crucial scene in which Blunt confronts the Queen. If they had done so, wrote Bamigboye, they would not only

'Disaster strikes as I'm doling out the tinned peaches.' Maggie Smith as Susan, the vicar's wife in *Talking Heads*, BBC, 1988. (BBC)

Lecturing and treachery as Simon Callow quizzes Bennett in
A Question of Attribution, National Theatre, 1988. (Donald Cooper/Photostage)

Bennett as seen by the *Observer*'s Jane Bown. (Camera Press)

'My Hamlet.' Griff Rhys Jones as Toad in *The Wind in the Willows*,
National Theatre, 1990. (Donald Cooper/Photostage)

Bennett as seen
by Snowdon, circa
Madness, 1991.
(Snowdon/Camera Press)

'Oh Jesus, help me.
For pity's sake. I am the
Lord's Anointed.'
Nigel Hawthorne as the
tormented king in *The
Madness of George III,*
National Theatre, 1991.
(Donald Cooper/Photostage)

'La Routledge.' The indomitable star of *A Woman of No Importance* as seen in *Talking Heads*, the stage version, Comedy Theatre, 1992. (Donald Cooper/Photostage)

Off to receive an Olivier award for
Talking Heads, April 1992.
(Mark Stewart/Camera Press)

As Graham, worrying about Mam, in
Talking Heads, April 1992.
(Rex Features)

Cherchez la femme. Anne Davies: Bennett's loyal friend down the years.

(MSI)

Derry Moore's famous mantelpiece shot: at home in Camden, 1994.

(Derry Moore/Camera Press)

The Maggie factor: Dame Maggie Smith, triumphant again, this time in
The Lady in the Van, Queen's Theatre, 1999. (Donald Cooper/Photostage)

Respectable, bespectacled: Bennett plus scarf and suede shoes, outside the former site of Miss Shepherd's front gate in 1999. (Jane Bown/Camera Press)

have sabotaged what went on to become the National's biggest hit of the year, but they might have lost Richard Eyre too, who threatened to resign if the play was censored. Eyre may not have wanted to be associated with an organisation that attempted to curb its writers' powers of expression, or which appeared to cower at the prospect of a run-in with the Palace, but there was a slightly awkward matter of timing too, since the theatre had only recently acquired the title 'Royal' National Theatre. However, Lady Soames, who was due to take over the chair from Lord Raynes in January 1989, went to see the play while it was still previewing. She evidently came away satisfied that the National hadn't fallen into the hands of crypto-Communists, and Eyre's threat remained unspent. There may have been a more self-interested motive to Eyre's gamble – besides not wishing to tarnish his fruitful partnership with Bennett – since he must have known that Bennett was handing him a sure-fire box-office smash which it would be madness to turn away or attempt to tone down.

After ten solidly successful weeks, *Single Spies* transferred to the Queen's Theatre on 28 February 1989. By this stage, America had seen little of Bennett's work. Only Bennett's beloved New Yorkers knew him well, and, at that, only those who had managed to crowd inside the Museum of Modern Art to see *A Woman of No Importance* shortly after it was shown in the UK in 1982. So it was a significant moment when Steve Lohr of the *New York Times* and *International Herald Tribune* made his way up the short driveway to Bennett's Camden house, not least because of the unofficial greeter who almost blocked his path. 'She is a shriveled old woman, wearing a tattered wool cap, hunched over in her wheelchair, accosting would-be visitors with vaguely threatening gestures and indecipherable grunts . . . Welcome to the gently eccentric world of Alan Bennett.'

By the beginning of 1989 Miss Shepherd, Bennett's sitting tenant, was beginning to show signs of age. Bennett didn't think that anything serious was wrong with her, but she was visited by various social workers, and in particular a kindly ex-nurse who lived near by. On 27 April she allowed herself to be borne away to a daycare centre for a full MOT. The scene must have been reminiscent of any number of similar scenes in Bennett's work, from *A Little Outing* to *Enjoy*, and *A Private Function* to *Kafka's Dick*, with anxious elderly relatives pleading with their sons or daughters not to have them taken away and put in a home. The following day, Bennett watched from his desk as the ex-nurse, Miss B, poked her head into the interior of Miss Shepherd's van. 'Miss B knocks at the door of the van, then opens it, looks inside and – something nobody has ever done before – gets in. It's only a moment before she comes out, and I know what has happened before she rings the bell. We go back to the van where Miss Shepherd is dead, lying on her left side, flesh cold, face gaunt, the neck stretched out as if for the block, and a bee buzzing round her body.'

It is a typical offstage Bennett death, with a bee tastefully taking the place of the fly which did for Miss Prothero. Typical, too, of many such deaths in that Miss Shepherd seemed braced for a new life, one involving sheltered housing and, possibly, a degree of cleanliness hitherto unknown. She had been Bennett's companion, the bee in his ointment, for twenty years. Bennett had, of course, been keeping a careful note of her eccentric activities, and sure enough *The Lady in the Van* was published in the *London Review of Books* later that year. It was to become his most famous piece of non-fiction. Of course, Bennett had been protecting a hunted species. It had been one of his many small acts of kindnesses to people in need, most of which will never come to light. But what cause was he actually fighting, and to what effect? The world was changing, and more and more people were driving – and parking – cars. Bennett's campaigns have often been long on idealism and short on pragmatism. Such hopefulness is fine, perhaps even necessary, when struggling to save a beautiful church or the appearance of a Dales village. But allowing one mad old woman with far-right ideas to station her clapped-out van in his drive was just one unilateral act of patronage. With the publication of *The Lady in the Van*, did that represent an amicable settlement? Miss Shepherd had lived off Bennett, it was true, just as numerous microscopic species had lived off her. But after her death his writing about her gave him financial compensation to which no one else in the street was entitled. Miss Shepherd's presence in the Crescent was little short of a health hazard. At one point a swarm of flies blew out through a window and made themselves at home in one of the neighbouring houses. There must have been many such intrusions and mini-emergencies which his neighbours had little choice but to accept. And yet none of the neighbours complained. Bennett's eccentricity went unchallenged and uncriticised. People refused to see anything other than charitable instincts in his maverick behaviour. He could no more shake off his reputation for kindness than his neighbours could remove the persistent stench of Miss Shepherd's turd-encrusted clothes.

Part Four

Into His Shell

17

National Teddy Bear

Poetry in Motion, The Wind in the Willows, 1990

Alan Bennett reviewed Russell Harty's life for the *Dictionary of National Biography, 1986–1990*. Bennett's anger still shows through in his account of Harty's death throes, and the part he felt the press played in his suffering, though the article also includes the claim that Harty's father 'introduced Blackburn to the avocado pear' and the judgement that Harty's gravestone is 'evidence of the vulgarity from which he never entirely managed to break free'. It is a tribute to Russell Harty that he inspired a better style of prose in his obituarist than he ever achieved in life.

At the dawn of the 1990s, Anne Davies, the woman to whom Alan Bennett had opened his heart, opened her doors to the public, and Café Anne, plum in the middle of Clapham, began to take in customers. The décor was like a life-sized blow-up of the mantelpiece over Alan Bennett's fireplace in London. On the walls was a seemingly infinite mass of postcards with faces, bodies and landscapes from all over the postcard-producing world, like an attempt to summarise the interests of the café's proprietress. The more elaborate meals, delicious when warmed, were bought in from outside suppliers. It was a welcoming place, and soon it became as familiar a landmark in the village as the local store, pub and the sprinkling of bed and breakfasts. What might not have been more widely known was that the £30,000 needed to launch it had been provided by a single donor: Alan Bennett.

Of course, if any of the villagers knew anything about the special bond that existed between the café proprietress and the local author, they were keeping silent. The patron would visit from time to time, so long as there was a less than remote chance of being spotted by enthusiastic readers or play-goers who, at the first sight of the retiring figure, might put off their hike to Scrogg's Wood, the River Greta, Crina Bottom or Slatenber for a few minutes to tell him how much they had enjoyed his latest offering. In April Mr Bennett would have been sheltering from the contented but determined reactions of Radio 4 listeners to his reading of *The Lady in the Van*. The response to this programme seemed to confirm the general impression that Bennett was moving into the realms of the untouchables. James Delingpole warbled in soft southern tones in the *Daily Telegraph* that 'What could have been a story of horrendous inconvenience was transformed by his soothing Northern tones into a warm and affectionate talk about a much-missed friend.' Elsewhere in the *Daily Telegraph* the revered radio critic Gillian Reynolds described it as 'like counting the colours in a rainbow while noting the build-up of black clouds'.

It was only when *The Lady in the Van* was published in book form in August that one or two brave souls ventured to depart from the standard text. Reviewing the book in the *Daily Telegraph*, Jeremy Lewis related the general outline of the story before concluding that 'the story is, alas, neither as touching nor – the odd flash excepted – as funny as one might hope. Bennett must have been the kindliest of friends over twenty years, but the sad truth is that however endearing they may be, the half-crazed ramblings of the likes of Miss S seem both pathetic and tedious.'

In 1990 two of Leeds Modern's brightest alumni – Alan Bennett and his contemporary Tony Cash – were reunited professionally when Cash directed a series for Channel 4 called *Poetry in Motion*. It is possible, too, that an outline of the programme might have crossed the desk of Channel 4's chief executive and Bennett's old defender from the days of *The Old Crowd*, Michael Grade. Bennett's favourite modern poets were, and had been for some time, Thomas Hardy, A.E. Housman, W.H. Auden, Louis MacNeice, and those two *On the Margin* stalwarts, Betjeman and Larkin. As with *Talking Heads*, the camera stayed mainly on Bennett's face. He was filmed with only a lectern and a carafe of water to assist him, in the intimate surroundings of the Art Workers' Guild Hall in Bloomsbury. Two series were made: one in 1988, when Bennett did all the readings, and another in 1990, when he shared the stage with Germaine Greer, John Mortimer and A.S. Byatt.

The Auden programme, which went out on 27 June, delighted the poet Peter Porter, but it did not please John Haffenden of the Auden Society. He criticised Bennett for being cowardly, for not trying to understand Auden, for showing a shallow interest in his better-known works, and for saying 'shallow and inconsequential' things about them. Bennett had more luck with Richard Last, who had reacted apoplectically to *The Old Crowd* in 1979. Mellowed perhaps by the passing of time, Last interviewed Bennett for the *Daily Telegraph* and found much to applaud in Bennett's stout views on the new multi-channel age, which, thanks to Rupert Murdoch, was just dawning. No doubt the *Telegraph*'s owner, the press baron Conrad Black, enjoyed reading Bennett's denunciation of his rival, too. Bennett's objection to 'niche' channelling, stemming from rainy afternoons in Leeds City Art Gallery, was that it banished serendipity, or the happy stumbling across something unexpected while looking for something else, as his parents did with the telly. 'They're made aware of programmes they weren't planning to watch – a documentary about Magritte, perhaps, when they were looking for Maigret – and their lives are made richer, more interesting, as a result.' Last also recorded one of Bennett's stinging remarks about how the government's onslaught on civilised values was diluting the TV companies. 'And now the death wish of accountancy is leaving it leaner, more competitive, and on its last legs.'

Poetry in Motion drew praise from an old admirer of Bennett's, Peter Lewis, the very man who had so enjoyed *Beyond the Fringe* in 1960. Writing in the *Sunday Telegraph*, Lewis applauded the choice of Bennett as the man charged with the tricky task of bringing poetry before a distant and suspicious public. Having described him as 'the national children's storyteller', thanks to his readings of *Winnie-the-Pooh*, *Alice* and *The Wind in the Willows*, he went on: 'The last TV poet/personality was Betjeman, and Bennett is a strong candidate as his successor – if not as Teddy Bear to the nation then at least as its favourite pessimist, its Eeyore.'

It was a useful comment for several reasons. First, because the National Teddy Bear title was about to be bestowed on Bennett officially, but also because Bennett had, since 1988, been working on the adaptation of a book, again for the National, which would bring him yet more garlands, and which had been first adapted by Eeyore's creator, A.A. Milne. If *The Wind in the Willows* is one of the nation's literary treasures, who better to adapt it for the stage than the man whom Richard Eyre described as 'one of our national treasures'.

By the winter of 1990, as the government's bold and exciting plans for the restructuring of arts funding in the UK went into top gear, a cash-strapped RSC Barbican – which had recently delivered very popular productions of *The Wizard of Oz* and *Peter Pan* – was forced to close down. Into this gap stepped the National, spearheaded by Alan Bennett's Christmas assault on theatre-goers young and old. *The Wind in the Willows* was the first book he had adapted since *Prick Up Your Ears*, and it had already defeated him once.

'I have tried to do a faithful adaptation of the book while, at the same time, not being sure what a faithful adaptation is,' he wrote in his introduction to the printed text. The challenge he had been set was a considerable one. He must have remembered the storm of protest that Jonathan Miller's Freudian version of *Alice* had provoked ('Sir,' wrote a viewer to *The Listener*, 'What a horrible travesty TV made of *Alice in Wonderland*. It was certainly a long way from Tenniel.'). If reading books for Radio 4 had taught him anything over the years, it was that BBC audiences knew their classics well and preferred them to remain classics, so he cannot have undertaken the project lightly. *The Wind in the Willows* is to many minds the ultimate evocation of an Edwardian childhood. It is the story of several riverbank friends who go out to discover the world. First is Mole the innocent, whose uncompromising 'Hang spring cleaning!' sets the tone for the book. Next is the poetically inclined Ratty, whom Mole initially looks to for guidance. Then comes the sadder and wiser Badger, and finally the wayward, unruly Toad, one of the great antiheroes in literature as well as one of the great comic creations. Together, though for periods without the incarcerated Toad, the friends embark on their various rites of passage into the world.

Bennett admitted in the introduction to the text that he didn't recall reading *The Wind in the Willows* as a child, 'or indeed any of the classics of children's literature'. He was later put off reading it because it had 'fans'. But once he had been properly introduced to the book, he fell in love with it, as most readers do.

The two most obviously stapled-on chapters – which were also the last Grahame wrote for the book – were both lost by A.A. Milne in his adaptation. One, 'Wayfarers All', a salty tale which Rat's seagoing cousin tells, Bennett also cut. The other chapter, 'The Piper at the Gates of Dawn', is similar in its imagery to Grahame's first collection of essays and stories, *Pagan Papers*, which first appeared in 1893. Bennett kept it, but sensibly reduced Pan to the level of an enigmatic aural presence.

'I ended up making the play the story of a group of friends, with the emphasis on Mole,' Bennett wrote. He gave Mole doubts where the others had none, and he made them less 'relentlessly nice'. He also felt that 'the atmosphere of the River Bank had to be less serene', so he injected a note of jealousy, in which Mole's arrival causes some jockeying for affections among the animals. Finally, there was the problem of Toad, a character with absolutely no 'dramatic arc'. As Bennett put it: 'Toad goes on his travels, but he does not go on a journey.'

Bennett tried to make Toad a sympathetic alien, writing him with half an eye on Tom Stoppard's cultured but slightly foreign accent, just as he had suggested for Daniel Day-Lewis's Kafka in *The Insurance Man*. Bennett felt that there was a little bit of Toad in all of us, but that we keep it hidden to get on in society. It soon emerged that, just as the audience for *The Madness of George III* didn't in the least mind that the King spent the final third of the play making a remarkable recovery, so, too, they were quite happy to know that Toad was simply impossible, and to leave it at that until his somersaulted change of heart in the final scene. It was all in the book, after all, and most of the audience knew the book well.

There are two enemies in *The Wind in the Willows*. First are the weasels, stoats and ferrets who inhabit the Wild Wood, seen by Grahame and many of his class as the urban proletariat who were threatening the genial way of life enjoyed by many in Edwardian Britain. A.A. Milne, who adapted *The Wind in the Willows* into the inferior, more sentimental *Toad of Toad Hall*, more or less followed Grahame's version, but, of course, such a constituency had all but taken over the reins of government by the 1990s. Bennett, with an inspired imaginative leap, turned them into more recent figures of hate: thuggish estate agents and property speculators. It is no surprise that the chief weasel is called

Norman. Norman Tebbit, later Baron Tebbit of Chingford, was still remembered for his time as Secretary of State for Trade in the first Thatcher government. Bennett's description of him as 'a sneer on legs' would be recognisable to anyone except a fervent admirer. Baron Tebbit of Chingford was also, one notes in passing, a popular and controversial columnist on the *Sun* between 1995 and 1997.

The other villain in Grahame's book, whose presence is felt on almost every page soon after Toad's arrival, is the motorcar. When Bennett spoke to Michael Ratcliffe in 1994, his most passionate plea was that 'If I ever sat next to the Prince of Wales I'd tell him to put a cycle track in Regent's Park . . . I know it might sound a bit wet, but it's not an eccentricity: if more people rode bikes, the world would be a lot nicer.' (When Norman Tebbit jeered at the unemployed to get on their bikes and look for work, we can assume that he was not trying to curry favour with the bicycling Bennett.) It was possible for Edwardian society to see the motorcar as romantic in those pre-Ford Cortina days and yet to know in a necessarily vague way that it was the harbinger of awful times to come. Throughout the book, Toad is the only supporter of the motorcar who is allowed to air his views. From the minute he sets eyes on it, all his previous loves seem like petty infatuations.

Toad, of course, is incorrigible, freewheeling from one wildly uncontrollable enthusiasm to another. Mole, if he had a handkerchief, would almost certainly have been stuffing it into his mouth in his delighted horror at Toad's waywardness. Mole, of course, 'wears NHS spectacles and though he is a mole he could also be an old-fashioned northern schoolboy'. The Wind in Bennett's Willows is thus felt largely through Mole's eyes, or his 'close-cropped black hair'. When Toad wrestles himself free from the authorities and returns home to Toad Hall, the last battle is for the control of his ancestral pile, which has been overrun by the Wild Wooders. Victory is eventually, and happily – and rarely, in Bennett's plays, but this *was* Christmas – given to the good guys, including Jeremy Sams, who adapted the music and wrote additional lyrics.

The National wanted a crowd pleaser for Christmas, and something which showed off the fancy new stage at the Olivier. Bennett, dependable as ever, provided it. The play, which opened on 12 December 1990, was a triumph, and was received with warm gusts of approval. Griff Rhys Jones, who first played Toad, later described the role as 'my Hamlet', and the reviewers were not far behind in their assessments. Peter Lewis in the *Sunday Telegraph* felt that, apart from one or two jokes in the second half which were 'a bit arch', the performances and the set were 'a delight', 'entrancing', 'brilliant' and 'beautifully judged'. Jack Tinker in the *Daily Mail* joined in the praise, describing it, as early as 14 December, as the runaway winner of the title Best Christmas Play. 'You will seldom see the structure of human society so deftly excavated in the name of Christmas fun,' he wrote. The only party pooper was Charles Osborne in the *Daily Telegraph*, who complained that nothing much happened, and wrote it off as 'innocuous Christmas entertainment'.

The play's success was not due just to its adapter, of course. The National had paired Bennett with a young director who would go on to be one of Bennett's outstanding collaborators, and who had already made quite a name for himself in the theatre.

Born in 1956 and educated at Manchester Grammar School and Trinity Hall, Cambridge, Nicholas Hytner's theatre credits ran from *Measure for Measure* with the RSC in 1987 to his West End triumph with *Miss Saigon* (Drury Lane Theatre and Broadway, 1989–91), in which a helicopter landed on stage. His charmed life through the mile-high club of modern stage and film would soon include a Tony for *Carousel* in 1994. It was Nicholas Hytner who directed *The Wind in the Willows* at the National Theatre, and Hytner who must take the credit for edging Bennett away from trying to draw in strands from Kenneth Grahame's life, many of which – such as the suicide of his only and much-loved son – would have been far too tragic for a Christmas pudding.

Bennett's irascibility with all sections of the press was gaining moment-um. He records in his diary that when Mrs Thatcher finally left office in November 1990, the *Guardian* telephoned him to record his reactions, and when his 'fairly uninspired comment' about not having much to say on the subject was printed, it was prefaced with 'Oo 'eck', and all his aitches were 'systematically' dropped. 'I suppose I should be grateful they didn't report me as saying: "Ee bah gum, I'm ret glad t'Prime Minister's tekken her 'ook",' he wrote. In a profile written for the *Guardian* in 1990, Nicholas de Jongh noted that Bennett had now 'grown bored of being interviewed and is girding himself up to become the Garbo of Primrose Hill, not only wanting to be alone, but refusing to face up to journalists whom he dislikes'. He also suggested that Mole, Ratty, Badger and Toad were essentially four single men, glorying in being bachelors. Just as with his use of his mother's Alzheimer's disease in the 'underrated' *Enjoy*, wrote de Jongh, 'his therapy has been our delight'.

In 1991, between fitful stabs at writing some more *Talking Heads*, Bennett had the chance to take a sidelong pop at another of his traditional enemies, Rupert Murdoch, when he played Lord Dacre, formerly Professor Hugh Trevor-Roper, in *Selling Hitler*. The book, by Robert Harris, told the amazing but true story of how a German forger called Conny Kujau in 1983 fooled the *Sunday Times*, and then *Stern* magazine, into publishing extracts from what he claimed were sixty surviving volumes of Adolf Hitler's diaries. Naturally, the non-Murdoch newspapers ran enthusiastic features about the programme. 'It's a great luxury,' Bennett told Jennifer Selway of the *Sunday Express*, referring to the cosseting and pampering that are traditionally handed out on film sets. 'That never happens to a writer.' The part of the Dirty Digger was played by Barry Humphries.

In the December 1991 edition of *Harpers & Queen*, Francis Wheen, the journalist and somewhat unlikely star of Radio 4's *The News Quiz*, acknowledged that a very important title had been conferred on Bennett. 'Two jobs became vacant when Sir John Betjeman died,' Wheen began. 'The Poet Laureateship (salary: £100 and a butt of sack) went to Ted Hughes . . . But the more important office – that of National Teddy Bear – was filled by Alan Bennett.'

As Wheen said, 'The only other candidate, Philip Larkin, was far too mordant. The National Teddy Bear is allowed (expected, in fact) to be gloomy, but his grumbles must be instantly defused by a wry smile and a self-deprecating shrug . . . With his [Bennett's] nostalgic bathos, his ear for the absurdities of everyday chitchat, his enjoyment of the petty paraphernalia of class distinctions and his fascination with dull suburban lives, he was a natural successor to Betjeman.'

Bennett's other qualifications for the job were that he had no apparent enemies. Wheen quoted Richard Eyre saying, 'It's terribly difficult talking about Alan without reeling off a litany of virtues. He's a really lovely man.' He added that though Bennett sometimes contradicted himself, life for Alan Bennett must feel like 'an extended scene from an Alan Bennett play'.

Wheen also claimed that Bennett 'hated nobody', a view which is harder to take seriously. There was the question of the former Prime Minister, for example. Peter Cook might have found Margaret Thatcher's posturings merely funny, unlike Dudley Moore who, ensconced in Marina del Rey, Los Angeles, probably only had a vague idea about who she was. But the two angrier ex-Fringers spoke out. Jonathan Miller, in a phrase that showed he had lost none of his satirical edge, said she had 'a voice like a perfumed fart', for example. Alan Bennett himself was too engaged with the real world to ignore the gruelling effects of Thatcher's reforms. But Wheen's characterisation of Bennett as the National Teddy Bear was decisive. If Bennett was bothered by this latest honorary decree, he probably knew that there were plenty more to come.

In September 1988 Bennett had written in his diary: 'I have started working on a play about George III, but I fear it may just have been brought on by being about to do another play in which royalty figures and that it will accordingly come to nothing.' Not for the first time, Bennett's predictions of his literary accomplishments were to prove wide of the mark.

18

I wish they'd leave him alone

102 Boulevard Haussmann,

The Madness of George III, 1991–1993

The name Marcel Proust is often invoked by Bennett as a kind of literary sofa, on to which he can collapse when he feels his knees begin to sag. Most recently, *Telling Tales* is replete with references to Proust. In one, he compares his own family's two-pronged Sunday walks in Yorkshire – whether to Guiseley or Lawnswood but which always came back to the same point – with Proust's Guermantes and Combray walks. In another talk, he has a Proustian moment on a trip to France, connecting a sudden smell of mimosa with the smell in his grandmother's front room, years before in Leeds. Proust casts a long shadow over any writer trying to describe the probings of the mind. Having suffered from asthma since childhood, Proust retired to a cork-lined room on the Boulevard Hausmann, where he slept by day and wrote by night, or occasionally ventured out to experience something of life that might fuel a passage in his novel. Bennett, having suffered from shyness since childhood, retired to a wood-panelled room in Camden, where he worked by day and occasionally ventured out to the Camden branch of Marks & Spencer or the matinée of one of his own plays, but otherwise sat at his desk, looking out of the window.

The attraction of Proust as a literary figure is fairly clear: Proust mined his own life, even his own relationships, to provide the subject matter for his great work *A La Recherche du Temps Perdu*. Bennett was engaged in a similar exercise, especially when foraging for material for his diaries. In Proust, all things point back to his childhood. Bennett's childhood is nowhere near as gilded, but remarkably resonant in its own way. Marcel Proust was homosexual, but he, like Bennett, wrote tellingly about heterosexual love. Proust was always falling in love and feeling hard done by. At times, Bennett must have felt the same.

There were significant differences too. In Yorkshire, Bennett still sleeps in the same bed that he and his brother were born in. (He even believed that the scratch marks at the bottom were gouged by his mother's toenails when she was in labour with his brother.) Proust, on the other hand, donated the furniture which had belonged to his dead parents to his favourite male brothel. Proust came from the upper echelons of French society but felt marginalised from it by his sexuality and, being half-Jewish, by religion. Kafka, Proust, Burgess, Orton: all were reborn in Bennett's work, and all were political exiles of some sort, whether the politics were religious, sexual or ideological.

At some point in 1916 or 1917, Proust attended a concert, at which he heard, for the first time, the César Franck String Quartet in D major, played by the Quatuour Poulet at the Concert Rouge in the rue de Tournon. The troupe included a young viola-player called Amable Massis, who was home on leave, having being wounded at the front – or, more accurately, halfway down the leg. Written in 1890, this new and challenging piece of modern music made a tremendous impact on Proust, and he yearned to hear it again. George Painter, in his masterly biography of the author, describes how Proust approached Massis and asked if he and his colleagues would be prepared to play the piece privately. A few days later, at what Painter describes as 'the Mephisto-phelean hour of midnight', Proust picked them up by taxi from their homes. 'Inside the taxi, while the chauffeur reassuringly winked and beamed, the alarmed Massis glimpsed a tureen of mashed potatoes, and a vast eiderdown beneath which Proust instantly crept'. All four arrived at 102 Boulevard Hausmann, Proust's famous address in Paris, where they were met by Proust's devoted housekeeper, Céleste. Then, in what the leader and first violin-player Gaston Poulet called 'the superlative acoustics' of Proust's cork-lined room, they played the piece. After they had finished it, Proust begged: 'Would you do me the immense kindness of playing the whole work again?' They broke briefly for potatoes and more champagne, and then took up their instruments once more. At the end, 'Proust, with cries of delight and congratulations, paid them on the spot from a Chinese casket stuffed with fifty-franc notes. Four taxis awaited them in the blacked-out street below.' The quartet were so charmed that they sent him a round-robin of thanks the next day.

This fragment from Proust's life was as resonant to Bennett – though at the opposite end of the scale in terms of interior décor – as the picture of Guy Burgess playing a scratchy record of 'Who Stole My Heart Away?' to Coral Browne in his shabby Moscow apartment. But from that juncture of musical obsessions, Bennett began to weave an alternative storyline. His took the plausible route that since Proust had fallen for Massis, he then gently disentangled Massis from his fellow players so that he could entertain the infatuated Proust on his own with selected works for the viola.

This fantasy became Bennett's TV film *102 Boulevard Haussmann*. There were other obvious comparisons with *An Englishman Abroad* in that Marcel was played with exquisite delicacy by a kiss-curled Alan Bates, and the Paris scenes were also shot in Scotland: Perth this time. Janet McTeer was the fiercely protective Céleste and Paul Rhys played the viola-player who stole the great writer's heart away. In Bennett's version, the infatuation was not entirely one-sided. Massis himself seems, to say the least, intrigued at having such a famous – or at least wealthy and sophisticated – man under his spell. In one exchange, several of the threads of the film are gathered together. 'Is the César Franck in your novel?' asks Massis. 'Not exactly,' says Proust, 'but then it'll do. Art does not correspond to life. It is life. For example, there's a violinist in my novel – or he could be a viola-player.' 'What's he like?' asks Massis. 'I don't think he's like you,' says Proust. 'He acquires a rich friend and patron whom I think he will abandon.'

After this invented loop, Proust hatches an ambitious plan to ship the whole quartet to Venice, where he would live in a palace and listen to their music while dawn broke over the Grand Canal. In real life, the war made such a plan impossible, but in Bennett's film Massis is misled into thinking that Proust has forgotten him, and so fails to reply to his letters. Mistakenly believing himself to have been abandoned by his inamorato, the asthmatic Proust takes to his bed, grey-faced, coughing and once again defeated in love. 'These young men,' sighs Céleste as yet another of Proust's emotional affairs goes awry. 'They take advantage. Money, favours, and they're not grateful. He's too soft-hearted. I wish they'd leave him alone. He'll end up getting upset. So then he works harder and it makes him ill. You think he'd have more sense.' Not for nothing had Bennett invoked the name of Proust at Russell Harty's memorial service.

When the unsuspecting Massis returns, viola in hand, to surprise his friend with a visit, he is met by the frosty countenance of M. Proust's housekeeper. As she opens the door, she makes no attempt to conceal the sight of another viola case, lying provocatively open on a side table. The shot is charged with as much sexual imagery as that of Midgley removing his glasses prior to his bed scene with Julie Walters in *Intensive Care* (perhaps more, in fact). We can even hear the sound of a viola being played. It is clear what has happened. The music has not betrayed anyone: only, in Proust's mind, the player. M. Proust has rallied, and has found a substitute.

Bennett's dialogue is superb, and there is a very funny running joke in which everybody who mentions the book confesses that they haven't read it, or at least not all of it. Sometimes, Bennett is unable to keep his own sense of humour out of the film, as when M. Proust is leading his band of players in triumph into the lift, and says, 'I must apologise for the lift. It dates from the period before lifts were invented.' Which may be the best anachronistic lift joke ever made.

102 Boulevard Haussmann made more of a ripple than a splash when it was broadcast, which is shameful because it is a beautifully realised TV play. Bates turns in a masterful performance, seeming to capture the essence of Proust as the aesthetic, athletically challenged artist, rendered pale and breathless as much by lilies as by a handsome musician. Over the years, Bennett has become something of a patron of the arts himself, generously helping out several struggling writers and artists with financial aid if he saw something he liked in their work. Midnight performances, we are left to assume, were not part of the deal.

Directed by Udayan Prasad, *102 Boulevard Haussmann* was the seventeenth collaboration between Bennett and Innes Lloyd, but it turned out to be their last, as Lloyd, who had been ailing for some time (though scarcely complaining to anyone, said Bennett) died in 1991. 'I can't believe that Proust was quite his cup of tea,' Bennett said at Lloyd's memorial service, and yet his enthusiasm for the project was typical of a man with a 'jumble of attitudes' in which 'you would ever find Kafka even in the same sentence as Bomber Harris'. This openness, said Bennett, had taken quite a battering in recent years, both in the corporation and nationally, and Bennett no doubt relished reminding his audience that Lloyd 'detested' Mrs Thatcher. What a shame, Bennett concluded, that the culture of the BBC had 'taken something of a battering' too.

There was sad news for Bennett in 1991 with the death of Coral Browne, who had been one of Bennett's dearest, and most gossipy, friends, since the night at the Mirabelle that set him planning *An Englishman Abroad*. Before she died, she sent back all the letters that Sir Alec Guinness had written her. In his diaries, Guinness quoted one of the letters, which contained a teasing reference to their mutual friend. 'I'm sending them back, for you to do with what you want,' she wrote. 'What we *don't* want is for Alan Bennett to get hold of them and knock them up into a play.'

Alan Bennett's diaries for the years 1991 and 1992 were not published, which suggests that he was in poor health – most recently, prostate cancer was mentioned – though it is hard to see when he could have found the time to be sick, since he was working flat out on a play that was markedly different in range and sweep from anything he had written before. Some time in 1991, an A4 package was dropped through the front door of Nicholas Hytner's home in Camden, containing the first draft. At the National Theatre, Richard Eyre, who was staring at a gap in his programming for the end of the year, read it and liked it. Hytner, who must have been between awards at the time, read it and liked it too. The play was scheduled to open at the National Theatre in November 1991, the same month in which *The Wind in the Willows* was relaunched, also at the National.

Bennett's health might have been poor, but by November 1991, too, the country was teetering on the verge of some sort of breakdown. Margaret Thatcher had been removed as party leader in 1990 after twelve years, but Neil Kinnock, 'the Welsh windbag', had not yet restored the Labour Party's fortunes to the point where it was a serious electoral alternative to the Tories. If Westminster was in turmoil, the atmosphere at Windsor Castle was even more unhappy. As the American writer Stephen Schiff put it in the *New Yorker* two years later: 'England's royals were in a state of almost unprecedented disarray, and the mortifying saga of Charles, Diana, and the ineffable Fergie seemed to reflect an even larger disgrace. The cynicism of the Thatcher years had given way to a kind of national self-loathing – a sense of lost empire, lost industry, lost civility and dignity and competence.' A new coronation might have given us something to celebrate, but the Queen seemed as robust as ever. How could Prince Charles, the current Prince of Wales, look anything other than impatient?

'I've always had a soft spot for George III,' wrote Bennett in his introduction to *The Madness of George III*. The affection sprang from the essay Bennett wrote about the mad King in his entrance exam to Cambridge in December 1951. George's name recurred periodically, but the dramatic potential of the period did not properly present itself until his attention was drawn, by Jonathan Miller and the medical historian Michael Neve, among others, to a series of publications that dealt with the medical background to the regency crisis of 1788–9. They develop the theory that, far from being 'mad', as is popularly supposed, George was stricken by porphyria, a condition which generates symptoms similar to madness, but which is physical rather than mental. 'From a dramatist's point of view,' wrote Bennett in his introduction to the play, 'it is obviously useful if the King's malady was a toxic condition, traceable to a metabolic disturbance rather than due to schizophrenia or manic depression.' Bennett set out to study the period – political as well as medical – in greater depth. Not since *Forty Years On*, over twenty years earlier, had he read so many history books.

The title of the play could be said to have suggested itself, but few writers would have dared to put it so bluntly as *The Madness of George III*. Not surprisingly, it generated a buzz of expectation. George III was popularly believed to have mistaken an oak tree for the King of Prussia, and the tabloid press had convinced the whole country that Prince Charles was habitually to be found talking to plants. Surely Bennett wasn't going to dare to suggest that the two eccentricities were by any chance related?

In Bennett's play, the King was seen first as a pepperish, nervously energetic man, battling to keep his lolling sons in tow and privately exchanging affectionate dialogue with 'Mrs Queen'. There is a premonition of the play's title when George is attacked by a madwoman in the first scene. She is mad at losing land: later, when the King suffers terrible torments, he was unable to stop babbling about the loss of the American colonies. The King goes on to describe the tortures inflicted on a man who attempted to assassinate the King of France: 'His limbs burned with fire, the flesh lacerated with red-hot pincers . . .' The King himself would soon be suffering similar torments.

George's irrational behaviour during his fits is graphically illustrated, whether attacking his own son, clumsily attempting to kiss one of the ladies of court or rousing his most loyal servants from sleep at four in the morning. Lavatories had always featured prominently in Bennett's life – through his mother – and work, whether through the Betjeman parody 'On Going to the Excuse Me' in *On the Margin* or with the graphic portrayal of Joe Orton fornicating in a public lavatory on the Holloway Road. Here, the King's stools are eagerly prodded, smelled and weighed by an alternative army of in-Palace doctors. And the diarrhoea is not just fecal. Words tumble from the King during his fits. Bennett had gone from writing a pilot programme called 'I Can't Help Thinking' to a stage play about a king who can't help talking. 'I am dragged at locution's tail,' he says desperately to his wife. Like a sufferer from Tourette's syndrome, it frees him to blurt out whatever passes through his mind. To hear him shout 'Push off, you fat turd' at Baker, the court doctor, is funny but also tragic. And meanwhile the plotting around court is seen, too, with the languorous Prince of Wales as greedy for snacks as for power.

There were five major attacks between 1765 and 1820 during which the King's symptoms ranged from tormenting cramps to foaming at the mouth and even delusions. George III's worst bout of insanity in 1788–9 provoked Charles James Fox's opposition party to put forward the 'reprobate' Prince of Wales, desperate to get his hands on the throne, as Regent, while the Queen was barred from seeing her husband, and Prime Minister William Pitt fought desperately to keep him on the throne. The politics are a vital part of the drama, of course, but the emotional heart of Bennett's play is with the struggle to restore the King to normality. The distinctly quackish medical profession knew next to nothing about the King's malady, and so he was for a while reduced to the status of a shuttlecock, being knocked around by whoever argued most strongly that they could cure him. (Bennett's horror at being examined, naked, by an insensitive consultant at the John Radcliffe Hospital some years earlier, while a gaggle of students took notes and sniggered, had scarcely abated.) Furthermore, while the King was in the grip of the symptoms, there was a paradox between this most unkingly figure – who, subsequent research suggested, understood what was happening to him while it was happening but was unable to control it – and a man in whom supreme power was vested, and who thus still demanded the subservience due to a king.

The only person who dared to challenge that rule was the most self-assured of the King's healers, the Revd Dr Francis Willis. He had his own private madhouse at Greatford in Lincolnshire, and for a while he became the King's in-house 'mad doctor'. Under Willis's regime, the King was frequently, and painfully, 'confined' or 'restrained' in the middle of an attack, which may have reduced the symptoms, or equally may have prolonged them. In the sensational climax to Act One, a howling George III is restrained by Willis's men and 'strapped into the chair, feet and arms clamped, his head held rigid by a band round his forehead'. The fevered King howls: 'I am the King of England.' Willis bends down to him and, through his teeth, hisses: 'No, sir. You are the patient.' The music swells: it is Handel's Coronation Anthem, written for George I. Once again, Bennett has found a subversive – and historically elastic – function for the chorus of 'Zadok the Priest'. Previously, it coincided with Joe Orton and Kenneth Halliwell becoming intimate for the first time with each other in 1953. Now, tragically and awfully, the poor mad King is the prisoner of his throne, the helpless, powerless patient of one of his subject's whims. The condition stabilises by the end of the play, which ends with his arrival at St Paul's for a service of thanksgiving on his recovery, but we are left with the uneasy foreknowledge that it will return.

In Bennett's attempts to balance his treatment of the King's condition and to set it comfortably in its political context, the play went through three major rewrites. The luxury of a ten-week rehearsal period also helped to streamline the drama. Hytner was, incidentally, re-rehearsing *The Wind in the Willows* at the same time, so, as Bennett noted, 'it was Pitt and Fox in the morning, Rat and Mole (and Fox) in the afternoon'. Bennett says he worked harder on *The Madness of George III* than on any of his previous plays, and it was certainly one of his most daring adventures in drama. In the earlier drafts, Bennett felt that the audience might have benefited from a fifteen-minute history lecture before the play began. They would have needed longer to recover if Bennett hadn't given them half a happy ending. As it is, the final third runs down slowly, as the relieved royalists in the audience are allowed to experience the knowledge that the King is himself again, but audiences were poleaxed by the scenes that preceded them. Madness and lunacy had not been so intertwined by a British playwright for years, and the spectacle of the royal retinue beginning to resemble Bedlam was terribly harrowing. Having presented Elizabeth II in such measured, and hilarious, terms in *A Question of Attribution*, it was a shock for audiences to find such a different side to royalty presented on stage. Luckily, there were many jokes along the way, and had it not been for Mrs Thatcher's recent removal, Bennett says there would have been even more. One that audiences enjoyed was Pitt's muttered comment that he just needed another five years, a threat which the Conservatives had made regularly around election time. One of the King's pages, Fortnum, said that he was off to become a grocer, which regularly raised a laugh, with most people assuming that it was one of Bennett's clever historical pranks. In fact, it was the truth.

In November 1991 Charles Nevin of the *Independent on Sunday* met Alan Bennett at the National Theatre during a blizzard of activity too intense even for tea to be offered. The headline and the stand-first set out the writer's pitch. 'Our National Treasure' was sub-headlined 'A playwright with a unique insight into the British, or a patronising voyeur?' Bennett, writes Nevin, agreed to talk to him only after a characteristic 'silence seething with dither'. When they met, Nevin was disappointed to find Bennett wearing suede shoes and not what he thought were the obligatory plimsolls. Nevin wrote that Bennett had been awarded 'Favourite Uncle' status, a reward denied the other *Fringe* members, of whom Miller was thought 'too clever', Cook 'too subversive' and Moore 'too much away'. Nevin runs through the main areas of Bennett's life. Shy, donnish and envious in *Beyond the Fringe*, cuddly and unfashionable in *Forty Years On*, too joke-dependent in *Habeas Corpus* and *Enjoy*. The name of Betjeman is invoked, but whereas Betjeman was the poet of the suburbs, Bennett is 'the playwright of the repressed and respectable working classes'. Since then, the ungregarious Bennett 'has left the Workers but refuses to join the Chatterers'. Nevin found him giggly and friendly but unable to help with most of his questions. Bennett seemed to have learned a new technique that was almost Gandhi-esque: non-violent non-cooperation. 'I can't see this relates to anything at all, really,' he said in response to one question, and

'I've got no feeling at all about that.' When asked if he was patronising, Bennett said, 'I don't care really what they think. I think I would have, once. Now I just get on with it.' Bennett challenged Nevin to talk to someone who didn't like him, but 'Unfortunately, Steven Berkoff was too busy.' So what of the 'Favourite Uncle' label? Nevin was forced to conclude, as has almost everyone else, that 'the label reflects only a fraction of his gifts'. Bennett's only concession – and it was a big one – was to admit to a fear that he was becoming a parody of himself in the same way that Betjeman became.

In conversation with Peter Lewis of the *Sunday Times*, Bennett had a good answer to the question of why he wrote plays. It was because 'I was always terrified of dons. I would have been a very bad one. I'm not good at precise, coherent argument. But plays are suited to incoherent argument, put into the mouths of fallible people. Drama,' said Bennett, 'is the backstairs of the intellect. Philosophers and historians go by the front door, but playwrights and novelists sneak up the backstairs with their more disreputable luggage.' Which leaves journalists, presumably, using the tradesmen's entrance – or perhaps the outside lavatory.

Bennett was still frantically tweaking the text two weeks before curtain up, but, the work finally done, *The Madness of George III* was first performed at the National's Lyttelton Theatre on 28 November 1991. It ran, pretty much selling out, for a total of 147 performances. Fans included Charles Spencer in the *Daily Telegraph*, who praised it as 'a piece that combines humour with deeply affecting compassion'. The editor of the *British Journal of Psychiatry*, Hugh Freeman, reviewing the play in the *Psychiatric Bulletin*, described Bennett's portrayal of the King's illness as 'impeccable', though, while regarding the 'blundering attentions' of the royal physicians as 'regrettable', he felt that it was wrong to portray Dr Willis as just another 'naive rural clergyman'. 'In the prevailing state of knowledge,' writes Freeman, 'Willis's management of the King was probably the most effective available.'

There was criticism too. Benedict Nightingale in *The Times* called it 'a dullish, crudish play' because of its minor characters, most of whom were mere caricatures. What all agreed on, though, without exception, was that Nigel Hawthorne's performance as the King was a triumph. 'The kind of performance that is going to be talked about for years,' wrote John Gross in the *Sunday Telegraph*. Michael Coveney in the *Observer* described Hawthorne as 'giving the performance of his life'.

'Hawthorne shines in the role like a cracked jewel,' wrote John Peter in the *Sunday Times*. Even Mark Lawson, enjoying a brief stint as theatre critic of the *Independent*, took time off from working his own jokes into the text to remark that Hawthorne is 'at the top of his form'.

If the theatre professionals reacted ambivalently, those people who paid for their tickets were emphatic in their approval. *The Madness of George III* became a massive word-of-mouth hit. The contemporary references delighted audiences, Mark Thompson's staging was beautiful, and Nicholas Hytner's production was universally admired. With their production of *The Wind in the Willows* now entering its second year at the National's Olivier Theatre, Bennett became the first contemporary playwright to have two productions in repertory on the South Bank at the same time: a major achievement. The press, though, like a concerned parent, was impatient to know what Bennett was going to write next. 'Oh, I'm toying, just toying, with the idea of dramatising those stories about the lady who came and camped in my drive in Camden for all that time,' he told Alfred Hickling of the *Yorkshire Post*. 'I think she owes me that.'

Kings lose countries; councils lose libraries. The text of *The Madness of George III* was published by Faber in 1992 and copies were duly dispatched to public libraries, including Bennett's own in Camden, but if any readers in nearby Belsize Park were hoping to get their hands on a copy, they would need to turn up on the right day. Labour-controlled Camden Council, facing debts of an estimated £700 million, had decided to take drastic measures to cut costs, which included sacking sixteen library staff with the further threat of twelve more jobs to go. These cuts seriously affected the little library at Belsize Park, in looks not unlike Bennett's own boyhood Armley Road library. As a result, Belsize Park was forced to close its doors for several days each week.

Bennett went on the warpath. A meeting was arranged under the banner 'Save Belsize library'. Bennett was the most illustrious Camden resident present. His words made the next morning's papers. 'Bennett Throws Book at Labour in Library Row', ran the *Express* headline on 26 September. Most of Bennett's anger was aimed at the Labour group which had been in power in Camden for twenty years. Employing the sort of language his father used, Bennett described them as 'a thick-headed lot'. 'I voted Labour at the last election out of conviction, because we had fourteen years of Conservatism,' said the former SDP sympathiser. 'But if it were possible to get this council out by voting independently, then I would do it. They have been in power too long. They have ceased to be sensitive in any way to public opinion. The more noise people make about libraries, the better.'

In a refrain that comes straight out of Bennett's book of common prayer, he went on: 'Once you start closing a library for two or three days a week, you destroy the whole ethos. It has got to be there, available all of the time – that's the point about libraries. It's a facility you shouldn't have to think about. It's part of civilised life.'

In one way, Bennett was making life even more difficult for librarians, by writing more plays. At least his next production had already been seen before, albeit on television. The stage version of *Talking Heads* opened at the Comedy Theatre on 21 January 1992, with Patricia Routledge – Bennett referred to her simply as 'the Routledge' – starring in both *A Woman of No Importance* and *A Lady of Letters*. Bennett, who also directed, performed *A Chip in the Sugar*. As the show circled the capital before hitting the West End, nerves were evidently getting to the author. On one night in Guildford, he lost his place twice and had to leave the stage to collect himself. Perhaps Bennett couldn't get out of his head the unsatisfactory year his family had spent there in 1944.

He had gathered most of his wits by the time of the opening night in the West End, with the exception of one night when he 'dried' – i.e. forgot his lines – three times. Once again it was only a partial hit with the critics. Nicholas de Jongh in the *Evening Standard* regretted that, without the 'deep probe of the camera's close-up, pathos gives way to stand-up social comedy'. The challenge with Peggy Schofield, the woman of no importance, was to portray her dying of cancer on stage. This, said de Jongh, was done brilliantly, as were the comic tones of Graham, the gay mother's boy. And yet, by the time 'the Routledge' returned to the stage, de Jongh 'began to tire of the relentless small scale and sense of confinement'. Television monologues, he felt, 'should know their place is ideally in the home, not on the stage'.

And yet Bennett had achieved the seemingly unimaginable triumph of having three plays on in London at the same time. Frank Rich, theatre critic of the *New York Times* and a man who, like a Roman emperor, was said to be able to close a show with a downturned thumb, came to London to report on this feat. 'In London, a Writer Has a Three-show Coup', ran the headline. Rich detected a 'hermetic vision of an eternal boyhood' in both Graham, of *A Chip in the Sugar*, and (Kenneth) Grahame. Rich felt that Mole and his friends, with their 'school gentility and unarticulated gay crushes', were reminiscent of the gentlemanly traitors Anthony Blunt and Guy Burgess. He didn't enjoy the 'lengthy recountings of Georgian political intrigues', but he correctly described Hawthorne's performance as 'the performance of his career'. As a suffering patient, wrote Rich, 'this King is nothing if not a direct ancestor of the wheelchair-bound, middle-class woman of no importance played by Ms Routledge in *Talking Heads*'. Rich concluded: 'Alan Bennett's comedies may be crowd-pleasers, but they are subversive ones, depicting lost souls who seem to emblemize an unhappy England that cannot diagnose, let alone cure, its ills.'

Bennett admitted to Alfred Hickling of the *Yorkshire Post* that it 'got a bit lonely' doing *Talking Heads*, unlike a major play which was 'a nice, big social occasion'. Still, there was a large crowd gathered to pay homage to him at the Olivier Awards on 26 April. At this, the theatrical gong show of the year, Patricia Routledge was nominated for Actress of the Year, though she narrowly lost to Juliet Stevenson in Ariel Dorfman's *Death and the Maiden*. *Talking Heads*, up against Jason Donovan in *Joseph and the Amazing Technicolor Dreamcoat*, among other shows, won two Olivier awards, for Best Entertainment and Best Actor for Bennett himself. It seemed that Bennett only had to enter a race to be declared the winner. 'Patricia Routledge bore the brunt of the evening,' said Bennett with well-honed award-accepting modesty. 'I was just the jam in the sandwich or perhaps the egg on the face.' Lest anybody forget that there were other plays by Bennett in the running, Nigel Hawthorne won Actor of the Year for *The Madness of George III*. 'It's a huge, huge accolade and it was quite unexpected,' Hawthorne said to the press after receiving his award from Hollywood star Kathleen Turner. 'I'd never in a million years expected to win it, and suddenly I found it so touching that I started to cry.'

On 25 May 1992 Alan Bennett wrote an article in the *Guardian* which seemed to mark a new low in the history of his relations with the press. It was a complaint about an interview he gave to Graham Turner of the *Sunday Telegraph* in 1988 about intellectuals and Mrs Thatcher. In essence, Bennett said that Turner had ignored his serious and heartfelt objections to Thatcher, and merely put in an off-the-cuff remark about the Thatchers being lowbrow but aspirational. Bennett was angry because this remark had found its way into Noël Annan's book, *Our Age*. Bennett felt misrepresented, and he was angry because he felt sure that the tone of Turner's article had been dictated on high from the paper's increasingly eccentric right-wing editor, Peregrine Worsthorne. Bennett's conclusion was that 'Not to be interviewed is the only answer'. As ever, though, this declaration to withdraw from the limelight was to prove only partly true.

There was another high spot in Bennett's career in 1992, when his recording of *Winnie-the-Pooh* and *The House at Pooh Corner* was released by the BBC on audio cassette. The part of Eeyore, especially, suited him down to the ground. It became, and remains, a bestseller, and was shortly joined by *Alice in Wonderland* and *Through the Looking Glass* (1993), *The Story of Dr Dolittle* (1995), *The Voyages of Dr Dolittle* (1998) and *The Wind in the Willows* (2001). What was significant about the first recording was that it was a conscious attempt both by the BBC and Bennett to put up a show of resistance to a perceived Disneyfication of a classic English children's book. Bennett was in the forefront of the campaign to reannex a revered section of British literary culture from American cultural imperialism.

Bennett may have associated himself even more strongly with a kind of Englishness, but he never lost his affection for New York, and so when he was approached by that city's most famous magazine, the *New Yorker*, he agreed to be profiled. The issue of the *New Yorker* for 6 September 1993 contained, for the first time, a critical profile of one of the original members of *Beyond the Fringe*. (The next occasion would be in 1995, with John Lahr's extraordinary death notice for Peter Cook.) Selling English authors to American audiences is not that easy, even when the editor of this journal was the British-born Tina Brown. The peg for the article was the imminent arrival in the States of *The Madness of George III*, with the full cast of twenty-five, beginning on 11 September in Stamford, Connecticut, and moving to the Brooklyn Academy of Music on 28 September, with Baltimore and Boston to follow. The staff writer Stephen Schiff, under his own column which bore the rubric 'Cultural Pursuits', was sent to London to write a critical profile. 'In England,' the introduction declared, 'the playwright Alan Bennett is regarded as a national treasure and a bit of a mystic – an eccentric, famously private writer who wittily articulates the grace and grit of what it is to be English.'

And so the piece begins. Bennett, wrote Schiff, 'represents something far-off and dear, a wee lost England of tea cozies and unspoiled country lanes and fair-haired schoolboys with skinned knees and heads full of Shakespeare – England before the Fall'. But then he pulls himself, and us, up, reminding us that 'this is also the man who wrote a play called *Kafka's Dick*, in which Kafka's father blackmails his illustrious son by threatening to reveal the diminutive size of the lad's penis'.

In other words, writes Schiff, 'There's a duality that runs through Bennett and through his work: an awareness that whatever we pretend to be on the outside is a deception; that underneath we are all weak, noisome, and, if we could only see it, deeply embarrassing. For all his apparent snugliness, he likes to make the bluenoses squirm.'

Bennett reveals some of his eccentricities to Schiff, such as his behaviour when he's writing. 'If you saw me, you'd probably think I was mad. I tend to act things out and stride about the room, saying the dialogue out loud. I don't know how you write with somebody else in the house if you do things like that – that's why I've always lived alone.'

Other eccentricities, though, Schiff discovered himself, such as the sponge attached to the hanging metal lamp over his desk, which an embarrassed and giggling Bennett explains as being there to prevent himself hitting his head on the lampshade. And how about the pencil hanging about the sponge? 'I'm becoming so eccentric,' he giggles. 'No, the lamp was too high and I still bumped my head, so I tied the cord around that pencil to shorten it.' The same eccentricity, Bennett claimed, was useful in keeping the press off your tail.

So far, so good. Schiff had described a man with a 'timorous image' who 'loves nothing more than shattering it', for example by 'scooting around' on the back of a motorbike driven by Jonathan Miller's son, Thomas. But he was about to reveal a side of himself which he had never before made public and one that would provoke a feeding frenzy among the British press.

19

A few unguarded remarks about my personal life

The Madness of King George, Writing Home, 1994

The bombshell was concealed towards the bottom of the third page of the article. 'Among other things, he'd imagined himself to be gay,' wrote Schiff. 'On being asked about his sexuality, though, he would generally turn cryptic. "There's been something of both in my life, but not enough of either" was one of his responses . . . Still, practically everyone he knew was astonished when, in the late seventies, he very quietly began a relationship with the darkly attractive woman who had been doing his house-cleaning.'

Schiff went on to describe Anne Davies. She was ten years younger than Bennett, divorced, with three sons 'all of whom took to Alan with alacrity, as most of his friends' children do'. Bennett told Schiff: 'I'd always been in love with guys, you see, but always unhappily. They were always straight, and it was always totally unfulfilled.' Bennett's explanation for what had happened with Anne was reassuringly frank. 'Just over ten years or so, you know, I just got to depend on her and just to like being with her more than with anybody else. And one enormous virtue was that she was not in the least interested in my work. She didn't want to be the artist's wife. And I like that, because I don't want to have to be explaining how far I've got with it every day.' As Proust said of his housekeeper in *102 Boulevard Haussmann*: 'Céleste has many virtues, and one of them is that in the two years she has been with me she has never asked if she has been put in the book.'

The interview appeared on 14 September. That same day, not entirely surprisingly, he found himself under siege. The man who had put up with a smelly but essentially harmless old woman in his front drive for twenty or so years now found some better-dressed but potentially more damaging visitors camped out in his driveway. Fleet Street's finest were hot on the trail, running up hundreds of pounds in mileage expenses as they swarmed between Camden and Clapham, North Yorkshire. In London, he told a *Daily Mail* reporter, 'I don't see that it's the concern of anybody. I don't want to talk about it.' To his diary he fumed: 'All you need to do if you want the nation's press camped on your doorstep is say you once had a wank in 1947.'

'How Alan Bennett's Charlady Swept Him Clean Off His Feet,' ran the headline in the *Daily Mail* on Wednesday 15 September. Reporter John Woodcock tracked Anne Davies down to her home in Clapham and asked for her side of the story. 'I suppose you could describe me as his common-law wife,' she seems to have told him. As Bennett had been subjected to the *New Yorker* style of profile, so Davies was subjected to the rather more clipped *Daily Mail* house style, such as: 'Drawing on a cigarette, she disclosed that their relationship is passing through a turbulent stage.' Woodcock wrote that their intimacy had 'not [been] helped' by the *New Yorker* profile. 'I wish he'd warned me about the article,' Davies told Woodcock. 'Alan has protected me, kept me out of the limelight for fourteen years, and I'll have to speak to him about what's happened. He really should have told me about this.'

So far as the British press were concerned, the fact that Bennett had mentioned the existence of a woman was an indication that he was prepared to talk about it. In their minds, he could not name his partner and then draw a discreet veil over the whole business. So they pursued him, and were greeted with a wall of silence. Bennett described the stakeout in his journal, observing them through his shuttered windows as they sat in their cars, waiting for the door to open and the tea to be offered. 'The woman is smartly dressed, hair drawn back, hard-faced and ringing the bell at this moment (and now rattling the letterbox),' he wrote. 'Madam periodically strides briskly up to the door and rings the bell as if it were the first time she has done it. She is at it again now, and clip clip go her little heels as she trips back down the path.' He was no more impressed with the other players in this little farce. One was 'a solid middle-aged man with bright white hair and glasses: a sports outfitter perhaps, the secretary of a golf club, even chairman of the parish council, though there is something slightly seedy or lavatorial about him'. The third 'slightly forlorn figure is a balding young man in a Barbour who rang the doorbell last night to say he was from the *Daily Mail*' – Bennett closed the door in his face – 'and now he is back, but with no car to sit in he stands disconsolately on the pavement, picking his nails. Meanwhile the phone rings constantly.'

Eventually, the balding young man started calling through the letterbox. 'I just want to clear up one or two misconceptions.' The photographer took photographs of the figureless house. They even took to dropping notes through the letterbox, one of which read: 'I don't want to make your life a misery.'

The reporters fared better in Clapham. Jim Oldfield of the *Mirror* claimed to have found Anne Davies in her café. 'I think he has done this because he fears losing me,' she is quoted as saying in the course of an article which mentions only *Talking Heads* among Bennett's credits, merely stating: 'He lives mainly in London at the hub of the stage, TV and film world.' Davies is quoted as adding: 'I think this is his way of declaring his love.' To the *Mirror*, and to many of its readers, after all, Alan Bennett *is Talking Heads*.

The *Mirror* reckoned it knew why Bennett had 'blabbed' to 'that glossiest of magazines, the *New Yorker*'. It constructed a possible scenario. 'She throws herself into the business 240 miles away . . . He now sees her only once a month – and he begins to fret. Despite being a writer of extraordinary insight, with a wit sharper than a surgeon's knife, he acts just like the rest of us might. He panics and blurts it out. Their love affair is laid bare.' So that's what happened . . . But Davies is quoted as saying: 'Alan is a reclusive person and he wants me to go away with him. He would like to move to a new part of England where no one knows us. But I have told him I can't. I am so busy with the business that I can't leave it now. I'm really making a success of it. It's ironic, I know, because he set me up in the business. I think he is frustrated by the situation and this could be his way of declaring his love.'

The *Mirror* said she was 'frantic' about the revelation. 'I have spoken to him several times over the phone and he is in a terrible state. He just says to me he doesn't know why he did it. He is a very private person, yet he has brought all of this on us. But it will blow over . . . and I'm not cross with him.'

On 17 September, the same day as the *Mirror* ran its story, the *Express* added its bit too, under the headline 'Curtain Up On Playwright's Leading Lady'. 'Yesterday,' reported Stephen Thompson, 'she played her part in his real-life drama by cycling barefoot through the Yorkshire Dales village of Clapham, where she runs a teashop next door to his weekend cottage.' Davies, who had almost completed her three-day crash course in media management, 'made an exit stage left without adding to the dialogue'. The reporters pitched up in the New Inn, where they established that 'Most evenings she walks down to the New Inn for glasses of lager which she chases down with measures of Famous Grouse whisky. She is an enthusiastic member of the pub pool team.' A follow-up story in the *Mail* used the same picture as the *Express* used of Davies on a bicycle, again with no further comment from her. Some of the villagers were as stunned as the newspaper readers. The *Evening Standard* produced the first named quote, from Richard Sexton, owner of the village craft shop. 'We just thought they were good friends,' he said. Which they still were, after all.

'All this,' Bennett wrote in his diary, 'is because . . . I made a few unguarded remarks about my personal life.' Bennett was, of course, protesting too much. He had played the media game for too long not to know perfectly well that his candid admission would presage a storm of publicity. He may have regretted being at the centre of it – referring to himself ruefully during this period as 'London's most prominent heterosexual' – but the more important question is to ask why he chose that moment to reveal the affair to Stephen Schiff.

There are various reasons: some pragmatic, others less so. To some extent the revelation about Anne was a Trojan horse. In all the media onslaught, the issue of his sexuality was more or less ignored. Bennett had managed to reveal that he was gay, in other words, but only as a by-product of his relationship with Anne. So the whole matter had been brought, relatively painlessly, into the open. Bennett may also have been rejoicing in the fact that, at last, he had a sex life to speak of. It reminds one of another famously highbrow figure, Stephen Fry, who after many years of unhappy emotional searching finally found the right partner and acknowledged with joy – this is not how he phrased it but it gives a flavour of how he was feeling – that he wanted to be a good shag as well as a good read.

There was also the question of Bennett's debt to Anne. There is no doubt that he owed a good deal of his peace of mind in recent years to her. She had been his loyal friend and partner for fourteen years. He wanted to thank her, to acknowledge her. Perhaps there was a temporary rift which he was trying to make good, but he also genuinely seemed to want more people to know how much he depended on her. So he chose to admit this intimate secret to a proper writer from a proper magazine. And the confession was properly buried at the foot of the third page, where it belonged.

Then again, did he mean to say as much as he did? A few months later, Schiff was responsible for another bombshell when he wrote a piece on V.S. Naipaul, in which Naipaul revealed for the first time the existence of a mistress and also of a past that included the repeated frequenting of prostitutes. Maybe part of the reason why Bennett had spoken so confidentially was because he felt relaxed in the company of a sympathetic writer.

The trouble with the British press, though, is that it always wants more. If journalists are people who are always trying to ask one more question, a celebrity – at least of a certain kind – is a person who is always trying to answer one less. Then again, it was typical of Bennett to grant an interview, cause a huge fuss, and then withdraw silently, complaining that he couldn't see what all the excitement was about.

With *The Madness of George III* enjoying a major success in the States, and further plaudits raining down on the head of Nigel Hawthorne, the next stage in the crowning of Bennett's success was unprecedented. There may have been attempts to film one of his plays before, but none got off the ground. This time it was different. The Samuel Goldwyn Company met Channel 4 Films, discussed the deal, liked each other's terms and produced a contract which both signed. Unlike the original *Prick Up Your Ears* discussions, there was no attempted Hollywoodisation of the personalities, with American producers hinting that George III should be played by Tom Hanks, or that the play be reset in 1950s Chicago. There were, inevitably, cast changes, either for reasons of cinematic expediency or because of previous acting commitments on the part of the original cast. Out went Janet Dale as Queen Charlotte, replaced by Helen Mirren. The Prince of Wales changed hands from Michael Fitzgerald to the cinematically more established Rupert Everett. Dr Willis's role passed from the very fine Charles Kay to Ian Holm. Julian Wadham kept his hands on Pitt, but Fox changed from David Henry to Jim Carter. Retained, of course, were Hawthorne and – understandably but still impressively given his previous movie experience (zero) – Hytner. For Bennett, these two names were a *sine qua non*.

There was one other change. The Goldwyn Company knew their market, and they seemed convinced that American movie-goers would be confused by the title *The Madness of George III*. In his introduction to the finished screenplay, Alan Bennett wrote that a survey had 'apparently shown that there were many movie-goers who came away from Kenneth Branagh's film of *Henry V* wishing they had seen its four predecessors'. It was agreed that the movie should be renamed *The Madness of King George*.

The film was produced by Sam Goldwyn Jr, and it was considered such a strong Oscar contender that it was rushed into a pre-Christmas release in New York and Los Angeles. There are some stunning scenes in the film. Alan Bennett could now exploit the magic of the movies to re-create his abiding interest in lavatories and bodily functions, as demonstrated by the scene in which the King squats against a wall to relieve himself, but the contrasts between external pomp and internal squalor are explored thoroughly. The scenes where the King flings open the door of the cupboard to reveal three sleeping pages crammed in together and hurtles down corridors, trailing equerries in his wake, are among the film's finest moments. Hytner keeps a strong grip on the film, ensuring that it loses little of its vitality.

Bennett had an enjoyable time during filming, which took place in settings as diverse as Windsor, Eton, Oxford, Banbury, Greenwich, Arundel Castle and Syon House. He made a fleeting appearance, as a meandering MP in the House of Commons, and during a break in shooting was asked by one of the other extras if he did much extra work nowadays. 'Not really,' says Bennett, happy to nestle in relative anonymity while his creation was brought to life around him. These visits to film sets brought back happy memories of *A Day Out*, twenty-two years earlier, and other such films where he would mooch around, chatting to the actors and watching with fascination as the camera crew moved in its mysterious ways. 'As always I'm pretty surplus to requirements,' he notes in his production diary, though he well knows that it is a rare privilege to be extraneous at a party held in one's honour.

In the first week of March 1994, Faber & Faber's chairman, Matthew Evans, made the successful bid in a three-way auction for the publication rights to Alan Bennett's journals. The selected works of Alan Bennett were published in October under the title *Writing Home*. The book, all 417 pages of it, was the perfect Alan Bennett reader, with his memorial addresses, prefaces to plays, *The Lady in the Van* complete with the original illustrations by fellow Gloucester Crescent resident David Gentleman, and the diaries themselves from 1980 to 1990, from the disappointment of *Enjoy* to the triumph of *The Wind in the Willows*. It was a fascinating ragbag. The essays were well worth the cover price alone, but what really made it a hit – and captivated most reviewers – were the diaries. Despite their having appeared in the *London Review of Books* first, and several national newspapers thereafter, the diaries made the reader feel as if Bennett's inner thoughts had become public property, and it was this, as much as *Talking Heads*, which made him more popular than ever.

Bennett, for so long the object of slightly cheapening interest from cub diarists on newspapers large or small, gave a master class in how to keep a diary. One should be able to open a good diary anywhere and find something entertaining or startling. Bennett provided just that. Overheard remarks: 'In the market today: "Listen, there's nothing you can teach me about road-sweeping." ' Notes on vulgarisation: 'Note that after a successful round even show-jumpers punch the air. Croquet next.' Notes on cultural impoverishment: 'In a bookshop in Ilkley – ASSISTANT: Is that *Geoffrey* Chaucer?" ' Notes on urban decay: 'To Leeds, where the decent cupolaed building on Woodhouse Moor that housed both the public library and the police station has been converted into a pub, The Feast and Firkin.' And groans about the press: 'The *Sun*'s headline this morning [about the IRA]: "String 'Em Up." ' There is observation of couples, and singles, and people going mad in Camden or New York. There are death notices for old friends, tinged with sadness, like Lindsay Anderson ('None of the obituaries mention how consistently and constructively kind he was'), as well as for old heroes ('Truffaut dies – an oddly personal loss'). And there is also, of course, self-deprecation.

'Watching Barry Humphries on TV the other night I noticed the band was laughing. It reminded me how when I used to do comedy I never used to make the band laugh. Dudley did, and Peter, but not me. And somehow it was another version of not being good at games.'

Even the index threw up a steady stream of jokes on the lines of 'College of Cardinals: cardboard urged on as material for papal crown' or 'Marcos, Ferdinand: AB's fellow feelings with'. A good index is like a come-hither look. Who could resist 'Lineker, Gary: thighs the talk of Harlesden'? How could one not want to know more about 'Thorndike Theatre, Leatherhead: lewd ingenuity of schoolboys at' or 'Hailsham, Lord: more humbug from' or, perhaps best of all, 'Wykehamists: improbable claims for genitals'?

If there is a hierarchy among Bennett's friends, then surely pride of place – apart from Mam and Dad, of course, and the rarely cited (or sighted) brother Gordon – went to those few persons whose presence in the text was implied by a single letter. There were London neighbours like 'J.', of course, for Jonathan Miller, and 'K.' in New York, for Keith McNally. And naturally under 'A.' was Davies, Anne.

Writing Home went straight to number one in the non-fiction bestseller lists, where it remained until Christmas. It was reviewed pretty much everywhere over the course of October, and it was interesting to see which Bennett groupies it flushed out. Hanif Kureishi, for example, in the *Mail on Sunday*, described it as 'delicious', and 'personal without being self-indulgent'. He looked forward to the day when the complete diaries would be published and 'hints of deeper feeling' revealed, though for now this was 'plenty to be going on with'. Sean French in *The Times* felt it was a better introduction to literature than most supposedly academic writing. Former Gloucester Crescent resident Fiona MacCarthy in the *Observer* admired it as 'wonderfully funny. What he is not is cosy . . . You finish this book liking Alan Bennett less than you imagined, but admiring him much more.'

Then there were the crusties. Keith Waterhouse in the *Daily Mail* read it with a generous and open mind. 'It's one of those books where, if the author's name had been unaccountably left off the jacket, you could open it at random and know at once who wrote it.' He found some of the opinions 'surprisingly angry for so mannered if waspish a public persona' and wondered, quite reasonably, if the many relatives quoted had received complimentary copies to make up for the raid on their thoughts. He concluded, however, that 'it throws little light on the secretive lifestyle of the author himself'.

As Waterhouse himself admits, one can tire of Bennett's pith, of the eavesdroppings which might have been improved somewhat for publication. A tetchy note creeps into the diary at times, of a man hard to please, quick to find fault, forever watching the telly, tutting and being irritated by the latter and yet continuing to watch. The sentiments are laudable – 'Our pillar box is now emptied at 9 a.m. not by the Royal Mail van but by a minibus marked Portobello Car and Van Hire' – but one sometimes wishes he wasn't so damned right all the time. He complains that entry to his college is now by swipe card. One agrees, but slightly resents oneself for doing so. He turns down an invitation to speech day at Giggleswick School on the perfectly reasonable grounds that the guest of honour is Lord Archer. But did he need to add in his letter that next year 'doubtless the guest will be Bernard Manning'? God help those who fall short of his high standards by using modern jargon, or taking an interest in things of which he disapproves. He can sound caustic, judgemental, pious – even prim, as he used to say of himself. An early glimpse of Chris Evans prompted the following, on 9 April 1993: ' "It's *Good* Friday!" shouts the ginger-haired young man who presents *The Big Breakfast*, as if the goodness of the day were to do with having a good time.' Which prompts the reply that Chris Evans, who might irritate many but is no fool, knew perfectly well that he was twisting the words. But also, what was Alan Bennett doing watching *The Big Breakfast* in the first place?

And yet if Alan Bennett can be frustrating at times, one only has to read his detractors to come running back to Bennett with renewed admiration. Richard Ingrams, writing in the *Evening Standard*, at first concedes that Bennett, although he was 'always considered the least brilliant' of the *Beyond the Fringe* quartet, 'has become a revered and respected figure – almost a sacred cow'. He describes Bennett as 'an acute observer of . . . the funny things we say on the bus or in the supermarket. Yet try as he might, he remains a minor talent. He has never really risen above his original role of writer of comic monologues and sketches.' Furthermore: 'Regrettably, like many funny men, when Bennett turns to more serious themes and ventures beyond revue material he is liable to fall flat on his face.'

Ingrams, a man who gave up the ghost in the 1980s but somehow forgot to die, describes the *London Review of Books* as 'that most dispiriting of magazines'. Bennett's diaries are derided as 'the world of a self-centred bachelor living in Camden Town'. And his final paragraph is taken up with a posthumous attempt to assassinate the character of Russell Harty, whom Ingrams describes as 'an unctuous, ingratiating snob', an imposed viewpoint which is irrelevant to a discussion of the book.

Ingrams may have lost his blush but at least he never turned as sour as Alan Clark. The *Guardian*, hopefully but mistakenly thinking to set one diarist on another, asked Clark to review *Writing Home*. The review is a grim reminder not only of how out of touch politicians are with anything that doesn't happen in Westminster, but also how they reveal their bumptiousness and humourlessness while trying to show the complete reverse. Clark's first line is: 'I must admit I thought Alan Bennett was dead.' How very amusing.

In his second paragraph he admits that 'there is a certain type that brings out the worst in me: all those old dears, comfily on the left'. Clark's belief, again preferring to opine rather than review, is that 'they all peaked back in 1968, and then got wiped out by the Falklands War'. He describes the Malvinas as 'the Black Death for all those wuffly intellectual queen bees'. He damns one or two of Bennett's lesser anecdotes, and derides people like Bennett who are 'pretty feeble as philosophers, political commentators or even columnar journalists'. Bennett's response was done for him. By March 1995 *Writing Home* had sold 200,000 copies, surpassing the wildest dreams of its publisher. The public seemed fixated on Bennett.

Those mocking critics might have done well to read a lecture by Paul Taylor, the drama critic of the *Independent*, which was commissioned by the West Yorkshire Playhouse and published in the *Independent* on 23 May 1994. In it, he hit back at the 'reassuring simplification' of Alan Bennett, which, he said, needed requalifying lest Bennett be seen as just 'a sartorially more subdued version of Victoria Wood, or else a lovably lugubrious Eeyore-figure lodged where the cuddly John Betjeman teddy bear once nestled in the nursery-wing of the Anglo-Saxon mind'. In fact, said Taylor, 'the work of this most English of writers is not cosy, safe, or in any way beholden to official thinking'. Taylor pointed to 'a stubborn ambivalence about England and Englishness' as evident in all Bennett's work since *Forty Years On*. Taylor compared Bennett's lack of recognition by the Establishment with that awarded to Tom Stoppard CBE, Alan Ayckbourn CBE and even Harold Pinter CBE. (If Bennett had hankered after a gong, he probably would not have written that 'If you can get a boiled egg down at ninety, they give you the Order of Merit.') Whatever the press deduced as Bennett's interests, Taylor described them as 'secrecy, treachery, people who, awkwardly straddled between groups, feel implicated in a double life'.

In May 1994, to celebrate Bennett's sixtieth birthday, his became the thirty-ninth name to appear in the *Independent*'s weekly Saturday magazine's 'The Good, The Great & The Ugly'. The only drawback to this was that one had to suffer the indignity of being drawn as a cartoon by one of the paper's cod cartoonists, Martin Rowson. The question-and-answer column listed Bennett's various sobriquets as Eeyore, Mole, Annabel Tent (an anagram) and The Garbo of Primrose Hill. What his scripts had in common, wrote the thumbnail sketch-writer, were 'Spies, animals, homosexuals, embarrassment'. The profile was well meaning, though the weakest line, cribbed from the *Guardian*'s Pass Notes section, was 'Least likely line after blowing out candles on Monday: "Christ, I feel good. Let's go hit the Ministry of Sound." ' Which just makes one appreciate the real Alan Bennett all the more.

The photograph accompanying Blake Morrison's review of *Writing Home* in the *Independent on Sunday*, on 25 September 1994, was a head shot of Alan Bennett taken by Derry Moore. Bennett wears his famous sleeveless cardigan, button-down collar and tie, one hand resting against the side of his face as photographers seem to like people to do. His hair is swept untidily to one side, one stray lock falling over his left eye. But what is significant is that behind him, reproduced in rich colour, is the mantelpiece of his home in Camden Town. This seems a substantial admittance into his private life. Here, caught for the first time on film, is the busy collage that caught the eye of so many interviewers in the less cautious, more accessible 1960s and 1970s, from the various pictures of 'Bennett and friend' (one male, one female) to a portrait of his father, a cobbled towpath, a railway bridge, and various art gallery-style postcards. (He became a trustee of the National Gallery in 1993.)

The *Independent on Sunday* had the Bennett photo of the year, but to the *Observer* went serialisation rights of the Bennett diaries, and an accompanying interview with their drama critic, Michael Ratcliffe, on 4 September. Ratcliffe is, of course, a fan. The section – from *Writing*

Home which he approvingly quotes in full – a lengthy description from December 1986 of the improvised decorations for a Christmas tree – is exactly that which Alan Clark attempted to attack so witheringly in the *Guardian*.

And so yet again, having made himself as clear as he wanted to be in the diaries, Bennett is probed for more. He reiterates the fact that, if he had had to pay his own way, he would never have gone to Oxford. And he returns to his hatred of Mrs Thatcher: 'What's so hard to forgive is the deliberate destruction of BBC morale simply because it stood up to her.' Ratcliffe's conclusion, conveniently overlooking Miller, who is still a substantial creative force, is that 'Originally the tortoise in the quartet, he has long since outrun both Cook and Moore.'

Poor Dudley Moore had more or less dropped out of the race, having suffered from a mysterious but degenerative malaise throughout most of the 1990s. The condition, which in 1999 was revealed as being a sinister offshoot of Parkinson's disease, slowly scraped away his physical coordination, and was gradually robbing him of the ability to walk, talk and – most cruelly – play his beloved piano. There was worse news for *Fringe* fans in January 1995, when British comedy lost one of its most influential figures with the death of Peter Cook. In his latter years, Cook had taken to dialling up radio talk shows, posing as a depressed Norwegian fisherman called Sven. If this was a kind of chamber music compared with the big-band comedy of his younger days with Dudley, it also represented a sort of *Writing Home*, since he could and often did inject considerable pathos into these miniature performances.

For thirty years, Bennett and Cook had lived a couple of miles from each other, Cook in a Queen Anne house in Hampstead. Even though Cook was an heroic drinker, most of his friends thought he was indestructible. Bennett must have been shocked, too, though in his diary he dwelt on Cook's apparent nihilism, how 'literature, music – it was all just the stuff of cocktail party chatter'. If Bennett was surprised at the acres of newsprint devoted to Cook and his self-destructive life, his friend Sir Alec Guinness felt the same way, wondering if even a royal death would have caused such a fuss. (He would have the answer to that question less than two years later.) Guinness asked Bennett why he felt it was. 'It's because he was a journalist,' Bennett responded, a little tartly, considering his shared past with Cook. Of course, Cook was in many ways the exact opposite of Bennett: impulsive where Bennett was measured; drunk or drinking where Bennett was sober; press-friendly where Bennett was press-hostile. Possibly Bennett was wondering in advance, with forgivable vanity, how many column inches his own death would occupy. A few months later, however, when he was asked by Lin Chong, Cook's third wife, to make an address at Cook's memorial service, he was more the master of his feelings. In some ways, the cautious, sober Lin was a sort of Bennett figure for Cook, just as the high-spirited, drink-loving Anne was Bennett's Cook figure.

The memorial service was a carefully controlled exercise by the deeply traumatised Lin, with Cook's first two wives not present. Bennett was there, though, and feeling more charitable to the old stage colleague about whom he used to write so often. He berated the media, as usual, for presenting Cook's death as some sort of settling of scores, and he dwelt on the picture of the young, handsome, effortlessly witty Cook which many of those present would have remembered, but in his ringing final sentence he declared that: 'In him morality is discovered far from its official haunts, the message of a character like Peter's being that a life of complete self-indulgence, if led with the whole heart, may also bring wisdom.'

There was another death later that year, more personal this time. Lilian Bennett died on 2 April 1995, and was buried, next to Walter, in the little cemetery in Clapham. The stone they share bears the inscription: 'In loving memory of Walter Bennett, Dearly Loved Husband of Lilian Mary Bennett. And father of Gordon and Alan. Also of the above Lilian Mary Bennett.' For Bennett, it meant more sorting out of family possessions, and re-encountering long-forgotten heirlooms. Having suffered the personality erasure of Alzheimer's disease, it had been years since Lilian had been able to remember anything significant. Bennett's tribute to her was to do the remembering for her, an exercise which bore fruit several years later, with *Telling Tales*.

Peter Cook referred to himself as an orphan after his own mother's death, and it could have been said to have prompted the renewed drinking which led to his death. As well as both being residents of the London Borough of Camden, Cook and Bennett had another thing in common: each had a grandfather who had committed suicide. If – and it is a big 'if' – this became manifest in Cook's personality through a propensity towards self-destructive drinking, Bennett had at least checked any such tendency within himself by giving up the juice at an early age.

He may have had a tendency to brood, but he also had the benefit of a Protestant work ethic to distract him from excessive melancholia.

Meanwhile, the build-up to the launch of *The Madness of King George* was under way. 'Film is drama at its most impatient,' Bennett wrote in his introduction to the script. 'There's a bit more leeway on stage . . . and more still on television . . . But with film, meandering is out of the question.' The result is that the film has a brisker feel to it, something which worried one or two observers. David Thomson, writing in the *Independent on Sunday*, called him the Prose Laureate of Britain. He described the film as 'an effective but rather sly adaptation'. And yet when the Oscar nominations were announced, there was Bennett in the line-up for Best Adapted Screenplay. The fuss even led to a profile of Bennett in *Time* magazine.

Bennett was meant to be the subject of a profile by the *Independent* in March 1995, but that was before he spotted a reference to himself in the same newspaper as the 'winsome Alan Bennett'. The *Today* programme reported on 16 March that he rang up straight away and cancelled the appointment, saying: 'Win some, lose some.' Maybe he had just had a bad day. Then again, it was becoming clear that he would latch on to any excuse to cancel a media commitment. And yet what was he trying to do? If he so disliked the British press, why did he read what they wrote, and – more to the point – why did he still care? Was he trying to be his own censor? The spat prompted an article in the *Evening Standard* by Sarah Sands. One of Sands's sincerest opinions was her admiration for the way in which the *Daily Mail* scared its readers, a fact which she inadvertently shared with the computer system – and therefore every journalist – at the *Evening Standard* just before she went off to scare the readers (and probably the staff) of the *Daily Telegraph*. Sands effectively accused Bennett of hypocrisy, of benefiting from publicity while claiming to shy away from it. And yet, with the masochism of a true hack, she could not help applauding the way he did it. The piece was headlined: 'Alan Bennett: Don't You Just Love Him?'

Bennett sat out the Oscars ceremony, dining with Sir Alec and Lady Guinness. When the verdict was announced, and the film received just one Oscar, for Art Direction, he said that the Guinness caviar was better than any Oscar. No doubt he would have been genuinely uncomfortable amid the glitz and glamour of an Oscars awards ceremony, with his privacy being periodically encroached on by roaming reporters and camera crews. The Guinnesses were almost parental in their affection for him, delighting as much in his company as he did in theirs. There was further comfort in the success closer to home of *The Madness of King George*, which won three awards at the *Evening Standard* British Film Awards in 1996.

Bennett's trilogy of films to date makes up a small proportion of his work, but each shows a very different aspect of his writing craft. Where *A Private Function* was comedy at its broadest, with social issues providing the compost, *Prick Up Your Ears* was a daring attempt to side-step his own reputation. *The Madness of King George* meshed these two trends, combining farce and serious topics. In his next major project for television, the shadows seemed to be gaining on him.

20

Bennett pens TV child sex drama

The Abbey, Talking Heads 2, 1995–1998

In December 1995 the BBC screened Alan Bennett's third collaboration with the documentary maker Jonathan Stedall in the form of a religious counterfoil to their first joint project, *Dinner at Noon*. In March 1993 they had also made *Portrait or Bust*, a study of some of Bennett's favourite paintings in Leeds City Art Gallery. *The Abbey* was Bennett's personal tribute to Westminster Abbey. It was also a study of the thousands of people who passed through it each day, and of the many guides who tried to convey, in basic English, something of its majesty. In a sense it was a departure for Bennett, the quintessential observer of the British, since so many of the tourists who came to visit were from abroad. The five months he was there, from October 1994 to February 1995, were also a chance to revisit some of the characters who had peopled his dramas. There were Pitt, Fox, Burke and Sheridan from *The Madness of George III*. There was the memorial to A.E. Housman, at whose dedication Bennett would give an address on 17 September 1996. And there was the Chapel of St Benedict, where the subject of his never-completed thesis, Richard II, was believed to have sought spiritual strength in times of crisis.

Bennett was seen peering through a keyhole at the crowds, or tiptoeing over the thirteenth-century Cosmati pavement in his stock-inged feet, a luxury not extended to the average visitor. A few months after filming, he returned to record his voice-over. 'Undiscouraged, in they come. The tribes of Adidas and Nike and Reebok . . . There they go, back to their hotels in Bayswater,' he sighed, as the tourists filed out of the Abbey before evensong. 'A chance to put their feet up before they go off to *Cats*, or *The Phantom*, not quite as long-running as Westminster Abbey but still, all part of the heritage.' Bennett stood knee-deep among the Japanese tour guides, Canute-like. 'The pilgrims came in the early days. But pilgrims are simply tourists on their knees.' Perhaps the boys at nearby Westminster School – 'Even at 9.15 a.m., armoured in their careful languor' – were more familiar with his name. And when the beautiful voices of the choristers filled the air, he declared: 'It's moving to see boys of nine or ten doing something supremely well, with a seriousness and professionalism one normally thinks come with age.' As for the memorials to the entombed: 'For all the banners, it's just a lot of middle-aged men who have done well behind a desk: but then, most of life is, these days.'

The programme was received, as ever, with due rapture. Brian Viner of the *Mail on Sunday* gave it a rave review, while also revealing his own Bennett war scars. 'When I called him recently and said I was from the *Mail on Sunday*, Bennett quite literally let out a shriek before putting down the phone.' Viner was disappointed, but his appreciation was in no way dampened. Meanwhile, up in Clapham, there was more shrieking when Anne Davies was banned from the New Inn, Clapham's one and only pub. The ban came about when a rowdy drinking game went wrong and some glasses were smashed. 'I'm pleased. He should have barred me years ago,' Anne said in the *Mail on Sunday*. 'Now I don't have to go there and spend lots of money.' The veil of anonymity that had protected Bennett and Davies over the years was slipping. One 'pub regular' said: 'She's great company when she's sober, but she's bad news with a few whiskies inside her.' It was a view that the papers eagerly endorsed. On her own, it would have been no more than a squabble in a pub, but the combination of Anne's waywardness with Bennett's famous reserve was irresistible. It put a whole new spin on writing about the nation's teddy bear.

The mercurial Anne popped up again in 1996. This time, the story even appeared in the *Guardian*. 'Village Vandal Strikes Again To Fight Change', ran its headline on 30 April. Anne Davies was in hot water again. She had been arrested.

The fuss came about because a sign proclaiming, 'Clapham – Jewel of the Dales' had been defaced with red paint. Davies herself wasn't able to respond to press enquiries for a little while, as she was in police custody, but she was released within an hour without being charged. The following Monday the *Daily Express* presented the arrest as a victory for a whispering campaign 'which has split the Yorkshire Dales village where she lives and led to her arrest as an alleged vandal'. The *Express* may have been the first paper to point out her dislike of footwear. 'Bennett affectionately refers to his friend as "a reformed hippy" and her Bohemian attitude distinguishes her from many other residents. Standing barefoot as she served coffee to customers, she said: "I've been here six years and still feel like an outsider to some. I don't know why someone identified me as being responsible, but I suspect there was some kind of petty jealousy behind it." '

While gossip continued to rebound around the village, at least the press had feasted enough for the time being. That was until a journalist called Mary Greene turned up on Anne Davies's doorstep one morning and introduced herself as having once worked in the café. Davies believed her, and they had a friendly drink. As Davies talked, Mary Greene listened, and at some point must have ducked into the lavatory to make notes. Anne may have thought it was no more than a chance to catch up with an old colleague, but the fruits of their conversation – at least, Anne's contribution – appeared in the *Daily Mail*, again, on Saturday, 12 April 1997, under the gaudy headline 'The Playwright, His Lover, Her Boyfriend And . . . A Very Private Passion'.

It was a horrible piece of writing. Greene tried to make a joke in the first paragraph, suggesting that Bennett's mum might have tried to excuse him from being a good mixer with a note. ' "Alan can't do bonhomie today," she might have written, "because he's forgotten his kit." ' But there was worse to come.

According to Greene, Davies said: 'Alan is the most exciting, the most inventive, the most considerate, the most imaginative lover I've ever had. And I've had plenty.' Greene gets some things correct, striking the right note, for example, in her description of Davies as 'Dark, fiery, gipsyish – her Hungarian blood evident in her striking looks'. The next quote sounds reasonable too: 'He is gay, but he doesn't want to be gay. Which is sad . . . I was the only woman he'd ever been close to. I shook him up. I was just like an earthquake, turning his life upside down with kids and lovers and mess. He didn't know what hit him – but I did him a lot of good. Well, I never did him any harm.'

And how about the daubing? Davies confessed all to Greene: ' "I'll tell you now," she crows. "I did it. I have a few whiskies and I get vulnerable . . . and they wind me up." ' Mrs Christine Cass, presumably one of the 'they' referred to, is quoted as saying, 'My guess is he sent her up here to get her out of his way', and yet straight away she adds, 'but don't say I said so'. Which, of course, Mary Greene did. Luckily, Alan Bennett still had plenty of work to concentrate on, and to distract him.

In June 1996 Bennett joined forces with another young star of the British stage, Sam Mendes, for a new production of *Habeas Corpus* at Mendes's home base, the Donmar Warehouse in London's Covent Garden. It was roundly praised. The tape of *Talking Heads* was declared the most successful 'talking book' of all time, with UK sales of 115,000. *Writing Home* had also sold over 750,000 copies, an extraordinary number, when it was reissued in March 1997. The memorial address for Peter Cook was added, as well as the introduction to *The Madness of King George*. Bennett visited Holland, Venice, New York and various top-security prisons, whether for pleasure or to promote his books. There were also trips to Chichester, to perform *Talking Heads*. In his diaries, Bennett rages against the drab, leaden soullessness of John Major's England. New York always cheers him: its unselfconsciousness, its classlessness and its vibrant sense of democracy.

Each December or January, the publication of Bennett's diaries in the *London Review of Books* had become a longed-for annual event, an easy news story when the papers could cherry-pick Bennett's loves or, more often, hates and add their own commentary. The *Independent*, under the headline 'That nice Alan Bennett takes the gloves off for Tory politicians, the Queen Mother – and Dennis Potter', felt that it said much about the real Alan Bennett, who had written in the first edition of *Writing Home* that he wanted to be 'liked and thought a nice man'. By the time the *Evening Standard* writer Mark Jones (an inveterate title – bestower) had scanned the reissued *Writing Home* in February 1997, he had coined another nickname for Bennett. The bulk of the article was concerned with the 'Curmudgeon Laureate'. 'This traditional accolade goes to the man – it has to be a man, it seems – who does most to cheer us up by being incessantly bad-tempered about everything and everyone.

The CL is disdainful, despairing and dyspeptic. His words are like the bracing rasp of rough tweed in the soft paunch of modern manners. The V-neck sweater he never takes off is a permanent "up yours" to Johnny-come-lately politicians, modern artists and ancient adversaries. He thrives on vendettas, regales against publicity-seekers, then writes private diaries and intimate memoirs for instant serialisation.'

Jones reckoned that Bennett, being 'fundamentally nice and liberal . . . hates his own niceness and despises his lapses into self-deprecation'. And yet, Jones concluded, 'he can't stop us displaying our affection, however much it may hurt him'. Jones's tone was knowledgeable and appreciative, and at least the piece was witty.

From his soapbox, or his high horse, Bennett also took a much-needed swipe at Classic FM, which had been piping out treacly classical muzak since 1992. In his diary for 1996, which the *LRB* published in December, he described the station's estimated 4.7 million listeners as 'Saga louts'. Bennett, said the *Sunday Times* arts correspondent John Harlow, 'is the first weighty cultural commentator to condemn both the station and its listeners'. In February 1996 Bennett wrote: 'I loathe Classic FM more and more for its cosiness, its safety and its wholehearted endorsement of the post-Thatcher world, with medical insurance and Saga holidays rammed down your throat between every item.' But the trouble was, he kept listening. As with many of Bennett's beefs, he knows what irritates him, and yet he keeps returning to it to be irritated, like a man unable to stop scratching an itch. Harlow phoned Bennett to ask for more of his views and was met with the refrain, which probably crops up as often as Beethoven's Fifth Symphony does on Classic FM: 'I am putting the phone down now, very nicely. Goodbye, goodbye.'

In November 1997 Bennett published another first, this time with a comic novella. *The Clothes They Stood Up In* is vintage Bennett. Its plot represents a return to the surrealism of *The Old Crowd*, his 1979 collaboration with Lindsay Anderson, but this time there are no disconcerting cutaways, or muted sex scenes, or references to the films of Luis Buñel. It begins, if anything, more dramatically, not with a dinner party but with a burglary. The highbrow, opera-loving Ransomes come home from Covent Garden one night to find that their flat, in an ox-blood Edwardian block near Regent's Park, has been burgled. Nothing has been left: all the furniture, the carpets, the curtains – everything, even the toilet roll and paper holder, has gone. Suddenly, the Ransomes realise that they are being offered the chance to make a fresh start. 'They had transported this paraphernalia with them across thirty-two years of marriage to no purpose at all . . . and now at a stroke they were rid of the lot. Without quite knowing why . . . Mrs Ransome suddenly burst out singing.'

Mr Ransome eats sweet potato for the first time, and Mrs Ransome sits on a beanbag in front of an electric fire. Dusty, a slightly lumpen 'counsellor', distantly related to Julie Walters in *Say Something Happened* from *Objects of Affection*, rings on the doorbell to offer them help and reassurance. Mrs Ransome watches TV programmes like *Oprah* for the first time, and doesn't think much of them at first. She struggles with the language, trying to understand daytime TV argot, like Miss Ruddock in 'A Lady of Letters'. It intrigues her. These guests are baring their souls, and awful and vulgar though it is, she feels a distant bond with them that could not have existed before the burglary.

No sooner have the Ransomes settled into their new routine than the carpet is once again pulled from under their feet when they receive a letter instructing them to go to Rapid 'n' Reliant Removals 'n' Storage in Aylesbury, where they find, to their shock, that their entire house has been reconstructed, exactly as it was before. Thus *The Old Crowd* gives way to the final scene of *Enjoy*, and history is recreated. Their possessions are returned, and life is back to normal, except that a corner has been turned, and life can never be the same again. Instead of listening to Mozart all the time, Mr Ransome listens on headphones to a tape of the love-making noises of the man and woman who looked after their possessions for all those weeks. 'We have never hugged, Maurice,' says Mrs Ransome to her husband, who at the end of the story suffers a stroke and is taken to hospital. 'We must hug one another in the future.' And, sure enough, as death surrounds her husband with a sweep of the ward curtain, Mrs Ransome thinks to herself, 'Now, I can start.' It was a brittle, biting little story, but was it also a last post for Walter and Lilian Bennett, and a coded recognition that they and their memories were now gone for good? It was the sort of story that could have been prompted by the spring-cleaning consequent on the death of a parent.

In his introduction to volume one of *Talking Heads*, Bennett wrote dismissively of the suggestion that any of his subjects should be concerned with anything as 'topical' as child abuse – 'My instinct is generally to take flight in the opposite direction' – so he cannot have been too pleased with the headline 'Bennett Pens TV Child Sex Drama' which appeared in the *Sunday Times* on 10 May 1998. 'The mind of a paedophile is to be explored by Alan Bennett, the playwright, in a new drama for BBC television,' wrote Nicholas Hellen, the paper's media correspondent, in his trademark style of barely suppressed hysteria. 'Bennett, widely regarded as the voice of liberal middle-class values, has written an intimate monologue spoken by a middle-aged man convicted of the sexual abuse of a girl.'

The news article was the run-up to what turned out to be a further bout of publicity surrounding the second series of *Talking Heads*, which figured heavily in the BBC's autumn drama season. Bennett's introduction to the text of the second series is as teasing as ever. He first apologises for not having produced more, sooner, saying that if he had carried on writing at the time of the first series he could have written another half a dozen, 'but seeing the first lot produced with a measure of success made the next batch harder to do'. He protests that he kept putting them aside, and even kept them in a drawer for a year when they were nearly finished 'as I felt they were too gloomy to visit on the public'. The gloom, Bennett claimed, was not deliberate, nor was it that as he got older he took a grimmer view of the world. 'It's simply that, though I may sit down with the intention of writing something funny, it seldom comes out that way any more.' Which seems to amount to the same thing.

He also records his reactions to seeing the first series of *Talking Heads* appear as an A-level syllabus subject. Bennett writes that he received dozens of letters from candidates 'wanting a low-down on the text'. He divided the letters into serious enquiries and those who felt that 'writing to the author was a useful way of getting their homework done', but in almost all cases wrote back in what is now a familiar device with 'a postcard saying that their ideas about the monologues were as good as mine and they should treat me like a dead author, who was thus unavailable for comment'.

In the opening monologue, 'The Hand of God', Eileen Atkins plays a woman called Celia who runs an antiques shop. She parts with a seemingly minor work for a mere £100, only to find that the buyer was 'some young blood from Christie's' who had identified it as a

Michelangelo sketch for the hand of God on the Sistine Chapel ceiling. When the press pounce on the young man from Christie's for finding the Michelangelo sketch, he describes her emporium as a junk shop, a phrase that Celia can barely bring herself to pronounce.

In 'Miss Fozzard Finds Her Feet', Patricia Routledge plays a spinster who discovers that she can give pleasure to her middle-aged male chiropodist Mr Dunderdale by walking up and down on his back in a variety of footwear. Meanwhile, she tries to help her brother Bernard recover from his first stroke, and an Australian nurse called Mallory helps herself to whatever is left of Bernard's savings by persuading him to write out cheques to her at the same time as conducting a short affair with him. This ends when Mallory runs off, and Bernard suffers a second, more serious stroke. Mr Dunderdale, though, is prepared to pay for the services of Miss Fozzard's feet, and so the arrangement continues – almost a happy ending.

It is the third monologue, 'Playing Sandwiches', and starring David Haig, that made the *Sunday Times* prick up its ears, as it tells the wretched tale of a convicted paedophile, trying to make a new start as a park attendant, whose attempts to turn his back on his past are thwarted when he is befriended in the park by a single mum and her young daughter, whom he eventually rapes. 'Playing Sandwiches' was directed by Udayan Prasad, who besides directing the adaptation of Hanif Kureishi's novel *The Buddha of Suburbia* ('featuring full-frontal nudity', wrote Nicholas Hellen in shocked terms) also directed *102 Boulevard Haussmann*, in which the blatant use of bedsheets and nightclothes went unreported by the *Sunday Times*. 'I am repelled by the self-righteous morality of gaols,' wrote Bennett in his introduction to the published scripts, 'and their hierarchy of offences whereby murder and grievous bodily harm are thought of as respectable crimes and sexual offences are not.' It is a strange plea for clemency. Wilfred the paedophile may have been punished for his former crimes, and he may be a dutiful park attendant, even a friendly figure for a little girl and her mother, but he is a habitual reoffender who is unable to prevent himself striking again when temptation looms.

'The Outside Dog' was Julie Walters's second appearance in *Talking Heads* and was, if anything, even darker than 'Playing Sandwiches'. Serial killers were very much on the newspapers' panic agenda at the time. Rosemary West was sent to jail for life in November 1995 on ten murder convictions, and her husband Fred had hanged himself in his cell on New Year's Day in the same year. They had buried their victims under the patio at their house in Cromwell Street, Gloucester. The case also had an eerie echo in the northern soap opera *Brookside*, which saw the murder of Trevor Jordache in May 1993 and – almost two years later, in early 1995 – the discovery of his body under the garden patio. Walters plays a woman whose husband is suspected of a string of murders of local women. In the end, she is unable to prevent herself coming across the evidence herself, though it is left ambiguous as to whether she will denounce her husband. Despite Bennett's claimed immunity to topical themes, these two monologues both feel more rooted in the spirit of the times than most of Bennett's writing hitherto. Bennett swore it was accidental: maybe so, or maybe the writer and the times he lived in were coming together. Whatever the explanation, watching 'The Outside Dog' is a tense, hot and rather suffocating experience.

'Nights in the Garden of Spain' is partly a female version of *Me, I'm Afraid of Virginia Woolf*. In this oddly touching story, Penelope Wilton plays Rosemary, a woman who finds friendship, maybe even love, with her neighbour Fran. The friendship is conducted at a distance, though, as Fran has shocked the neighbourhood by being sent to prison for shooting her husband, a man who had been part of an enthusiastic group of local fetishists, roping in (quite literally) his own wife as well as Rosemary's husband Henry. But like Irene Ruddock in 'A Lady of Letters' in the first *Talking Heads* series, Fran's imprisonment is no obstacle to her having a soul-mate. The final fade-out reveals Rosemary, transported to Spain's Costa del Crime, mourning the death from cancer of her new friend, and despondently contemplating seeing out her days with her husband.

The final one of the six is another triumphant vignette for Thora Hird, playing a decade-older version of the woman she portrayed in 'A Cream Cracker under the Settee'. In 'Waiting for the Telegram', Hird, now in hospital and unlikely to emerge, looks back tearfully on her life, on the unconsummated passion she had for her fiancé who was killed in the Great War, and on the friendly male nurse who is himself swept away in the Great Plague of the late twentieth century, AIDS. Thora Hird won the Best Actress award in the 1999 BAFTA ceremony.

If the tone of *Talking Heads 2* is angrier, darker than the first series, the general tone of the introduction is more beleaguered than ever: wherever he looks, Bennett finds that standards are slipping. Antiques shops have been ruined by Christie's, Sotheby's and the *Antiques Road Show*. Department stores are not as elegant as they used to be, nor are Camden's shoe shops, or milk deliveries (formerly by horse and cart), or potpourri (once rather stylish), or housekeeping (these days rather scanty), or women's legs (no longer mottled), or the Vale of York (now 'prairified'), or women's prisons (deprived of educational resources), or the number 16 tram route (with flimsy houses replacing the decent old back-to-backs). And, of course, journalists are called in for a talking to as well: 'I find I now make no distinction between reporters from the *Daily Mail* or journalists from the *Guardian*: they are more like each other than they are ordinary human beings.' It all sounds rather desperate.

The programmes themselves were received with delight, not least at Oxford University, the university with the longest history of talking heads in the country. At sixty-four, as he approached the age when working men begin to think about retirement, Alan Bennett's contribution to English literature was about to be recognised – or at least offered recognition – in the highest terms. Bennett had already accepted the honour of a fellowship from his old college, Exeter, in 1987, but eleven years later came recognition on an altogether larger scale. On 17 November 1998 he wrote: 'Out of the blue, a letter comes from Oxford offering an honorary degree. This distinction is what Larkin called "the big one".' However, 'Murdoch's is not a name with which Oxford should have associated itself. So eventually I write back saying no and explaining why. Of course I am aware that writing (and publishing) this may be sneered at as showing off, and that if one does turn something down it's proper to keep quiet about it. But this refusal isn't for my own private satisfaction: Murdoch is a bully and should be stood up to publicly and so, however puny the gesture, it needs to be in the open.'

It was an extraordinary act of renunciation, and seemed to take his curmudgeonliness to new heights. After all, CBEs and the whole New Year's Honours List gong show were by now a slightly degraded currency, but turning down an honorary degree from Oxford was supremely maverick. If his parents had been alive they would never have forgiven him. This was the place where, in 1960, he had expected to spend the rest of his life. Could Rupert Murdoch really be blamed for discrediting the entire currency of academic awards? Was there not something about Oxford which even Murdoch could not pollute?

Perhaps the dons should have studied *Writing Home* more closely. The clue was there, in the index: 'Murdoch, Rupert: University of Oxford truckles to'. The problem was a chair. Specifically, it was the Rupert Murdoch Chair in Language and Communication, whose first incumbent was Professor Jean Aitchison. Bennett's indignation had been so great that when he was invited to a fund-raising dinner at Merton on 10 August 1990, he had turned it down. 'Perhaps they ought to approach Saddam Hussein to found a chair in Peace Studies,' he fumed in his letter of reply.

To Bennett, and any other Murdoch-allergics, Professor Aitchison was a defector. One look at the title of her 1981 book *Language Change: Progress or Decay?* would have been enough for them to conclude that her idea of academic study was to deconstruct a copy of Murdoch's *News of the World*. Her arrival at Oxford was Bennett's nightmare: his beloved alma mater sipping from the same cup as his ultimate bogeyman, the owner of the newspaper which, he felt, had chased Russell Harty into an early grave. No wonder he was angry.

And yet, hadn't Bennett's fightback started too late, now that millions of houses wore the Murdoch membership badge of a satellite dish, and no one laughed at cricketers on the telly wearing pyjamas? If Bennett were to conduct the same sort of ethical cleansing on all his professional contacts, he would probably never have been able to work with anyone again. 'Is there a little bit in the corner of your life? I know there is in mine.' There is, to some extent, a little bit in everyone's.

A week before Christmas, on 19 December 1998, Bennett was forced to receive another laureateship. This time it was the *Independent*'s 'Accidental Heroes of the Twentieth Century'. Bennett had improved his poll rating of 1994 and was now in there at number nineteen. The article was a short one, running in six shallow paragraphs across the page with a picture at the side showing Bennett looking like a suitably nonplussed don. The writer was much taken with one of Bennett's jokes from *Writing Home*: 'I get pleasure out of being able to do simple, practical jobs – replacing a fuse, changing a wheel, jump-starting a car – because they are not generally associated with a temperament like mine. I tend to put sexual intercourse in this category too.'

Next, the *Daily Express* – never one to let someone else's idea go uncopied – followed suit on 24 January 1998 when he was awarded the title of 'National Treasure No. 69' by the paper's gossip columnist, the pseudonymous William Hickey. Bennett, he told us, was now 'the Pepys of his day'. Which was a nice thought, though he then spoiled the effect by adding: 'He effortlessly elevates the most common of everyday speech to high literature and makes the factual humdrum as compulsive as John Grisham's fiction.' High praise indeed.

On 18 October 1998 the National Theatre released the results of a questionnaire in which 800 playwrights, actors, directors and arts critics voted on who they thought was the greatest playwright of the twentieth century. And the winner was . . . Arthur Miller. Harold Pinter came second. There was no place in the top twenty for Steven Berkoff, or David Mamet – or Alan Bennett. It was as if, in some sense, Bennett was still perceived as marginal: adored by many but still lacking the gravitas of the big hitters. Was it because his concerns were not seen as universal enough? Or possibly, as Miss Shepherd might have said, because Mr Bennett cannot resist making jokes?

21

The part of Alan Bennett will be
played by . . .

The Lady in the Van, Telling Tales, 1999–2001

The idea of turning *The Lady in the Van* into a stage play became a serious prospect in March 1999, when Bennett, Dame Maggie Smith and Nicholas Hytner approached the theatre producer Robert Fox. (One notes in passing that the producer of Edward Albee's *Who's Afraid of Virginia Woolf?* was finally getting to work with the writer of *Me, I'm Afraid of Virginia Woolf.*) This was to be Bennett's first original stage play since *The Madness of George III* in 1991, and he had been trying unsuccessfully to adapt his journal for it ever since. The production cost £400,000 to mount, but given the anticipation with which it was greeted, it seemed almost inappropriate to describe the play's backers, in the normal theatre terminology, as 'angels'. In the circumstances, anyone with a few thousand to spare would probably have invested them, Bennett being the nearest thing to blue chip that the London theatre has. Their faith was justified. It was announced that Maggie Smith was going to play the part of Miss Shepherd. The result was box-office bingo: before the press night, the play had taken £750,000 in advance box-office sales alone.

When Michael Ratcliffe interviewed Bennett for the *Observer* on 4 September 1994, he had briefly described Miss Shepherd's residency, and the success of Bennett's original prose version of *The Lady in the Van*. He knew at the time that Bennett thought it worth trying to dramatise the story, but that the project was stalled. 'There is one puzzle,' wrote Ratcliffe. 'The second most important character is Bennett himself, so who exactly, he will have to be asking, is that?'

Alongside a *Sunday Telegraph* profile of Bennett from January 1992 entitled 'Shy Observer Of The Bittersweet' was a cartoon drawn by Collet which featured one bespectacled character parting the stage curtains, and another bespectacled character looking on. Just in case there was any confusion, the observer's head was stamped with the words 'Alan Bennett'. Two Alan Bennetts. It was just such a trick that Bennett produced seven years later.

During his years with Miss Shepherd, Bennett had felt there were two versions of Alan Bennett operating side by side. One was the Alan Bennett who came into daily contact with the smelly old lady. The other was Alan Bennett the writer, looking on, wondering how he could exploit this promising situation for his own literary benefit. For his stage version of *The Lady in the Van*, the two Alans were played by two actors, Nicholas Farrell and Kevin McNally. 'I'm the Alan with slightly more conscience,' said Farrell to Kate Bassett of the *Daily Telegraph*, 'and Kevin's has a bit more ruthless creativity.'

Nicholas Farrell's Bennett, Bennett the man, was the resident of Camden, fighting a heroic battle with Camden Council against encroachments on civil liberty like single yellow lines, parking meters and residents' parking. He was also trying to prevent a deranged spinster from suffering the constant persecution of being harried from one spot to another because she didn't fit the profile that Camden wanted, of nice people in proper jobs with secure sources of income and properly planned domestic arrangements. Kevin McNally's Bennett, on the other hand, is the Bennett who, soon after she comes to rest like Noah's Ark on the top of Mount Ararat, begins to see a literary character emerging in his drive, and who, with a combination of voyeurism and exploitativeness, wants to extract as much of her eccentricity as he can. He thinks there could be a book in this, and he takes careful notes of her strange behaviour, which the first Alan criticises when he isn't clearing up Miss Shepherd's mess.

Bennett's play charts a fairly orthodox passage through his previously published account of the unlikely marriage of Mr Bennett and Miss

S. His concern for Miss S is, to some extent, a foil for his inability to care for his failing mother, but when Bennett attempts to suggest a deeper tragedy at work in Miss Shepherd's life, he fails to convince. Despite living alongside each other for so many years, Bennett was only ever allowed to glimpse Miss Shepherd from the margin. Bennett may be famously private, but compared with Miss Shepherd he is a rank self-publicist. Her steadfast non-disclosure may have made good occasional diary entries, but Bennett is unable to grasp her inner core, and so is compelled – perhaps for the first time since Julie Walters's unsuccessful porn actress – to 'make up' much of her character. Miss Shepherd's over-regard for toilet matters may be a Bennett joke to which he has often returned, but having so little else to clutch on to Bennett can hardly leave it alone, and any play that spends this long in the lavatory begins to feel airless after a while. It also didn't help that the Alan Bennetts on stage made Bennett sound more effete than he is in reality.

The play opened at the Queen's Theatre on 19 November 1999. Nicholas Hytner, the boy-wonder director, was showered with praise, but most of the wow factor went to Dame Maggie, whose performance as the mad lady sent some critics into a spin. It was as if, having made the point himself that the play was exploitative, Bennett had eluded further criticism. Nicholas Farrell was on stage to voice our own doubts about the morality of this exercise, though no one is on stage to ask if it is an act of vanity for a playwright to write two parts for himself, and whether the Miss Shepherd story was like an old van which had been pushed too far. No one suggested that, since duality and ambivalence are so much parts of the human condition, it was simplistic and stylised to have two Alan Bennetts on stage. No critic thought it distasteful to see a predominantly middle-class, middle-aged audience – many of them probably from somewhere near Camden itself – laughing their heads off at an elderly, infirm, mentally sick woman whom few would have allowed anywhere near them, let alone in their driveways. When Charles Spencer said of *The Madness of George III*, 'In less sensitive hands one could imagine the play becoming a distasteful spectacle in which the audience, like seventeenth-century visitors to Bedlam, are invited to laugh at lunacy', he had unwittingly predicted the overall tone of Bennett's next play. Of course, Miss Shepherd herself was dead and so could not be hurt. And, of course, Bennett had been very kind to her, and perhaps he deserved to get something in return. But did the mere fact of her death free him to write this type of a play?

There were other questions of taste too. For one thing he had released the details of his address to an entire theatre audience, six nights a week. How did the other residents of his street feel about that?

Among the critics, opinion was again split. Writing in the *Daily Telegraph* (in December, mark you), Charles Spencer's verdict was quite clear. 'This was, without doubt, the best new play of the year,' he said. Nicholas de Jongh in the *Evening Standard* begged to differ: 'a soufflé, all dressed up to reveal the meal it is not,' he wrote. Voicing a criticism not heard since *Forty Years On*, his objection was that we were back to a 'revue-style format'. All in all, it was 'a display, not a play', culled from an inadequate thirty-page diary entry.

In the *Guardian*, *London Review of Books* old girl Susannah Clapp acknowledged that 'There's some blurring round the edges' and called Hytner's production 'over-perky', with some 'sketchily written characters – floridly pretentious neighbours and a drab social worker'. But at the centre, she said, referring to the two Bennetts, 'are a further pair of brilliant and telling impersonations'.

By the time of the Saturday matinée on 27 November 1999, Nicholas Farrell's wife was in labour, and Farrell had no option but to duck out. The theatre manager walked to the centre of the stage before the play started and began by saying that he had an apology to make. 'Nicholas Farrell will be unable to perform the role of Alan Bennett today, as his wife is having a baby.' There was a concerned hum from the assembled theatre-goers. 'However, the part of Alan Bennett will be played by . . .' – a slight pause – 'Alan Bennett.' Delight and smiles all round. Bennett referred to the script while playing the part, but few penalised him for that. It was for the *Daily Telegraph* diarist to note that: 'Some would say Alan Bennett has been impersonating himself ever since he first came to public attention. But never quite so obviously as at Saturday's matinée.'

Another set of theatre-goers who enjoyed the play were Prince Charles and Camilla Parker-Bowles, who came to see it on 17 January 2000. Bennett recorded that whereas normally the presence of royalty 'is guaranteed to put a frost on the audience', Prince Charles is one of the few royals who 'actually laughs, and loudly too', so that 'gets the audience going'.

In December 1999 Bennett's short story 'Father! Father! Burning Bright', which had grown up around the TV play *Intensive Care,* was published in the *London Review of Books*. In a note, Bennett said how he had 'put it away in a drawer in 1982 where it has remained ever since. I've dusted it off and publish it now, I suppose, as part of an effort to slim down my *Nachlass* and generally tidy up.' *Nachlass*, in German, means 'unpublished works', but it also has a slightly morbid sense of clearing the shelves, or of putting one's affairs in order.

In the September 1999 issue of the *London Review of Books* it was announced, tersely, that 'Alan Bennett is working on a series of autobiographical sketches to be called "Untold Stories".' When these were broadcast on BBC Television in November 2000 they had mutated into ten and were known, more teasingly, as *Telling Tales*. Though the setting could not have been simpler – it was a series of single takes of Bennett in a head-shot – two directors were used, reuniting him with different aspects of his working life: Patrick Garland (*On the Margin*, *Forty Years On*, *Getting On* and *Talking Heads 2*) and Tristram Powell (*Talking Heads 1* and *2*). This was Bennett's *Phantom Menace*, the prequel to his subsequent dramas, which foregrounded the reader in the writer's pre-, mid- and post-war Leeds. Each monologue was a slab of autobiography, anywhere in length from eleven to fourteen minutes, in which Bennett discussed in forensic detail aspects of his earliest years. As the camera moved from take to take, slowly a larger and larger area of the wall behind him and the room around him came into shot. His memories were almost shockingly fresh, and the emotion with which he talked about his parents revealed a more tender side than he had ever chosen to reveal before. It was, in several senses, vintage Bennett, talking about one of his favourite periods, when he had hardly impinged on the world at all, but when his parents – happy, laughing and, most important, *there* – impinged on him. This was *Talking Heads*, but with a twist. There was no dramatic pretence here, no characterisation, and yet the intensity of feeling was highly charged, and each tale somehow never ended where it might have been expected to settle. The title cleverly alluded to what might have been some qualms Bennett had about discussing other people – not a problem he had struggled with too violently in the past – and yet, with the exception of his brother, every person he mentioned, in all ten programmes, was now dead.

Bennett's 2000 diary records the loss of some more good friends.

Gielgud died on 21 May, prompting some affectionate reminiscences which he had decided not to vouchsafe to 'various programmes, including the *Nine O'Clock News*'. Bennett noted that an *Omnibus* tribute programme a few days later contained no reference to *Forty Years On*: an extraordinary oversight, and perhaps an indication of further dumbing down at the Beeb. And then in August there was more sad news with the death of Sir Alec Guinness, whom Bennett had seen only two days before he died. People, he wrote, kept ringing up to comfort him. 'It's like being consoled for the destruction of a view or the disappearance of a part of the landscape.' Only a few months later, Bennett was noting the death of Guinness's wife for sixty years, Merula Salaman. Meanwhile, Bennett was still cycling grumpily into central London, still swimming in friends' pools, still complaining about this or that programme on the telly, and still taking sandwiches with him as he wandered around the country, intent on exploring Britain's shrinking assortment of rural treasures, and still flitting over to New York, where he notices on the faces of New Yorkers 'that sense of fun and occasion so seldom generated in London except when licensed by the passage of royalty'.

Accolades continued to rain down, unwanted and frequently uncollected. Bennett became one of the most popular voices on Radio 4's impressionists' topical comedy show, *Dead Ringers*. The sketches, written by Nev Fountain and spoken by Chris Nallon, usually began: 'I was taking a pot of Earl Grey with Thora Hird . . .' Bennett had suffered a similar treatment at the hands of the *Spitting Image* puppeteers some years earlier, though this time the monologue rapidly went off the rails as Thora revealed to Bennett how she had joined a 1980s rock band, or assassinated President Kennedy, or bought some tabs of Ecstasy in a club. Though it played on a very hackneyed and one-dimensional view of Alan Bennett, and one that he simply did not fit, the combination of Bennett's tweeness and Dame Thora's unexpected slide into surreal or psychotic behaviour always drew gales of laughter from the studio audience.

Then, in January 2001, Bennett was presented with a Lifetime's Achievement award at the British Comedy Awards. These days Bennett is touchy about the sweep of such awards, regarding them as almost tantamount to being measured up for a coffin. He accepted the award, though he didn't collect it in person, preferring to send Nigel, now Sir Nigel, Hawthorne. It was, in a way, a very British version of the furore created by Marlon Brando at the Oscars ceremony in 1972 when Sasheen Littlefeather stood up in his place to collect his Oscar (awarded for *The Godfather*) and then made a speech about the treatment of American Indians. Littlefeather, whose real name was Maria Cruz, was listened to in angry silence by the Academy, whereas Hawthorne was heckled by the actress and writer Caroline Aherne, who was known by the tabloids to have a flair for drinking. But it was a typically quirky gesture from a man whose penchant for such gestures remained as strong as ever.

On 16 November 2000, an article in the *Daily Telegraph* media section listed some of the most favoured names to take over the post of editor of Condé Nast's *World of Interiors* magazine. One of them, the magazine's deputy editor and – it added casually – 'the boyfriend of Alan Bennett', was called Rupert Thomas. On 23 January 2001 Rupert Thomas was officially appointed *WI*'s editor, and was interviewed in the *Independent*. The article quietly revealed that he lived in Camden Town 'with his partner, the playwright Alan Bennett'. Thomas and Bennett had been together for several years after his relationship with Anne Davies ended, though Bennett and Davies remained extremely close. Thomas's first specific appearance in the *LRB* diaries was through a casual remark on 3 January 1996, when he was assigned the letter 'R', formerly reserved for Russell Harty. Thomas, thirty-four, had a degree from the Courtauld Institute, and was a lecturer at the Winchester College of Art. He is also the co-author with Eglé Salvy of *Antique and Flea Markets of London and Paris*. He is, of course, a respected design journalist and not a Wapping hack. But what an exquisite and wholly appropriate irony that Bennett should end up sharing his own world of interiors with a man who was quite comfortable in the world of glossy – albeit 'glacially stylish', to quote the *Telegraph* – magazines.

What Bennett does next remains to be seen. But the sincerity, combined, of course, with the subtlety of *Telling Tales* is not a bad place to leave him for the time being. In 1978 Nicholas Wapshott described Bennett as 'a model Englishman, at once bluntly straightforward and reserved; enthusiastic yet difficult to impress; a private person who loves to perform; holding strong views on everything but with no logical framework; a hard-working professional who likes to make out that he is merely a lucky amateur'. And in 1984 he spoke for himself in the

Observer when he said: 'I'd rather the public have an image and not quite fit it. It'll do to play with. That way, you're free.'

One of Bennett's few public appearances of recent years came on 8 August 2000 when he agreed to be winkled out of seclusion for the launch of Humphrey Carpenter's book *That Was Satire That Was*. The scene for the symposium was the Cottesloe Theatre on London's South Bank, which was set for the National Theatre's production of Arthur Miller's play *All My Sons*. As the distinguished former satirist, now sixty-six, made his way gingerly down the steps at the rear of the stage, brushing fronds of foliage out of his face, a warm and appreciative burst of applause swelled the room. It was clear that most people were here not to refine their definitions of satire but simply because they wanted to see Bennett in the flesh. And Bennett, faced with an audience of readers, play-goers and admirers, rather than newspaper journalists or potential biographers (although there was at least one that night), seemed as relaxed and happy to chat as ever. The old anecdotes were requested, and then dutifully rolled out. Bennett claimed to have some difficulty in remembering some of them, but once he got into the swing of it there was no stopping him. If his confidence had relied on the warm glows on the faces of the audience, he could have been there for hours. It might even have been what he used to refer to as one of his 'our Alan' performances. As it was, he and Carpenter chatted for about forty minutes, and then took several questions – further requests for old anecdotes, mostly – from the floor. For an hour, he didn't even touch his glass of water. And at the end, the cherished figure retraced his steps to the back of the theatre, walked through the door and was gone. And everyone stood up, put on their jackets and went home happy.

Bennett had given away almost nothing about himself, and yet he had entertained a room full of people. No one had attempted to pin him down too hard about his writing, or about his characters, and he had flourished. Forty years on from *Beyond the Fringe*, away from journalists and prying lenses, he had given the people what they wanted, which was how to seem like Alan Bennett. If some bright spark had thought to bring a few boxes of the British Library's literary chocolate bars, they could have shifted a lorry-load that night.

Postscript

The Futile Pursuit

In 1998 I wrote to Alan Bennett to ask if I could interview him for a book which I had been commissioned to write on the subject of two of my favourite comedians, Peter Cook and Dudley Moore. I received a polite, handwritten note on a small slip of paper two days later suggesting that he didn't really do interviews, but that if I posted a few questions to him he would try to answer them if he felt he had something to say. Encouraged, I agonised for several months over the wording, and then posted half a dozen questions. He never really replied, but when, some months later, I sent him a copy of the book, I was delighted to receive another friendly note from him saying how much he had enjoyed it, especially, he said, the somewhat poignant final chapter in which I had flown to Los Angeles in a vain attempt to meet Dudley Moore. It seemed a suitably friendly note on which to close our brief correspondence.

Some weeks after that, I was approached by another publisher and asked whether I would consider writing a biography of Alan Bennett. I pondered the wisdom of endangering what had seemed, until then, an almost friendly relationship with such a famously retiring figure, but eventually I plucked up the courage to write to him.

Again, two days letter a small slip of paper arrived. The tone was not hostile, but it left me with the clear impression that Bennett was flatly opposed to a biography, and anyway that there was something of a queue. With the myopia of naivety and optimism, I interpreted this as his way of leaving the door ajar, or at best of not slamming it shut on my foot. Of course he would like me, I told myself. I was a fan of his work. Besides, I was a keen cyclist: we'd get on fine, if and when we eventually met. I signed the contract and sent it back to the publishers.

I started swotting up on the plays and TV films which I'd not seen, and then I sent out my first letter, to Mary-Kay Wilmers, editor of the *London Review of Books* and one of Bennett's best friends.

Her reply was not as prompt as Alan Bennett's, but more emphatic. She wrote that she took a pretty dim view of biographies of living people, and so was unable to help me. Several other letters started arriving that made similar points. We'd love to talk to you if it's authorised, they said: can't wait, lovely man, lots of happy memories. But if it isn't authorised . . . sorry. At first it was a trickle, then a flood. I had a vision of dozens of elderly actors, some of them with only months to live, raising themselves up in their beds to make the effort to write just one more letter, to assure me that I couldn't talk to them.

I spoke to a few authors who had written authorised biographies. Don't do it, they said. Authorised biographies are a nightmare. Just think of all those hours of original interview material, and all those personal journals that no one has ever seen, to say nothing of the spouses, siblings and children who all want to talk to you to make sure that they come out of it well. And when I checked to see if they were laughing at me, they swore they weren't.

Whenever I spoke to any of my friends, the subject of the Bennett book tended to come up. Their response was always the same. 'That sounds interesting,' they would say. 'Have you spoken to him yet?' It was as if, in their eyes, I needed only to reach out for the phone, ring up and say, 'Alan, hi, I'm writing your biography. Can we have a chat?' And within minutes the kettle would be on, the pot warming and the teacakes out. No, I said patiently, it's not quite as easy as that. And yet deep down I knew that they were right. If I wasn't talking to him, what was I doing writing a book about him?

My wife, as usual, spoke the truth. It was no wonder that I was making no headway, she said. Alan Bennett didn't know who I was. Barring an inarticulately shouted greeting during a heavy shower of rain one dark night fifteen years earlier, which I vividly recalled but which he could not possibly have remembered, and just because he had been momentarily entertained by my *Pete & Dud* book, there was no reason why he should trust me. My only chance was to make contact with someone who could persuade him of my bona fides. So one day, early in the year 2000, on the premise that I needed to purchase one or two back copies, I cycled to the offices of the *London Review of Books*.

Would it have helped my case more if I hadn't stuttered quite so much? No. What would have helped would have been a signed letter from Alan Bennett introducing me as his official biographer and saying that he had no objection to anyone talking about him, but I knew and Ms Wilmers knew that I didn't have that. Dejected, I walked away empty-handed.

Meanwhile, the steady drizzle of refusal letters puddled my doormat every morning, and I could see a pained, beseeching look on the face of the postman, urging me to stop writing to people. At one point I convinced myself that I had received refusals from more people than I had originally written to, but maybe paranoia was taking over. Having written at the start of this book that I wasn't taking Bennett's refusal in 1986 to talk to me personally, I now realised that I couldn't help it: for all the worst possible reasons, I was taking it extremely personally. Once again, I tried to find someone to mediate on my behalf. Was there one person I could turn to, someone even closer to Bennett than Mary-Kay Wilmers? Well, it had to be worth a try. I rang the Arbutus House bed and breakfast in Clapham, North Yorkshire, and booked a family room for one night. At least they returned my call.

I drove up to Leeds on my own and got lost at every junction in its horrendous one-way system. Briefly emerging on to a section of road that hadn't been carved into an urban motorway, I met some students in Halliday Place who had vaguely heard that the house which now contained their vast collection of videos and computer games had once been occupied by Alan Bennett. I nosed round the Gilpins too, and various other surviving outcrops of pre-war Leeds like Upper Armley Road Library. I also spent two fascinating days reading back copies of the Bennett school magazine, *The Owlet*, in Leeds Central Reference Library, interrupting my studies to drive to the *Yorkshire Post* for an interesting root around the library. Then I set off for Leeds Station to collect my wife and children.

We drove along the edge of the Dales. Bennett always said that when he travelled north he could feel the tension lift from him, but as we neared his parents' dream cottage I found it was having the opposite effect on me. We spent one night in Settle and visited Russell Harty's grave in Giggleswick. Then we drove to Clapham. The village was, pretty much, as the newspaper reports described it. We noted Anne's Café, but went first for a walk up to Ingleborough Nook. We made it as far as the famously deep pothole of Gaping Gill, where it started to rain. There, the Bradford Potholing Club did not endear themselves to us by refusing to let our children – then aged three and one – have so much as a glass of water. Then, finally, we returned, carrying our sleeping children over the slippery rocks, and sought out Anne's Café. Anne herself emerged, looking sleepy but unmistakable. It was mid-afternoon and she was, of course, barefooted and smoking. She immediately took to our children, and displayed her famously relaxed attitude by urging their fretful father not to fuss so much as they climbed over the tables. We chatted about the walk, and the weather, and the shameful xenophobia of the Bradford potholers. Then she asked us what we were doing. I took a deep breath and, feeling not unlike a potholer myself, plunged in.

As I talked, for the first time in months I could feel the weight slipping from my shoulders. I didn't apologise for sounding emotional. I knew that, whatever happened, I had done the right thing by coming to see Anne. At least she was giving me the hearing I thought I deserved, and she seemed just as sympathetic as the media profiles had claimed. She listened to my tale of angst, and then she said, 'Well obviously he doesn't want to talk to you. He doesn't know you.' Just as my wife had said. 'You should come up when he's here. He lives next door.' I knew that, of course. 'Come up next weekend, and I'll introduce you.' I couldn't, I said; he won't talk to me. 'He might not,' she said. 'We can only try.' I tried to refuse again, for politeness' sake, but she was having none of that. 'Look,' she said, 'if you don't want to, don't, but the offer's there.' I began to wonder if it might be possible: perhaps at last I was about to achieve the breakthrough I so desperately sought. I even started fantasising about a new line to go on the cover: 'Written with the reluctant compliance of Alan Bennett'. I knew it was my last chance. Wife, children and I went back to our B&B and walked across Malham Gorge. The scenery was awe-inspiring, yet gentle: cows wandered over to us, offering unsolicited friendship. On the way back we even allowed ourselves the rare indulgence of a brasserie meal at the Devonshire Arms, Bolton Abbey. They were posh but friendly, and they didn't seem to mind when Fergus accidentally smashed an ice-cream goblet, for which I was very grateful.

And so I set off again, the following weekend, alone. The train was delayed, of course (broken rail outside Doncaster), and I sat stewing for a further two hours, my chest once again rigid with tension as I weighed up the possibilities. As I saw it, there were two possible outcomes. Either (and more likely) it would all end in ignominious failure, or, at best, Bennett would half-open his door and listen with a long-suffering expression as I blurted out a less halting version of the speech I had tried to make to Mary-Kay Wilmers on the subject of media intrusion, namely that if for any reason he was uneasy about the book, well, he shouldn't be.

Anne collected me from Clapham station and could not have been friendlier all weekend, introducing me to some of her sons and being very hospitable. I also met her boyfriend Rob, with his stonewall-builder's hands, and the three of us visited the pub together, and regulars said what a nice man that Mr Bennett was, and yet how very private too – had I noticed that? And I nodded and said, funnily enough, I had.

Eventually, several hours and an awful lot of drinks later, I asked Anne if she felt there might be any chance that Mr Bennett might want to talk to me. Telling me to wait in my room, she went next door. She came back a few minutes later. The answer, it seemed, was no. Not 'No, thanks' or 'No, not at this particular moment.' Just no. And it occurred to me, not for the first time, that, as Alan Bennett's biographer, I should have known that that was what he would say.

Later that evening, as a favour to Anne, whose driving might by now have been a matter of concern to the North Yorkshire police, I drove some of her son's friends in her large car – via the kerb, but only once – to a cold, damp rave in the middle of a moor. The people appeared friendly and chatty, and seemed not to have seen each other since the last cold, damp rave the previous weekend. When I told them what I was doing up there they looked interested, and then someone said: 'Have you met him?' And I looked defensive and said: 'Er, no.' And someone else said: 'Well, of course he won't want to talk to you. You're a reporter.' And I said, 'No, I'm not, I'm an author.' And she said:

'But you write for the papers.' 'Well,' I said, 'not as a reporter; as a comedy critic.' 'Well, anyway,' she said with a shrug, 'you're all the same.' 'No, we're not,' I said. 'I do not write for the *News of the World*.' 'Same difference,' she said.

And I wanted to say: 'Look, we are not the same. You might as well say that Anne's Café is the same as McDonald's since they both serve hot food.' But I didn't say anything. After all, had not Alan Bennett himself written in his introduction to *Talking Heads 2* that he no longer made any distinction between the *Guardian* and the *Daily Mail*?

At the same time, I was fighting hard to stifle some sense of indignation. Was he not at least curious to hear my side of the story? Had he really been through the mill so many times that he just didn't care what anyone wrote?

After an uneasy night's sleep I woke up early the next morning. The house was silent, so I made myself a coffee and went and sat in the back garden. I was still thinking of fresh ways of defending my approach. If anything, I felt it was cowardly for a writer to wait until someone was dead, and then, while the body was still warm, rush into print with every lurid story they had gathered. (Lurid? Alan Bennett? So far as that was concerned, staring out of a Camden window was about as lurid as it got.) Wasn't it more courageous to let the subject answer for himself? He had continued to talk to journalists even after the *New Yorker* interview in 1993. Why not me? And as I sat there, mulling over all this, I saw a branch tremble above the low wall that divided the two gardens, and there, just a few feet away from me, holding a small camera and training it on the rear of the little cottage, which his parents moved into in 1966, was Alan Bennett.

Slowly I rose to my feet. I waited for a second or two, sure that he must notice me. He did seem like a man who had thrown away the cares of the south, a respectable elderly gent taking a modest pride in his garden. And as I stood there, with the first stirrings of speech still gathering at the back of my throat, he suddenly looked to his left – like Guy Burgess, a part of him remaining 'watchful and alert', even here in Yorkshire. And without a word, a gesture, or a nod – apparently without even any movement – suddenly he had vanished. I was left holding a mug, with the words 'Good morning' still forming on my lips.

A few seconds later I heard a door slam, and events rapidly turned farcical, as if we had gone from *The Old Country* to *Habeas Corpus* within seconds. I crossed through Anne's house to the front door and walked out on to the road. He was getting into a car. Not only that: he was getting away. I took a few steps towards the car, and in a voice that may have been just shrill enough to disturb the Sunday-morning calm of that little village exclaimed: 'I'm not trying to be difficult.' As I did so, Bennett's expression seemed to undergo a minor convulsion. I just caught the outer husk of the letter 'N' – as in 'No', I am forced to assume, rather than 'Nice idea' – and then he drove off. I briefly considered trying to race after the car, or cutting across the lovely babbling stream and spread-eagling myself across the bonnet as it turned left outside the Old Manor House, but reason soon returned to me. This was Yorkshire, after all. I thought of the balding *Daily Mail* reporter, after the Anne Davies story broke in 1993, calling through the letterbox: 'I don't want to make your life a misery.' At the time I had thought: What an idiot you are. What an incredibly stupid, pathetic thing to do. But that was me, now, give or take a receding hairline, frustrated and foiled by Bennett's vanishing act, doing a rather odd impression of someone trying not to make his life a misery.

I went back inside to Anne, and rather plaintively said goodbye to her, and thanked her for trying, and apologised again, and wrote her next-door neighbour a note which he may or may not have read on his return, in which I apologised for disturbing him, and assured him that I hadn't been staking him out, and expressed the sincere hope that the whole matter had upset me more than him. And I decided that when the book came out, I would conceal a stealthy dedication to Anne, perhaps in the postscript, to thank her for trusting me, or at least for letting me talk. And then, with my stomach churning and my chest tight with anxiety, and praying that the broken rail outside Doncaster had been fixed, I took a series of trains back south again, during which I read very few pages of *Writing Home*, and stared out of the window a lot. And if I ever wrote another book, I thought to myself, I should set myself an easier target. I began to think of possible titles: one that suggested itself was 'Several Long Intimate Chats with J.D. Salinger'. I arrived in London several hours later, knowing that that really was the end of my story. There was no alternative now but to write the book.

Acknowledgements

I am grateful to the following people who agreed to speak to me, whether specifically about Alan Bennett or merely for background: Jonathan Miller, John Bassett, Roland McLeod, Sydney Lotterby, Stuart Burge, Bishop Eric Kemp, Bill Mitchell, Philip French, Humphrey Carpenter and Stephen Schiff. Thanks also to the following people and institutions, which were enormously helpful: Gavin Henderson of the West Yorkshire Archive Service, Julia Chadwick of Exeter College Library, James Codd of the BBC Written Archive, Dick Fiddy and Kathleen Dixon of the British Film Institute, Louise Ray of the National Theatre Archive, Eric Roberts of the *Yorkshire Post*, the Associated Newspapers Library, the British Library, the Family Records Office, the National Sound Archive, the Bodleian Library, the British Newspaper Library, Colin McLaughlin of the National Library of Scotland, Colin Speakman of the Yorkshire Dales Society, Terry Fletcher of *The Dalesman*, Jeremy Mackrell of the Diocese of Bradford, Mr and Mrs David Kingsley of Arbutus House B&B, Clapham, Jo Lockhart of the Shakespeare Birthplace Trust, Chris Campbell of the British Council, Richard Mangan of Mander & Mitchenson, Andrew Spreckley of the AQA examinations board and Geoff Schofield of the Royal Grammar School, Guildford.

Thanks also to Graham McCann, Ronald Bergan, Matt Wolf, Tom

Sutcliffe, Lisa Martland, Iris Hunter, Karin Mochan, Tony Marshall, Dominic Cotton and Harry Pye. For spiritual uplift, unsolicited thanks go to Walter Becker, Donald Fagen, Paddy McAloon and Ian MacDonald.

Among the inner circle, thanks to Lindsay Symons of Headline Book Publishing, and to Mal Peachey of Essential Books, whose idea this was in the first place. Thanks, finally and most personally, to my children Fergus and Edie, without whose interruptions this book would have been written much sooner, and to my wife Esther Selsdon (whose father, incidentally, *did* have a chain of dry-cleaners) without whose support and advice it might never have been written at all.

The author wishes to thank the following (dead or alive), extracts of whose articles or other publications have been cited: Baz Bamigboye, John Barber, Godfrey Barker, Julian Barnes, Kate Bassett, Michael Billington, Mark Boxer, Alan Brien, Susannah Clapp, Alan Clark, Alistair Cooke, Peter Cooke, Terry Coleman, Michael Coveney, Mary Crozier, W. A. Darlington, Sean Day-Lewis, Nicholas de Jongh, James Delingpole, William Douglas-home, Kenneth Eastaugh, Sydney Edwards, John Ennis, Daniel Farson, Margaret Forwood, Michael Frayn, Hugh Freeman, Sean French, Richard Gott, Mary Greene, John Gross, John Haffenden, Alex Hamilton, John Harlow, Russell Harty, Hugh Hebert, Nicholas Hellen, Alfred Hickling, Michael Hickling, Andrew Hislop, John Higgins, Philip Hope-Wallace, Richard Ingrams, Ian Jack, D. A. N. Jones, Mark Jones, Herbert Kretzmer, Hanif Kureishi, Richard Last, Mark Lawson, Bernard Levin, Jeremy Lewis, Peter Lewis, Steve Lohr, Fiona MacCarthy, John McEntee, Barbara McMahon, Frank Marcus, Adam Mars-Jones, Blake Morrison, James Murray, Charles Nevin, Benedict Nightingale, Barry Norman, Jim Oldfield, Charles Osborne, Michael Owen, Jill Parkin, Peter Paterson, John Peter, Thompson Prentice, Michael Ratcliffe, Michael Redgrave, Gillian Reynolds, Stanley Reynolds, Frank Rich, Sarah Sands, Rosemary Say, Stephen Schiff, Jennifer Selway, Charles Spencer, John Stevenson, Tom Sutcliffe, Paul Taylor, Howard Tabuman, James Thomas, David Thomson, Stephen Thompson, Jack Tinker, Kenneth Tynan, Shaun Usher, Paul Vallely, Brian Viner, Alexander Walker, John Walker, Nicholas Wapshott, Irving Wardle, Keith Waterhouse, Richard Watts, John Wells, Francis Wheen, John Woodcock.

The extracts mentioned above appeared in the following publications: *Guardian, Observer, Daily Express, Sunday Express, Daily Star, Daily Mail, Mail on Sunday, Evening Standard, Daily Telegraph, Sunday Telegraph, Independent, Independent on Sunday, Mirror, Sunday Mirror, The Times, Sunday Times, Sun, News of the World, Yorkshire Post, Reynolds News, New York Times, New Yorker, New York Post, International Herald Tribune, New Statesman, Spectator, Listener, Country Life, Auden Society Newsletter, Harpers & Queen, British Journal of Psychiatry.*

Sources

PRIMARY WORKS
Plays (theatre)

1968 *Forty Years On*. Apollo Theatre, London, directed by Patrick Garland

1971 *Getting On*. Queen's Theatre, London, directed by Patrick Garland

1973 *Habeas Corpus*. Lyric Theatre, London, directed by Ronald Eyre

1975 *Habeas Corpus*. Martin Beck Theater, New York

1977 *The Old Country*. Queen's Theatre, London, directed by Clifford Williams

1980 *Enjoy*. Vaudeville Theatre, London, directed by Ronald Eyre

1986 *Kafka's Dick*. Royal Court Theatre, London, directed by Richard Eyre

1988 *Single Spies – An Englishman Abroad* (also director) and *A Question of Attribution* (also actor) National Theatre; Queen's Theatre, London, directed by Simon Callow.

1990 *The Wind in the Willows*. National Theatre, directed by Nicholas Hytner

1991 *The Madness of George III*. National Theatre, directed by Nicholas Hytner

1999 *The Lady in the Van*. Queen's Theatre, directed by Nicholas Hytner

Plays (television)

1972   *A Day Out*. Director Stephen Frears, LWT
1975   *Sunset Across the Bay*. Director Stephen Frears, LWT
1977   *A Little Outing*. Director Brian Tufano, BBC TV
1978   *A Visit from Miss Prothero*. Director Stephen Frears, BBC TV
1978   *Me, I'm Afraid of Virginia Woolf.* Director Stephen Frears, LWT
1978   *Doris and Doreen*. Director Stephen Frears, LWT
1978   *The Old Crowd*. Director Lindsay Anderson, LWT
1979   *Afternoon Off.* Director Stephen Frears, LWT
1979   *All Day on the Sands*. Director Giles Foster, LWT
1979   *One Fine Day*. Director Stephen Frears, LWT
1982   *Intensive Care*. Director Gavin Millar, BBC TV
1982   *A Woman of No Importance*. Director Giles Foster, BBC TV
1982   *Our Winnie*. Director Malcolm Mowbray, BBC TV
1982   *Rolling Home*. Director Piers Haggard, BBC TV
1982   *Marks*. Director Piers Haggard, BBC TV
1982   *Say Something Happened*. Director Giles Foster, BBC TV
1983   *An Englishman Abroad*. Director John Schlesinger, BBC TV
1986   *The Insurance Man*. Director Richard Eyre, BBC TV
1988   *Talking Heads*, six monologues. Directors Stuart Burge, Alan
       Bennett, Giles Foster, BBC TV
1991   *102 Boulevard Haussmann*. Director Udayan Prasad, BBC TV
1998   *Talking Heads 2*, six monologues. Directors Stuart Burge, Patrick
       Garland, Udayan Prasad, Gavin Miller, Tristram Powell, Slow
       Motion Ltd/BBC TV
2000   *Telling Tales*, ten monologues. Directors Patrick Garland,
       Tristram Powell, Slow Motion Ltd/BBC TV

Screenplays

1984   *A Private Function*, Director Malcolm Mowbray
1987   *Prick Up Your Ears*, Director Stephen Frears
1994   *The Madness of King George*, Director Nicholas Hytner

Performances (theatre)

1962   Archbishop of Canterbury in *Blood of the Bambergs* by John
       Osborne, Royal Court Theatre
1964   Reverend Sloley-Jones in *A Cuckoo in the Nest* by Ben Travers,
       Royal Court Theatre

1968   Tempest in *Forty Years On*, Apollo Theatre

1974   Mrs Swabb in *Habeas Corpus*, Queen's Theatre

1976   *A Poke in the Eye with a Sharp Stick* a.k.a. *Pleasure At Her Majesty's*, Her Majesty's Theatre

1988   Tailor in *An Englishman Abroad* and Blunt in *A Question of Attribution* in a double bill *Single Spies*, National Theatre and Queen's Theatre.

1992   Graham in *Talking Heads*, Comedy Theatre

Performances (film)

1982   Justice Shallow in *The Merry Wives of Windsor*, Director David Hugh Jones

1987   The Bishop in *Little Dorrit*, Director Christine Edzard

Performances (television)

1965   Various roles in *My Father Knew Lloyd George*, Director Jack Gold, BBC TV

1966   *On the Margin* (comedy series; also writer), Director Patrick Garland, BBC TV

1979   The Mouse in *Alice in Wonderland*, Director Jonathan Miller, BBC TV

1982   Midgley in *Intensive Care*, BBC TV

1986   Mr Posner in *Breaking Up* by Nigel Williams, Director Stuart Burge, BBC TV

1987   Lord Pinkrose in *The Fortunes of War* by Alan Plater, Director Sir James Cellan Jones, BBC TV

1988   Graham in *A Chip in the Sugar* (one of the *Talking Heads*), BBC TV

1991   Professor Hugh Trevor-Roper in *Selling Hitler*, Director Alistair Reid, Thames

2000   *Telling Tales*, BBC TV

Documentaries (television)

1988   *Dinner at Noon*, BBC TV

1988   *Poetry in Motion*, Channel 4

1990   *Poetry in Motion 2*, Channel 4

1993   *Portrait or Bust*, BBC TV

1995   *The Abbey*, BBC TV

Recordings

1993   *Alice in Wonderland* and *Through the Looking Glass*
1995   *The Story of Dr Dolittle*
1998   *The Voyages of Dr Dolittle*
2001   *The Wind in the Willows*

Publications

1978   *The Old Country*, Faber & Faber
1981   *Office Suite* (*Green Forms, A Visit from Miss Prothero*), Faber & Faber
1982   *Objects of Affection and Other Plays for Television* (*Our Winnie, A Woman Of No Importance, Rolling Home, Marks, Say Something Happened, A Day Out, Intensive Care, An Englishman Abroad*), BBC publications
1984   *A Private Function*, Faber & Faber
1985   *The Writer in Disguise* (*Me, I'm Afraid of Virginia Woolf, Afternoon Off, One Fine Day, All Day on the Sands, The Old Crowd*), Faber & Faber
1987   *Two Kafka Plays* (*Kafka's Dick, The Insurance Man*), Faber & Faber
1987   *Prick Up Your Ears*, Faber & Faber
1987   *The Complete Beyond the Fringe*, edited by Roger Wilmut, Mandarin
1988   *Talking Heads*, BBC Publications
1989   *Single Spies* (*An Englishman Abroad, A Question of Attribution*), Faber & Faber
1991   *Plays One* (*Forty Years On, Getting On, Habeas Corpus, Enjoy*), Faber & Faber
1991   *The Wind in the Willows*, Faber & Faber
1991   *The Madness of George III*, Faber & Faber
1994   *Writing Home*, Faber & Faber
1995   *The Madness of King George*, Faber & Faber
1997   *Writing Home* (revised), Faber & Faber
1998   *Talking Heads 2*, Faber & Faber
1998   *The Clothes They Stood Up In*, LRB/Penguin
1998   *Plays 2*, Faber & Faber
1999   *The Lady in the Van*, Profile Books
2000   *Telling Tales*, BBC Publications

OTHER WORKS

Marcel Proust: A Biography by George Painter, Chatto & Windus, 1956

The Presentation of Self in Everyday Life by Erving Goffman, Doubleday, 1959

George III and the Mad Business by Richard Hunter & Ida Macalpine, Allen Lane, 1969

The Pendulum Years by Bernard Levin, Jonathan Cape, 1970

More or Less by Kenneth More, Hodder & Stoughton, 1978

Prick Up Your Ears by John Lahr, Allen Lane, 1978

From Fringe to Flying Circus by Roger Wilmut, Eyre Methuen, 1980

In My Mind's Eye by Michael Redgrave, Weidenfeld & Nicholson, 1983

The London Encyclopaedia edited by Ben Weinreb & Christopher Hibbert, Macmillan, 1983

A Small Thing – Like an Earthquake by Ned Sherrin, Weidenfeld & Nicholson, 1983

The Dictionary of National Biography, Oxford University Press, 1986

Blessings in Disguise by Alec Guinness, Random House, 1986

Because We're Queers: the life and crimes of Kenneth Halliwell and Joe Orton by Simon Shepherd, Gay Mens Press, 1989

Beyond the Fringe . . . And Beyond by Ronald Bergan, Virgin Books, 1989

Stick it Up Your Punter: The Rise and Fall of the Sun by peter Chippindale & Chris Horrie, William Heinemann, 1990

Language Change: Progress or Decay? by Jean Aitchison, Cambridge University Press, 1991

Murdoch by William Shawcross, Chatto & Windus, 1992

The Kenneth Williams Diaries edited by Russell Davies, HarperCollins, 1993

A Biographical Dictionary of Film by David Thomson (revised edition), Andre Deutsch, 1994

Fight and Kick and Bite by Stephen Gilbert, Hodder & Stoughton, 1995

Six Contemporary Dramatists by Duncan Wu, Macmillan, 1995

Cary Grant: A Class Apart by Graham McCann, Fourth Estate, 1996

Something Like Fire edited by Lin Cook, Methuen, 1996

Alan Bennett: In a Manner of Speaking by Daphne Turner, Faber & Faber, 1997

A Kentish Lad by Frank Muir, Bantam Press, 1997

Michael Palin: A Biography by Jonathan Margolis, Orion, 1997

Dudley Moore: The Authorised Biography by Barbara Paskin, Sidgwick & Jackson, 1997

Lindsay Anderson: Maverick Film Maker by Erik Hedling, Continuum, 1998

Radio Times Guide to TV Comedy by Mark Lewisohn, BBC Worldwide, 1998

Understanding Alan Bennett by Peter Wolfe, University of South Carolina Press, 1999

Talking Heads: York Notes by Delia Dick, Pearson Education, 1999

That Was Satire That Was by Humphrey Carpenter, Victor Gollancz, 2000

Index